2002 Men's Health® TOTAL FITNESS GUIDE

Edited by Leah Flickinger

Notice

The information in this book is meant to supplement, not replace, proper exercise training. All forms of exercise pose some inherent risks. The editors and publisher advise readers to take full responsibility for their safety and know their limits. Before practicing the exercises in this book, be sure that your equipment is well-maintained, and do not take risks beyond your level of experience, aptitude, training, and fitness.
The exercise and dietary programs in this book are not intended as a substitute for any exercise routine or dietary regimen that may have been prescribed by your doctor. As with all exercise and dietary programs, you should get your doctor's approval before beginning.

Mention of specific companies, organizations, or authorities in this book does not necessarily imply endorsement by the publisher, nor does mention of specific companies, organizations, or authorities in the book imply that they endorse the book.

Internet addresses and telephone numbers given in this book were accurate at the time this book went to press.

Printed in the United States of America
Rodale Inc. makes every effort to use acid-free (∞), recycled paper ♻.

ISBN 1-57954-556-4 hardcover

2 4 6 8 10 9 7 5 3 hardcover

Visit us on the Web at www.menshealthbooks.com, or call us toll-free at (800) 848-4735.

WE **INSPIRE** AND **ENABLE** PEOPLE TO IMPROVE THEIR LIVES AND THE WORLD AROUND THEM

2002 Men's Health
TOTAL FITNESS GUIDE

Staff

EDITOR-IN-CHIEF, *MEN'S HEALTH* MAGAZINE
David Zinczenko

EDITOR
Leah Flickinger

ASSOCIATE EDITOR
Kathryn C. LeSage

EXERCISE ADVISOR
Michael Mejia, C.S.C.S.

CONTRIBUTING WRITERS
Mickie Barg; Ethan Boldt; Jeff Bredenberg; Kenneth Winston Caine; Steve Calechman; Adam Campbell, C.S.C.S.; Brian Chichester; Jack Croft; Marc Davis; Debora Dellapena; Doug Donaldson; Ron Donoho; Matt Fitzgerald; Kimberly Flynn; Kelly Garrett; Stephen George; Ron Geraci; Brian Good; Thomas Incledon, R.D., C.S.C.S.; Lisa Jones; Douglas Kalman; Joe Kita; John Lacombe; Richard Laliberte; Jon Lewis; Noah Liberman; James Mack; Michael Mejia, C.S.C.S.; Deanna Portz; Kenton Robinson; Lou Schuler; Todd Severin; Howard M. Shapiro, D.O.; Marie Spano; Bill Stieg; Duane Swierczynski; Andrew Taber; Zachary Veilleux; Elizabeth Ward, R.D.; Fred Zahradnik

COVER AND INTERIOR DESIGNER
Susan P. Eugster

RESEARCH EDITOR
Deborah Pedron

SENIOR RESEARCHER
Deanna Portz

EDITORIAL RESEARCHERS
Bernadette Sukley

LAYOUT DESIGNER
Jennifer H. Giandomenico

PRODUCT SPECIALIST
Dan Shields

INTERNATIONAL EDITORIAL COORDINATOR
Charlene Lutz

Rodale *Men's Health* Books

VICE PRESIDENT, WORLDWIDE PUBLISHER
Edward J. Fones

FITNESS DIRECTOR
Lou Schuler, C.S.C.S.

ART DIRECTOR
Charles Beasley

CUSTOMER MARKETING MANAGER
Matt Neumaier

CONTENT ASSEMBLY MANAGER
Robert V. Anderson Jr.

OFFICE MANAGER
Alice Debus

ASSISTANT OFFICE MANAGER
Marianne Moor

ADMINISTRATIVE ASSISTANT
Pamela Brinar

Contents

V Introduction

PART ONE: SIZE UP THE SITUATION

2 **MH QUIZ:** Is Your Gut Too Big?

ESSENTIAL READING

5 **Bust Your Gut**

8 **Get Primed to Get Pumped**

12 **TRAINER'S FORUM** with Michael Mejia

14 **MH LIST:** Make Your Doc Date Count

PART TWO: TOUGH IT OUT

18 **MH QUIZ:** Will You Wimp Out?

ESSENTIAL READING

20 **Why Your Workout *Isn't* Working**

25 **Get the Most from Your Gym**

30 **Exercise Made Easy**

38 **You *Can* Take It with You**

43 **TRAINER'S FORUM** with Michael Mejia

45 **MH LIST:** Let Your Shorts Hide Your Shortcomings

PART THREE: BUILD MUSCLE

48 **MH QUIZ:** How Fit Are You?

ESSENTIAL READING

50 **Stretch Your Assets**

55 **Muscle in a Minute**

60 **Abs for Anyone**

69 **Home-Grown Muscle**

76 **Look Great Naked**

78 **TRAINER'S FORUM** with Michael Mejia

80 **MH LIST:** Take Your Workout on Vacation

BONUS SECTION:
THE COMPLETE IAN KING WORKOUTS

84 The King of All Workouts

PART FOUR:
FEED THE BEAST

150 **MH QUIZ:** Do You Eat Right?

ESSENTIAL READING

152 **Laws of Leanness**

158 **Get into the Drink**

163 **The Hard-Muscle Diet**

169 **Eat More, Weigh Less**

174 **TRAINER'S FORUM** with Michael Mejia

177 **MH LIST:** Feast Lean on World Cuisine

PART FIVE:
CONQUER THE COMPETITION

180 **MH QUIZ:** Are You a Winner?

ESSENTIAL READING

182 **Shoot and Score**

190 **Be a Two-Wheel Wonder**

196 **Golf like a Pro**

202 **Better *Run***

207 **The Strongest Man Wins**

224 **TRAINER'S FORUM** with Michael Mejia

226 **MH LIST:** The Best Gear for Your Game

PART SIX:
STAY IN THE GAME

230 **MH QUIZ:** Will You Get Hurt?

ESSENTIAL READING

232 **Fix Your Broken Body**

238 **TRAINER'S FORUM** with Michael Mejia

240 **MH LIST:** Be Prepared

241 **Credits**

242 **Index**

Introduction

Questions, Anyone?

The cool thing about my job is that I get to talk to the smartest trainers in the world, guys who train Olympic and professional athletes. I get to browse magazines and the Web, snooping around for new and unusual workout and weight-loss ideas. I get to peruse scientific journals, and among the graphs and tables and snappy turns of Latinate phrase—which is mostly Greek to me—I find nuggets of information about exercise technique and diet choices that could really make a difference in a guy's life. (If I could find a way to get free shoes, too, it would be pretty close to a perfect gig.)

I do my best to communicate this stuff to you by translating it and then printing it in *Men's Health* magazine so you can use it. So it surprises me that month after month, you come back to me with questions I know I've already answered.

The problem? We don't have a failure to communicate so much as a failure to assimilate.

The reason is clear: The wealth of information packed into each issue of *Men's Health* is more than any guy can keep straight—even if he's a loyal and careful reader.

So welcome to the *Men's Health Total Fitness Guide*, our first-ever comprehensive look at exercise, weight loss, fitness, and sports performance.

Between these covers, you'll find all the information you need to start and stick with a serious exercise program. You'll find state-of-the-art nutrition and weight-loss tips. You'll find rock-solid guides to getting into and getting better at running, bicycling, basketball, and mountain biking, plus injury-prevention tips for every game you might want to play.

Many of the stories in this special publication come from the pages of *Men's Health* magazine and books. The heart of this volume, for example, is the complete Ian King workout series that originally ran in the magazine from January to August 2000. It was by far the most popular weight-lifting program in the magazine's history, and this is the first time the series has been published in its entirety.

But many other sections and articles were created expressly for this guide. To highlight just one, we asked our exercise consultant, Michael Mejia, C.S.C.S., to answer (once and for all!) some of the questions that come up over and over from our readers. His takes on these familiar topics appear throughout the guide.

Put it all together—the stuff that was published but that you may have missed, plus the new information—and you have a handy reference you'll go back to again and again.

If you still have questions that this volume doesn't answer, they must be pretty good questions. We'll be happy to answer them in the next *Total Fitness Guide*.

Lou Schuler

—LOU SCHULER, FITNESS DIRECTOR, *MEN'S HEALTH*

SIZE UP THE

PART ONE

When it comes to comes to weight control, you've got a few million years of evolution working against you. Your body is hard-wired to store fat in anticipation of lean times. But with a fast-food joint on every corner and pizza just a phone call away, lean times are hard to come by.

Back when biology installed your fat-storing program, it never considered the modern lifestyle. Your daily activities just don't burn fat the way your ancestors' did. When was the last time you chased a woolly mammoth for 11 miles? Or dragged its hairy carcass back home?

But getting in shape doesn't have to be a mammoth task. In this section, we'll give you all the prep work you need to get fit. And getting fit is all you really want to do, right? So put down the pizza, and let's go.

SITUATION

MH•QUIZ

Is Your Gut Too Big?

Lately, you've started to wonder whether your gut is getting the best of you.

Possibly it's because the last time you bought pants, you couldn't fit into your old size. Or perhaps it's just the way your stomach hung out over your swimsuit the last time you went to the beach. Or maybe you've noticed that it's suddenly gotten harder to bend over and tie your shoes.

If any of these things have happened to you, chances are your gut is too big. In fact, the simplest answer to the question "Is my gut too big?" is "If you think it is, it probably is."

If you're still in doubt, take this quiz to see how your middle measures up.

1 My dog is fat.
☐ True ☐ False

2 I want to get in shape, but I can't find the time to exercise.
☐ True ☐ False

3 Television? Oh, I guess I watch a couple hours a day.
☐ True ☐ False

4 Sure, I nosh while watching the tube, but I stick to low-fat snacks.
☐ True ☐ False

5 And, uh, while you're up, I could use another beer.
☐ True ☐ False

6 I've had to let my belt out a couple of notches since college, but hey, hasn't everybody?
☐ True ☐ False

7 I used to be able to see all the way down to the ground, but lately my belt—and my feet—seem to have disappeared.
☐ True ☐ False

8 All of my friends make more money than I do.
☐ True ☐ False

9 I'm married.
☐ True ☐ False

10 And speaking of my wife, nowadays she always wants to be on top.
☐ True ☐ False

WHAT YOUR ANSWERS SAY ABOUT YOU

1. Owners of fat dogs tend to be fat themselves, says Karen J. Wolfsheimer, D.V.M., Ph.D., associate professor of veterinary physiology, pharmacology, and toxicology in the School of Veterinary Medicine at Louisiana State University in Baton Rouge. This is not surprising, really, because if Bowser isn't taking any walks, neither are you, and both of you may be putting on the pounds.

2 and 3. "I just don't have time to exercise" is the most popular excuse for not doing it. And yet, Nielsen Media Research has found that the typical American man manages to find enough time to watch about 3¾ hours of television a day.

In addition, research has shown that the more TV you watch, the fatter you're likely to be. One study of more than 6,000 men found that those who viewed the tube more than 3 hours a day were twice as likely to be fat as those who viewed less than 1 hour.

4. Researchers have noted that even though we Americans are eating less fat than ever, we're still getting fatter. The reason, at least in part, may be that we're stuffing so much other stuff into our faces. Even if you're conscientious about eating nonfat or low-fat foods, they still have calories, and extra calories lead to pounds.

5. Research reveals a sad truth: Of all the alcoholic beverages, beer is the highest in calories. Given the choice between a shot, a glass of wine, or a brew, you who choose the brew will add more rubber to your spare.

6. According to the U.S. Departments of Agriculture and Health and Human Services, if you've gained more than 10 pounds since reaching your adult height (since high school or college, say), you probably have the makings of a weight problem.

Of course, it's possible that you were a string bean in high school and have since worked out, adding about 10 pounds of muscle mass to your frame. But in most men, extra pounds don't come from muscle. Further, being 10 pounds too heavy today has an unfortunate way of turning into 15 pounds (or 20 or 30) next year.

TOUGH TALK

"If you don't feel bad about missing a workout, you won't continue it no matter how easy it might be. And the older you get, the harder this is."

—JOE MONTANA

7. One way to gauge the state of your gut is to look at it when you're sitting down. If it engulfs your belt, you have more gut than one man needs.

A more scientific way is to measure your waist-to-hip ratio: Take a tape measure to your waist and then to your hips. Divide your waist measurement by your hip measurement. If the number you get is 0.85 or greater, your belly is too big.

8. It may be an unfortunate commentary on the role physical appearance plays in our society, but research has shown that fatter people tend to make less money. A study of business-school graduates found that men who were 20 percent or more overweight made $4,000 less a year than their thinner classmates.

9. Beware: Wedded bliss can turn you into a wedded blimp. A Cornell University study found that married men were twice as likely to be obese as single or divorced guys.

There are two theories about why this is so. It may be that married men eat more regularly because they have women feeding them. Or perhaps it's simply that having "caught" wives and stepped out of the dating pool, they're more willing than their single peers to let appearances slip a bit.

10. If your wife wants to be on top, she's probably tired of your crushing weight bearing down on her. Not that there's anything wrong with her being on top. But sex can be even better the smaller your gut. Studies have shown that when people lose weight, they feel better about themselves, and their sex lives often improve. In fact, one study found that when men started an aerobic-exercise program, they started having sex about 30 percent more often than they had before.

—KENTON ROBINSON

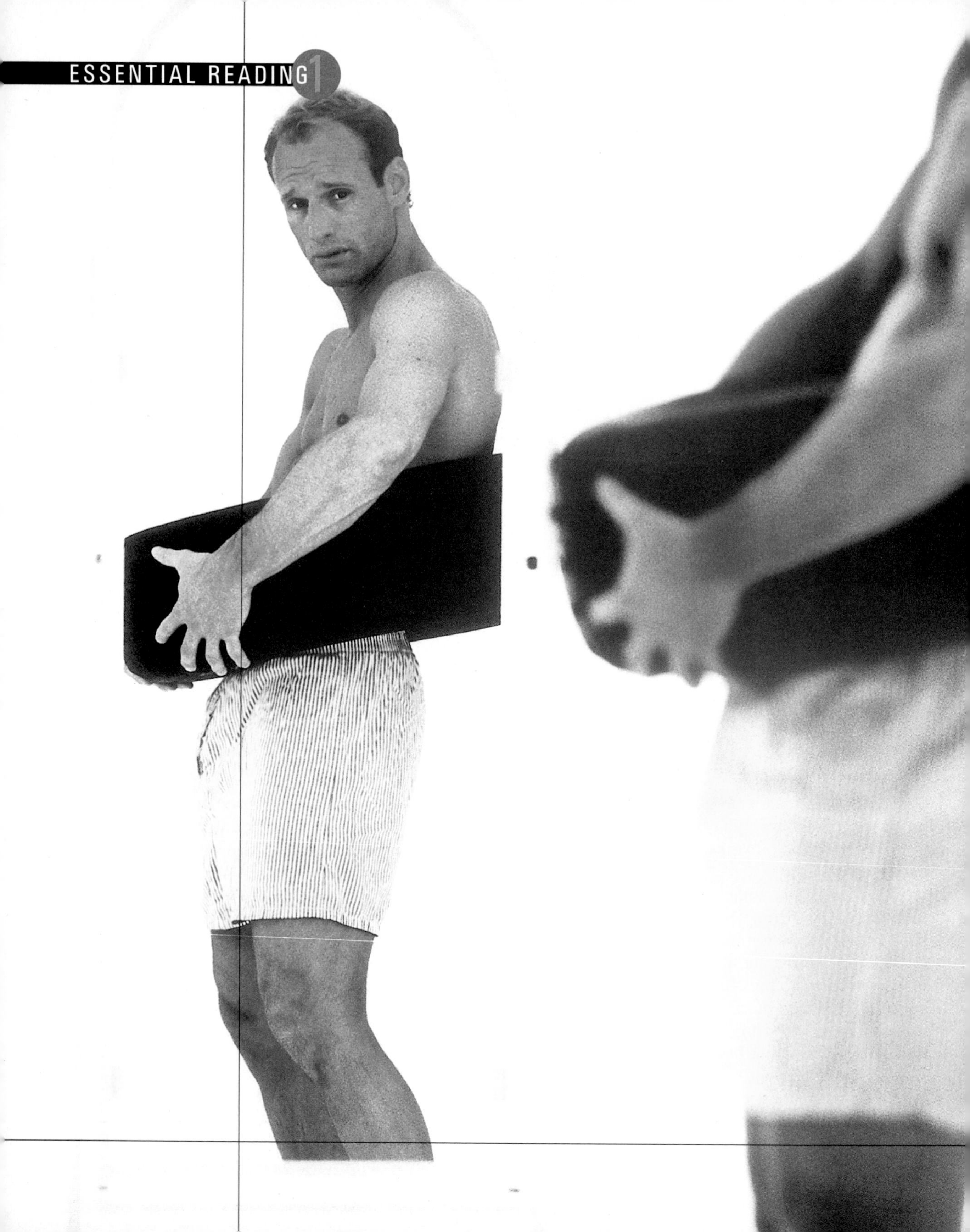

BY KENTON ROBINSON

Bust Your GUT

Never go back to your old weighs

If there's one thing all fitness-and-weight-loss researchers agree on, it's this: The only way you're ever going to tame your gut and keep it tamed is to make permanent changes in the way you live day by day.

You have to change the way you eat, and you have to make exercise a regular part of your life.

"Both those things have to change," says Janet P. Wallace, Ph.D., associate professor of kinesiology and director of the adult fitness program at Indiana University in Bloomington. "It has to be a total change in lifestyle. You're not just doing it to lose weight, because once you stop, you're going to gain the weight back."

Indeed, your biggest challenge is keeping that belly at bay. It's a lot like quitting smoking. Any smoker will tell you that it's easy to quit; he's done it dozens of times. The hard part is quitting once and for all. Same thing with getting rid of your gut: The "easy" part is losing the pounds; the hard part is keeping them off.

Here are the basic principles.

Wake Up and Write It Down

When you're trying to trim down, the first step is to increase your awareness, says Kelly Brownell, Ph.D., co-director of the Yale University Eating and Weight Disorders Clinic.

Start by keeping a daily log of everything you eat. You'll be surprised at how much you actually put away. Fact is, most of us grossly underestimate how many calories we consume on any given day. And evidence suggests that the bigger your gut, the more you underestimate your caloric intake—sometimes by as much as 30 to 40 percent.

Once you have a handle on how many calories you're taking in each day, what kind of calories they happen to be (carrot or Twinkie calories, for example), and where and when you're consuming them, you'll have a good idea of what, where, and when you can cut back.

Don't worry, you won't have to count calories for the rest of your life. Instead, focus on unconscious eating patterns—

Six Axioms of Gut Busting

Any successful and lasting reduction in the size of your gut depends on diet and exercise. With the help of Charles T. Kuntzleman, Ed.D., adjunct associate professor of kinesiology at the University of Michigan in Ann Arbor, we've cooked up six axioms to guide you.

When it comes to exercise:

1. Anything is better than nothing.
2. More is better than less.
3. Faster is better than slower.

When it comes to diet:

4. Nothing is better than anything.
5. Less is better than more.
6. Slower is better than faster.

Before you start starving yourself and running like a rat on a treadmill, allow us to explain.

1. If there's just one message researchers wish we would get, it's this: Get off your duff and do something. Take a walk. Play tennis. Do the hokeypokey. Anything you do will burn more fat than sitting still.

2. The greater the intensity of your workout, the more you'll burn. Simple enough.

3. Not only that, the faster you go, the more calories you'll use.

Now, on the diet side of the equation:

4. We're not suggesting that you fast. What we are suggesting is that when the hors d'oeuvre tray comes around, you let it pass right on by.

5. Which brings us to our central diet axiom: You can carve away some of that gut by carving extra calories out of your diet.

6. Finally, it is better to both eat slowly and lose weight slowly. The slower you eat, the sooner you'll feel full, which means you'll eat less. And when it comes to losing pounds, research has shown that you're much more likely to keep weight off if you take it off slowly and steadily.

mega-helpings, fast-food addictions, candy habits—that add excess fat to your diet (and your midsection).

You also need to gauge your level of physical activity. What kind of exercise, if any, are you getting every day? Again, keeping a daily log will give you a better handle on this.

Change Your Ways

Once you have a better sense of how you eat and what you do every day, you have to retrain yourself with a whole new set of habits, says Brownell. For example, instead of coming home every night and flopping down in front of the TV, take the dog out for a brisk 30-minute walk. Instead of downing your daily Danish, switch to a plain bagel.

Losing weight for the long haul involves more than just doing a few things differently, says anthropology professor Anne Bolin, Ph.D. of Elon University in North Carolina. "It can't be just, 'I'm going to change my diet, and I'm going to make myself exercise.' It has to be a life change," says Bolin. "Whatever you're doing on a routine basis has to be gradually changed so that you have something else that becomes part of who you are. This isn't just something you're doing; you're creating a new identity."

Do What You Like

Finding an activity or combination of activities that you like doing is a critical part of any weight-loss plan. A lot of people force themselves to do things they don't really enjoy—stationary bicycling, say, or jogging before work—with predictable results: About half the people who get into an exercise program will drop out in the first 6 months, says Wallace.

When Wallace studied exercisers, she found that the ones who were most successful at staying with a program were those who "did what excited them."

Find an activity that you enjoy, because then it will be something that you look forward to and stick with, she says. If you hate your exercise routine and do it only because it's good for you, you won't do it for long. If running is fun, run. If swimming is it for you, swim.

Once you've found something you really like doing, make it part of your new definition of yourself. Tell yourself (and others), "I'm a runner." Or "I'm a swimmer." Or "I'm a weight lifter."

"What it means is finding the athlete in yourself so that you become that athlete," says Bolin. "Once you've become that athlete, that's who you are."

PEAK performance

Don't Just Sit There

Canadian researchers found that 16 men who exercised an hour a day for 3 months lost as much weight—16 pounds—as men who dieted instead. Even better, the exercisers also lost 27 percent more body fat.

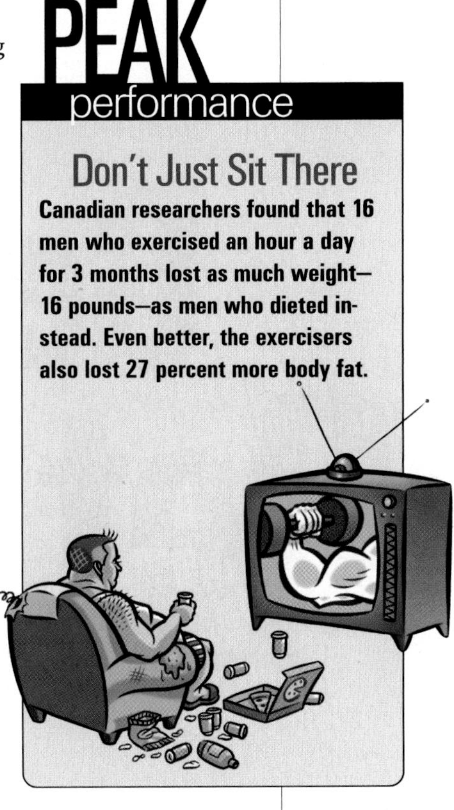

BY RICHARD LALIBERTE

Get Primed to Get Pumped

How to get started on your way to total fitness

Triathlon legend and three-time Ironman champion Scott Tinley sums it up: "Do nothing you're not prepared for."

It's worth remembering the following tips as you change your life one muscle at a time.

Seek expert guidance. A gym staffer or personal trainer can tell you if your goals are unrealistic, guide you on proper form, and tailor your program to your needs. Don't worry that you're signing on to a long-term dependency. "Even if you buy just one session with a personal trainer, it will be 25 to 50 bucks well-spent," says Alan Mikesky, Ph.D., director of the Human Performance and Biomechanics Lab and associate professor at Indiana University–Purdue University in Indianapolis.

Make an investment. Any money you spend on your fitness program will increase the value of what you're doing, providing a strong (but not fail-safe) motivation to keep active. Beyond trainers and gym memberships, it's hard to resist the allure of cool, expensive equipment.

There's a dilemma here, however: If you're new to something, how do you know you'll like it? If you're taking up biking, should you immediately blow as much as you can afford on a new steed? It's a tough call that's ultimately yours to make, but here are some thoughts to guide you.

▶***Rent first.*** It's probably not a good idea to spend gobs of dough on big-ticket items without a few trial runs. Start with day-long excursions with a bike (or kayak or snowboard or skis) from a local outfitter. If you enjoy your experience, you'll keep coming back for more, and the financial advantage of owning your own gear will quickly become apparent.

▶***Get good gear.*** When you do buy, invest in quality that's appropriate for what you intend to do, advises sport psychologist Kate Hays, Ph.D., founder of The Performing Edge, a Toronto performance-enhancement training company for athletes, performing artists, and business people. "You won't get full value out of equipment without a certain investment," she says. If you take up running but start with inferior shoes ("just until I know I like it"), you'll feel lead-footed and possibly pained. That won't be encouraging. "A moderately priced pair of shoes can make all the difference," says Hays. "You need good-enough stuff, but it doesn't have to be top of the line." If you're buying a bike, don't spend $2,000 on an elaborate rig, but don't spend $200 on a discount-department-store special either.

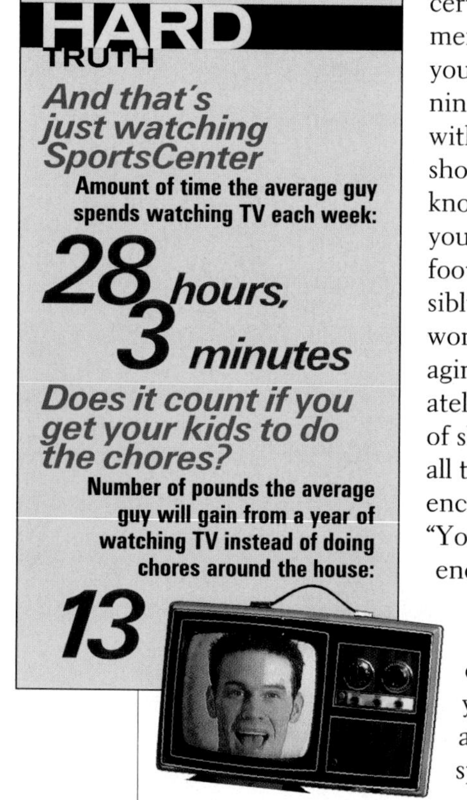

HARD TRUTH
And that's just watching SportsCenter
Amount of time the average guy spends watching TV each week:
28 hours, 3 minutes
Does it count if you get your kids to do the chores?
Number of pounds the average guy will gain from a year of watching TV instead of doing chores around the house:
13

▶***Consider buying used.*** Stores that sell pre-owned gear are becoming more common. Or check the classifieds for people who bought more hardware than they were ready for—and are now ready to sell.

Include your friends. You're not in this exercise thing alone. It helps to have someone around to share your progress, enthusiasm, and disappointments. Part of this involves what sports psychologists call values clarification. "If you tell someone, 'This is what I'm planning,' you're more likely to actually do it," says Hays. And who should this someone be? "A friend—it might be your wife or girlfriend—who will be interested in your plans or reasons for exercise."

Choose workout partners carefully. Though a male workout partner can help foster motivation, "sometimes guys get so competitive with each other that exercise becomes a contest instead of a process," says Hays. Make sure competition doesn't end up making the whole experience unpleasant or tougher than you really want. Remember, exercising should be fun.

Fortify against intimidation. Starting a new sport, joining a gym for the first time, trying a new activity—all can initially be intimidating. You notice only the people who seem much more proficient than you. There's a certain dork factor that's determined by how you feel and think about yourself. To feel more comfortable, work on listening to the negative things you tell yourself, and substitute some internal cheerleading, says Hays. Instead of saying, "I'll never be able to do that," say, "In a week, I'll be doing better than I am now." Anticipate the times and places where you'll feel the most self-conscious, and think of positive words to tell yourself ahead of time.

Build armchair enthusiasm. One way to feel more at ease with a new sport is to learn more about it. Read magazines or books. Talk to people at shops that sell gear. Learn the ins and outs of an activity before committing your ego to actually doing it in public.

Mark your calendar. You're psyched, you're pumped, you're ready to go. At least *now* you are. Two to 4 months from now? A different story. Count on it. In fact, plan for it. Studies show that half the time, regular exercise programs fizzle within 6 months, with most people dropping out after 4 to 6 weeks.

This isn't necessarily bad: Incredible gains can be made in 6 weeks, and it's possible to hit many of your goals in that amount of time. Figure that you'll eventually get bored and apathetic, but take it not as a sign to bail out but as an opportunity to set new goals and do something more interesting—and demanding. Persistent progress requires persistent effort. "Nothing's for free," says Tinley. "If there's no sacrifice, there's no reward."

Start low, go slow. "Guys like to hammer themselves when they do something," says Mikesky. It feels great immediately afterward. Then you get sore. "Most people can't stand hammering themselves every workout," says Mikesky. "After a few times, you lose your enthusiasm—or you get injured." If you're just beginning or have laid off a regular program for more than 6 months, start by doing less than you think you can. Slowly raise the demands you make on yourself, increasing the intensity, duration, or frequency of your exercise no more than 15 percent per week.

PEAK performance

When Should You See the Doc?

If you've been moderately active and otherwise healthy, and you're planning to add only a leisurely walk around the block to your daily regimen, you probably don't need to see a doctor.

According to researchers at the National Institutes of Health, you should get checked out if one or more of the following apply to you.

- **Heart problems**
- **High blood pressure**
- **Frequent chest pains**
- **Faintness or dizzy spells**
- **On prescription medications**
- **Bone or joint problems, such as arthritis**
- **Another serious health condition not mentioned here**
- **Over age 40**

Trainer's Forum

with MICHAEL MEJIA

WHAT'S WRONG WITH ME?

Q What are the advantages of hiring a personal trainer? Couldn't I just as easily work out by myself?

P. K., GLOUCESTER, MASSACHUSETTS

A You could. The question is, how effective would it be? Think about it: Aside from difficulty getting motivated, what's the other reason most people give up exercise? Lack of results.

After several weeks of sweating it out with nothing to show for it, lots of guys get disgusted and figure exercise doesn't work for them. In all likelihood, what isn't working is the haphazard way in which they approach their workouts.

In order for exercise to work, you have to do it systematically. You can't just indiscriminately lift weights and do cardio with no set plan and expect to see long-term results. Sure, if you're a novice, you'll probably see short-term benefits—after all, even unstructured exercise is better than no exercise. Trouble is, after a while your body adapts and progress comes to a screeching halt.

This is where a trainer comes in. He (or she) can help you avoid this inevitable plateau by carefully planning your workouts and, later, altering them as your fitness level improves. A trainer will also make sure you're using proper form and can even teach you subtle ways to make your exercises more effective.

Perhaps the most important advantage: A trainer can give you concrete feedback on your progress by carefully tracking your body composition, strength levels, flexibility, and cardiovascular fitness. No matter how diligent you are, that's pretty difficult to do on your own.

HARD TRUTH

Get fit and save on your heating bill

Indoor temperature above which you may get lethargic:

72°F

POP QUIZ

Invest in Yourself

Got a minute? No? Well, at least you have time to answer this one question: If you could make an extra $5,000 every week simply by working an extra 5 hours, would you do it?

A. No. I just told you, I don't have any time.

B. Where do I sign?

If you answered A, either you're one of those multigazillion-dollar CEOs who thinks nothing of spending $5,000 on a handkerchief, or your name is Andy Capp. More likely, though, you answered B. That means you do have the time to exercise—you just have to recognize that getting fit is every bit as important as getting rich. Though it'd be nice to have it both ways.

WEIGHT LOSS

Score Your Chores

You spent the weekend doing odd jobs around the house, and you didn't have time to get out and exercise. Don't sweat it. You may have already sweated enough—and burned more calories—doing chores than you would have engaging in your favorite weekend sport. Check out the chart below. All figures are based on calories burned per hour by a 180-pound male.

CHORE	CALORIES BURNED	SPORT	CALORIES BURNED
Washing car	270	Sex	240
Carpentry	270	Volleyball	396
Trimming hedges	378	Golf	411
Painting	378	Brisk walking (3.5 mph)	432
Chopping wood	414	Tennis (singles)	522
Mowing lawn	486	Inline skating	550
Gardening	576	Bicycling (15 mph)	600
Digging with shovel	701	Cross-country skiing	666

PEDAL VERSUS PUMP

Q I just want to get in shape. Should I focus on cardiovascular/aerobic exercise or weight training?

A. J., HALF MOON BAY, CALIFORNIA

A Let's start by clarifying what "get in shape" means. Most people equate getting in shape with losing weight—pretty silly when you consider that you can lose weight simply by restricting your caloric intake. Eat like a hummingbird and do absolutely no exercise, and I guarantee you'll lose weight. Does that make you more fit? No. From a professional point of view, getting in shape really means improving your overall fitness level in order to perform daily tasks more easily and efficiently.

There's also more to it than cardio versus strength training. Such minor tasks as carrying groceries up a few flights of stairs, sprinting to catch your morning train, or picking up your 2-year-old can seem monumental without muscular strength and endurance, cardiovascular fitness, and, yes, flexibility. You need all three for peak performance in any arena.

Your best bet is a three-pronged approach that includes equal parts strength training, cardiovascular conditioning, and stretching for 20 to 45 minutes for a minimum of three times a week. After 4 to 6 weeks, you should start noticing changes in your overall fitness level (you'll be less winded, your clothes will fit more loosely). Then you can begin to specialize more in a certain aspect of training, depending on your individual goals.

Make Your Doc Date Count

8 Ways to Get the Most from Your Checkup

You already know this, but we'll tell you again: If you're overweight and out of shape, you're at greater risk for a bellyful of serious conditions: heart disease, diabetes, and stroke, to name just a few.

That's why it's important to get checked out by a doctor at least once a year, says David Levitsky, Ph.D., professor of nutritional sciences and psychology at Cornell University in Ithaca, New York. Early detection of a health problem gives you a much better chance to prevent it from getting serious.

Here's how to make your annual visit last all year.

1 Be first. Always try to lock in the first appointment of the day, says David Power, M.D., of the department of family medicine at the University of Minnesota Medical School—Minneapolis. There's less chance of a backed-up schedule, so you'll be out sooner. The first opening after lunch is a good second choice. Avoid Mondays and Fridays.

2 Give blood early. A week before your appointment, drop by the doctor's office to give a vial of blood and grab any paperwork, advises Leann Michaels, R.N. This will eliminate hassles on the day of the exam, and your doctor can discuss the blood-test results during your physical.

3 Forgo the morning coffee. A cup or two can spike your blood pressure by as much as 5 points, which is enough to get you misdiagnosed as hypertensive, says Michaels. Ask the nurse to check your blood pressure at the start and the finish of the exam to make sure the readings match.

4 Get the finger over with. Many doctors save the most embarrassing tests for last. Ask for the digital rectal exam for prostate and colon cancers first so you won't have to dread it for 20 minutes. "Most doctors will be glad to alter their routine if you ask up front," says Isaac Kleinman, M.D., associate professor of family and geriatric medicine at Baylor College of Medicine in Houston.

5 Confess everything. Men usually report symptoms such as chest pain or dizziness but omit more obscure symptoms, says Dr.

Kleinman. "Spots in front of your eyes, ringing in your ears, and unexplained weight loss can also indicate serious problems." Bring up the stab wounds, too.

6 Get your shots. While you're there, make sure that all your immunizations are up-to-date. Ask the doctor whether you need a booster shot for measles, mumps, rubella, chicken pox, tetanus, or diphtheria. Look on the bright side: You probably had at least some of these as a kid, so you won't have to face all six needles.

7 Use drug samples wisely. If you need only a week's worth of medication, ask for free samples. For longer treatments, request a prescription for a generic version of an appropriate drug. "Most samples are for new, expensive drugs," says Jeff Susman, M.D., professor and director of the department of family medicine at the University of Cincinnati. Once the freebies ran out, you'd probably need to keep taking that same drug—and it'd be pretty pricey at the local pharmacy.

8 Put yourself through the mill. If heart disease runs in your family or you have other risk factors, ask for a cardiac stress test. A treadmill test can detect heart disease years before symptoms develop, but it's seldom part of a regular checkup.

—BRIAN GOOD
AND ZACHARY VEILLEUX

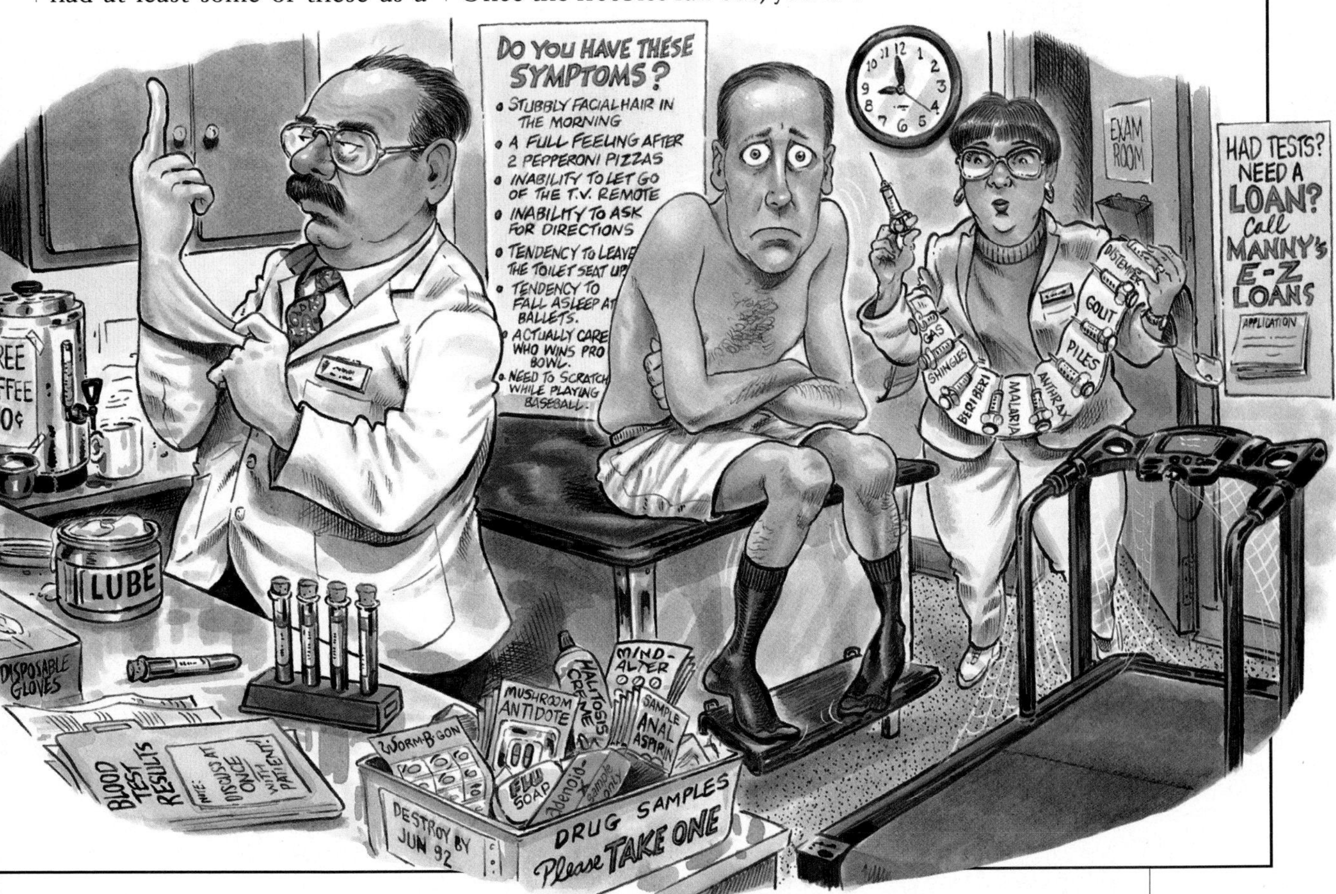

TOUGH IT

PART TWO

It's no secret why men's best fitness intentions so often fail: Guys march to the gym like lemmings because their wives or their girlfriends or an infomercial hard-body told them to. They start fitness programs with the zeal of cult converts—and 6 weeks later, they're more burnt out than Crosby, Stills, and Nash. So they bail.

Truth is, a guy rarely drops out of his own personalized fitness program. But he'll ditch somebody *else's* regimen faster than he can say "Jazzercise!"—because he never felt comfortable with it in the first place.

So take control. Your time, your life, and your body all belong to you. Your fitness choices should, too.

You just need to make 'em. Keep reading to find out how.

MH•QUIZ

Will You Wimp Out?

Committing to a fitness program isn't so hard. It's staying motivated for the long haul that's the killer. You know how it goes: The first day or so is a no-brainer. Pass on the fries—easy. Dust off the treadmill—30 breathless minutes later, you feel pretty good.

Now it's been a few days. Your muscles hurt. You still bust out of your dress shirt. The fries beckon like Heidi Klum's eyes. The treadmill . . . what treadmill?

Will you keep your eyes on the prize? Take our test to see whether you'll suck it up or wimp out.

1 I can't pass a mirror without checking myself out.

☐ True ☐ False

2 I'm too busy to commit to a fitness program.

☐ True ☐ False

3 I never lose a bet.

☐ True ☐ False

4 Goals are for losers.

☐ True ☐ False

5 My doc would tell me if I needed to exercise and change my eating habits.

☐ True ☐ False

6 The bike I bought last spring is still in pieces in the box.

☐ True ☐ False

7 I like to work solo.

☐ True ☐ False

8 I'll try, but I know I'm going to fail.

☐ True ☐ False

9 I've used the same toothpaste for 20 years.

☐ True ☐ False

10 Now I'm going to sit back, relax, and admire my new lean-and-fit body.

☐ True ☐ False

WHAT YOUR ANSWERS SAY ABOUT YOU

1. Research shows that guys who really care about their looks are better able to stick to a fitness program. Subscribe to *Men's Health*. And wear gym clothes that reveal your progress. It's motivating to see muscles emerging when you're working out, says Courtney Barroll, a certified personal trainer and medical exercise specialist at Equinox Fitness Club in New York City.

2. If you can figure out how to easily fit your workout into your lifestyle, you'll be more likely to stay motivated and stick with it. Play music you like, join a gym with a lot of good-looking women, work out with a friend . . . you get the idea. Soon, you'll want to make time for fitness.

3. You'll be more likely to stick with a fitness program if you have money riding on it, says researcher and epidemiology professor Robert W. Jeffery, Ph.D., of the University of Minnesota School of Public Health in Minneapolis. A study at Michigan State University found that people who bet $40 that they could maintain an exercise program for 6 months had a 97-percent success rate. Among those who didn't take the bet, fewer than 20 percent were able to stay with their routines.

4. Big-business gurus are right: Goals are for winners. They challenge, focus, and motivate. Most important? They make you want to succeed.

But they help only if they're attainable. "Some people run into inevitable failure because their weight-loss goals were unrealistic and could not have been maintained, even if achieved," says Paul R. Thomas, R.D., Ed.D., former staff scientist with the Food and Nutrition Board of the National Academy of Sciences. Set small, feasible goals such as "I want to lose at least 4 pounds this month" rather than "I'll lose 50 pounds by next year."

A good way to tell whether you're making progress is to benchmark your achievements. For example, keep a log of how many more pounds you can bench press and how much weight you've lost. On days when you don't feel like working out, look back on your achievements for motivation. Reward yourself for success.

5. In a recent survey of adults who had seen a doctor during the previous year, only 34 percent said the doc had recommended exercise. People most likely to hear this suggestion? Women, the elderly, and people with heart disease. Among men, it seems the fit guys received more advice on exercise than others. Our advice? Don't take no news as good news.

6. False? Good. You're a guy who can finish what he starts. And there's a good chance you won't let anything stand in the way of sticking to your fitness program. Persistence and time management are your allies. Use them to your leanest, hardest advantage.

7. Studies show that people are most successful at meeting their fitness goals when they do it with someone else, says Jeffery. Recruit a friend to be your lifting buddy. Or turn your dog into a running partner. Can't find a fitness buddy? Go after a woman. To class, that is. A fitness class or weight-loss group is jam-packed with support—and you'll be outnumbered. That's a good thing.

8. True? Start playing head games. Psychologists at Springfield College in Massachusetts studied 24 junior tennis players during tournament play. Players who berated themselves with cries like "Why can't I serve?" and "I'm so sloppy today!" followed with poor performance.

Anxiety and negative thinking can also translate into physical problems like nausea and headaches. They can cripple your athletic performance or deflate your spirit to the point that you abandon your goals.

Adopt an optimistic mindset and you'll be a step ahead in changing behavior, says Jeffery.

9. Either answer works. If your motto is "If it works, why change it?" keep your program simple and uncomplicated, says Jeffery. Focus on a fitness routine that's as automatic as hopping out of bed and brushing your teeth.

If you've switched from Crest to Colgate to Aquafresh, you may be easily bored by routine. Vary your schedules, activities, and goals. Search out new gyms, equipment, or biking and running trails. The trick is to find what's right for you.

10. True? Great. You've made progress, but you can still wimp out if you're not careful. You need to be committed over the long haul. Tough it out. You will be rewarded.

—**MICKIE BARG**

BY LOU SCHULER

Why Your Workout *Isn't* Working

When you sense your workout should be going better, here's what could be going wrong

Now and then, everybody has a day like this: You walk into the weight room feeling like the King of All Barbells but end up performing more like the Queen Mum. Dumbbells you handled easily in your previous workout seem to have put on weight. Rather than mastering the iron, you feel as if your body were three-quarters rust.

What makes your muscles go from 60 to zero so suddenly and unexpectedly? We found eight possible reasons and eight solutions. Put these into practice and you may go the rest of your life without another bad day at the gym.

1. You're Stressed

Stress is to your workout what Janet Reno was to religious compounds. Emotional upset unleashes a hormone called cortisol, "and cortisol is not a friend of the lifter," says exercise physiologist Dave Pearson, Ph.D., C.S.C.S., assistant professor at Ball State University in Muncie, Indiana.

Cortisol helps your body relieve stress, but it also suppresses testosterone. Lower testosterone means fewer results from your workout.

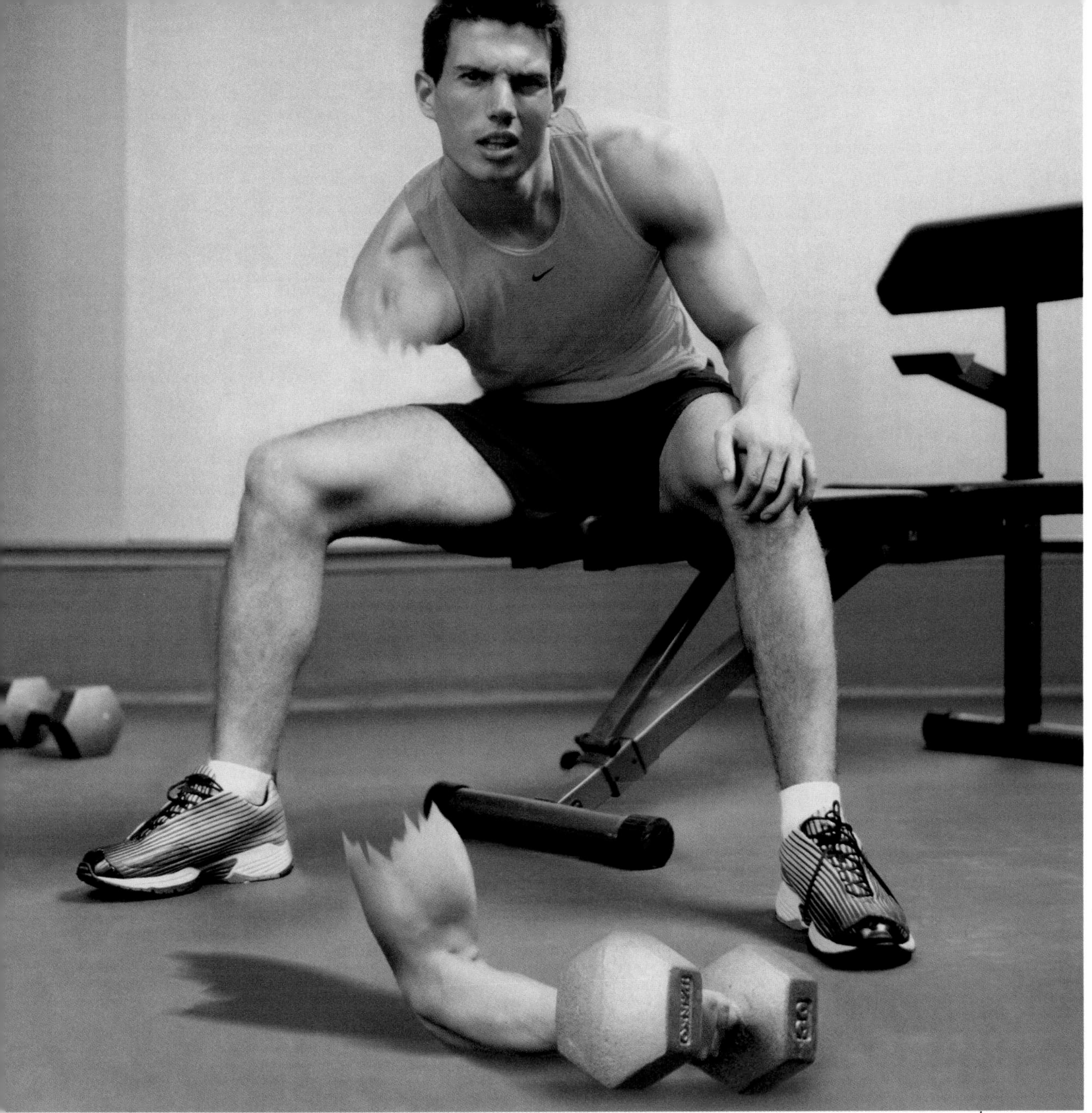

Worse, stress causes most men to tense the muscles in their upper backs, says Atlanta exercise psychologist James Annesi, Ph.D. And a tense muscle is easily injured.

Fix it. Relax before you work out. When you arrive at the gym, take a few deep breaths—the kind that make your stomach protrude when you inhale. (That means your diaphragm is dropping to let maximum air into your lungs.) Then shrug your shoulders as high as you can, hold for a few seconds, and very slowly lower them as you continue to breathe deeply.

Continue tensing and relaxing other muscles—chest, shoulders, back—until you feel less stressed. Then you're ready.

2. You Live at the Gym

Stress can also originate inside the gym. "When you're exercising too much, your level of anxiety rises," says Annesi. The excess stress (cortisol again) leads to muscle breakdown instead of buildup.

Fix it. Here are a few ironclad rules to lift by.

1. Unless you're a pro athlete or you have to be in shape for your job, never do more than four weight workouts per week.

2. Never lift on more than 2 days in a row.

3. Never do a high-intensity technique like drop sets (consecutive sets with progressively less weight and no rest breaks) for more than 3 weeks without giving your body a break and shifting to less taxing workouts.

3. You Drank Too Much

Drinking a lot the night before a workout can leave you dehydrated, and dehydration makes your workout suck. Every weight feels heavier, and you tire faster, says Chris Rosenbloom, Ph.D., R.D., associate professor of nutrition and dietetics at Georgia State University in Atlanta.

Many men are dehydrated even without the beer. If the only liquids you drink are coffee, tea, or sodas with caffeine, you're probably a liter or two light on body fluids.

Fix it. If you need to work out the day after a bender, slam down a sports drink a half-hour before your workout. Then drink more every 10 to 15 minutes, Rosenbloom suggests. The carbohydrates in the sports drink will help keep the water in your system (without them, you'll urinate a greater percentage of the fluid you take in), while the sodium will make you thirstier for more fluids, thus helping your boat float again.

4. You're a Cold, Cold Man

A productive workout is highly dependent on your state of arousal, says Tom Seabourne, Ph.D., C.S.C.S., a sports psychologist in Texarcana, Texas. And arousal, in the physiological sense, is dependent on body heat. Unfortunately, many of us have no choice but to work out when we have naturally lower body temperatures: early morning, late night, early afternoon.

Fix it. You've probably heard of this thing called a warmup. Start moving until you break a light sweat, yada, yada, yada.

A hot shower can also raise your temperature, says Seabourne. You still need to take your body into light-sweat land before you start lifting, but you'll get there a lot faster.

5. You're Not Emotionally Erect

Sometimes, the success or failure of a workout depends on how well you do on one or two sets when you're trying to lift more than you have before. This requires not only arousal but also single-minded focus. The gym, though, can be a tough place to focus: the music, the people, the heated philosophical debates.

Fix it. Wear a towel around your shoulders between sets, says Australian strength coach Ian King, C.S.C.S., who has trained Olympic and professional athletes. When you're ready to lift, pull off the towel. The sudden feeling of cool air on your sweaty shoulders will trigger a fight-or-flight response, increasing your level of arousal.

For focus, Seabourne recommends having a ritual before you begin a set. Go through the same sequence every time: how you set your hands, how you place your feet, how you square your shoulders and align your head. Follow this ritual with two deep breaths.

6. It's Thursday

Men tend to eat more on weekends than on weekdays, says Pearson. So on Monday, your body is well-fueled for a workout. But as the week goes on, you may miss a breakfast or two, work through a lunch, go to bed without a dinner. Toward the end of the week, your energy reserves are depleted, and you're gassed before you set foot in the gym.

Fix it. Well, eat. Try for some carbohydrates and protein in five or six meals and snacks a day. Dairy products are great because they contain both carbohydrates and casein, a protein that helps build muscle and strength. But eat them more than 2 hours before a workout; lactose (the sugar source in milk products) and casein are both slow to digest.

7. You're Just Plain Sick

But you don't know it yet. Often, a terrible workout is the first sign you're coming down with something, says Manhattan sports-medicine specialist Scott Reale, M.D. One indication that you may be sick: You do one good set of an exercise and then can't come close to repeating it. This could mean your immune system is redeploying your energy reserves to battle the illness.

Fix it. You can't do much about an illness once you're sick, except leave the gym and give your body time to recover.

8. You Should Drop By More Often

So let's say you're not sick, stressed, overexercised, underfed, or dehydrated. And yet you still have a lousy workout. Could be that you're undertraining—not exercising enough for the benefits you expect.

It works like this: If you work out hard, the immediate effect is that your body is broken-down and weak. But within a few days, your body has recovered and is actually stronger than it was before your hard workout. It may hold these new powers for a day or two, but then your strength starts to slip. Wait long enough between workouts and you could easily get weaker instead of stronger.

You won't notice this problem from one workout to the next. Most likely, you'll just feel that you're not making any progress.

Fix it. Work out either harder or more frequently. A few guidelines:

1. Train two or three times a week if you're doing total-body workouts, three or four times a week if you're doing split routines (lifting with your upper body one workout, lower body the next, for example).

2. Increase weights 5 to 10 percent per week. When you can't do this anymore, you've peaked on the exercises you're doing and need to change to new ones.

3. After six to eight workouts using one system of sets and repetitions, switch to another.

PEAK performance

Just Tape It

Given a choice between exercising for a half-hour and watching their favorite TV shows, most men will remain glued to the tube. Ask them why they don't work out, and they'll say they don't have time. We've got a trick for you: Use your remote.

According to Paul R. Thomas, R.D., Ed.D., former staff scientist with the Food and Nutrition Board of the National Academy of Sciences, that little control box is the secret to having it both ways: You'll have time to work out and watch your favorite shows.

"Tape the program, then watch it later and zap the commercials," advises Thomas. By fast-forwarding past the ads, you can save almost a half-hour for every 2 hours of television. "There's your half-hour to get some activity in," he says.

BY ETHAN BOLDT

Get the Most

1
2
3
4
5
6
7
8

from Your Gym

23 ways to build a brand-new body in the same old place

Your average gym is 25,000 square feet of black iron and polished wood, with more mirrors than Barbra Streisand could break in a lifetime. You pay a lot of money to go there, so make the most of it. Here's a blueprint to help you use everything your gym offers, from the lat bar to the snack bar. We'll show you how to save time, save money, burn fat faster, and build muscle better. The only thing we can't do is get you the phone number of the Pilates instructor. We tried—it's unlisted.

1 **Parking lot.** Ride a bike to the gym and you're warmed up before you arrive, saving yourself 5 to 10 minutes. Use the easiest gears, and go for high rpm.

2 **Rehab equipment.** This gear can rehabilitate injuries, so use it to prevent injuries, too. Strengthen your ankles by standing on the wobble board for a minute. When that's easy, do light dumbbell exercises while balancing on the board.

3 **Aerobics studio.** When the women clear out, use the cushy floor for your calisthenics: Jump rope for a minute, do 25 pushups, do stepups on the platforms for a minute, then do 25 crunches. Repeat three times.

4 **Climbing wall.** The key to climbing is using your legs, and the key to that is having shoes that fit. Buy climbing shoes that fit your bare feet so tightly you can stand but not walk comfortably. They'll give you optimal control on the wall. The wall also offers the best vantage point to (safely) ogle the babes.

5 **Yoga class.** Yoga improves flexibility and posture. But here's the best reason to get twisted: Women are suckers for centered guys.

6 **Sauna.** Dry skin? Skip the sauna. But if your gym offers a coed sauna and she's in there, wrap the terry loosely. And sign up for the lifetime membership.

7 **Juice bar.** When you're working out to lose weight, remember that a post-workout shake is your meal. Go for a shake made with low-fat milk or yogurt (for calcium), bananas (for potassium), and blueberries (for vitamins and that cool purple color). And don't forget the protein powder for muscle recovery.

8 **Shower.** Protect yourself by wearing shower shoes or flip-flops. But make sure you wipe them off with your towel when you're finished. Otherwise, your shoes will grow the same nasties that you just avoided in the shower.

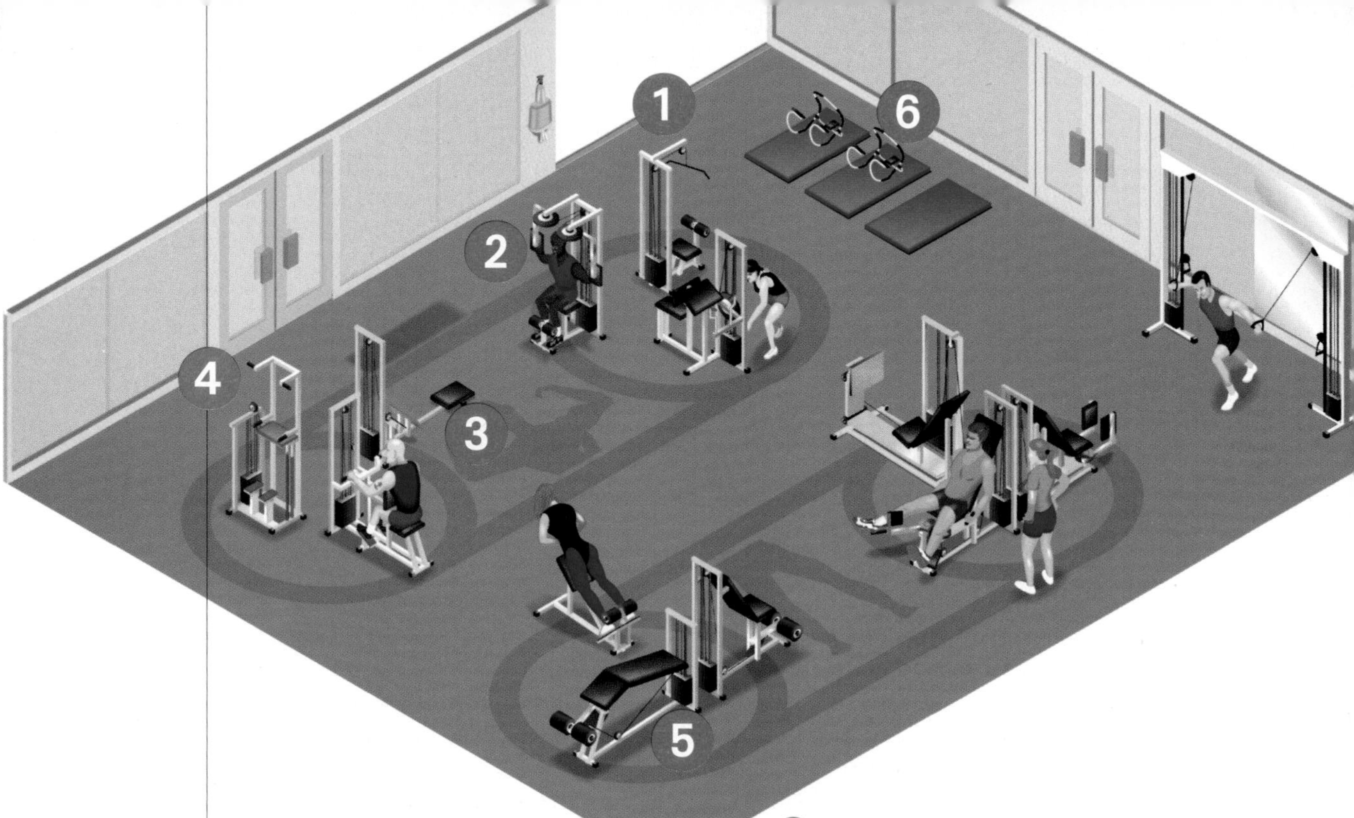

Weight Machines

1 Lat-pulldown machine. Most guys are stronger on one side than the other. You can even things up by doing one-armed lat pull-downs. Remove the bar and use a stirrup handle instead. Pull the handle down with one hand until it's even with your shoulder. Try one to three sets of eight repetitions on each side.

2 Butterfly machine. When you use this, you should always be able to see your upper arms in your peripheral vision. If you have to turn your head to see your upper arms, you're bringing them back too far.

3 Seated vertical-rowing machine. Instead of using a full rowing motion, keep your arms straight and simply pull your shoulder blades together in back. This strengthens the middle trapezius, an important muscle for upper-body posture.

4 Assisted-pullup/dip machine. To make pullups on a machine more like real pullups, kneel as far forward on the platform as you can, and concentrate on arching your back. Also, every workout, decrease the amount of help the machine gives you. You want to advance to the real thing as quickly as possible.

5 Leg-curl machine. Here's a way to make an easy, comfortable exercise a little harder—and a lot more effective: Raise the weight with two legs, but lower it with just one. Take 5 full seconds on the way down. Do one to three sets of six to eight repetitions per leg.

6 Ab roller. If you've had neck or upper-back injuries, an ab roller make it easier to do crunches without straining neck muscles. Healthy guys, steer clear: You don't need it. If you're hurting your neck during crunches, it's probably because you're pulling on the back of your head. Cross your arms on your chest instead.

Free Weights

1 Stiff-legged deadlift. Instead of doing hyperextensions and leg curls for your lower back and hamstrings, you can do this one move to produce the same results in half the time. Keep the bar as close to your body as possible throughout the exercise. And you don't need to lower it all the way to the floor: The middle of your shins should do the trick.

2 Lateral raise. The more you bend your elbows, the more weight you can lift. But that's not a good thing, says Eric Ludlow, C.S.C.S., senior personal trainer at World Gym in New York City. You'll use too much weight, leading to injuries. Try lifting with almost straight arms, and start with the weights beside your hips, not in front of your body. Even if you use just 5- or 10-pound dumbbells, you'll still work your shoulders harder.

3 Preacher curl. Next time you do preacher curls, try a reverse grip. You'll use more forearm muscles as well as your brachialis, a muscle that adds thickness to your upper arms. And use a wide grip; the narrow one is too tough on your elbows, says T. R. Goodman, owner of Pro Camp, a fitness-training company for professional athletes in Venice, California.

4 Incline press. The flat bench sees more use, but the incline press is the most functional chest exercise. The sports moves that involve your chest, triceps, and shoulders—throwing a punch, blocking a defensive lineman, or firing up a prayer from half-court—are all done with your body bent forward at the waist. Lower inclines—30 to 60 degrees from the floor—are easier on your shoulders, says New York City–based personal trainer and strength coach Michael Mejia, C.S.C.S.

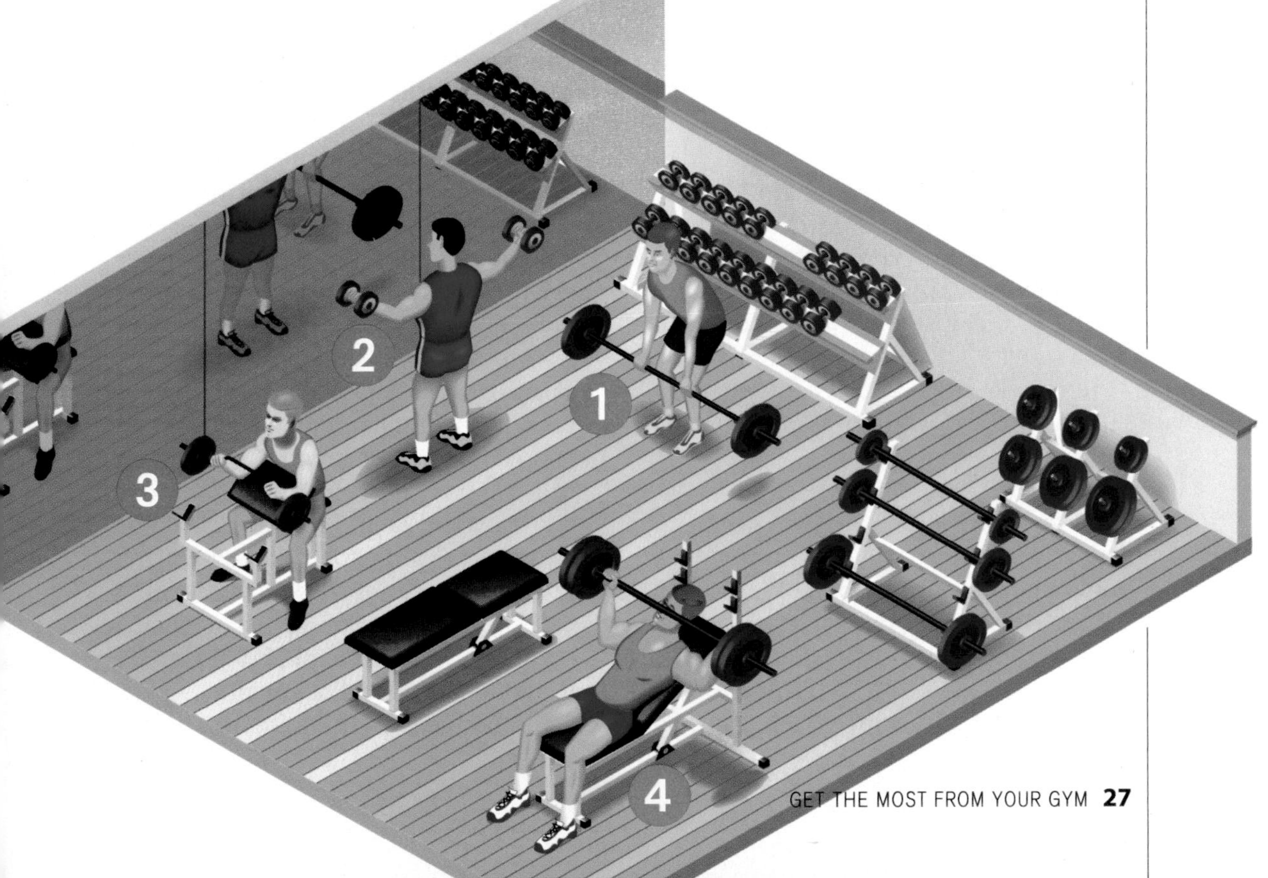

Aerobic-Exercise Room

1 **Stationary bike.** If you want to burn fat, avoid the program that says "fat-burning." It's just a long, slow workout. You'll burn more calories if you do the interval workout instead, working at varying intensities. In the long run, you'll chew up more fat.

2 **Spinning bike.** Can't make it to a class? Order the same tapes the instructors use, through Power Music (www.powermusic.com) or Dynamix, and hold your own session. When the music slows down, increase the tension on the bike; when it speeds up, decrease the tension.

3 **Treadmill.** Maybe your gym won't let you dribble a basketball while you run, but that doesn't mean you can't find other ways to make a treadmill more interesting. Set the machine on "manual" and alternate between walking at high inclines and running fast at low inclines. Finish with a "retro run": Slow the machine, then jog backward for 5 to 10 minutes. That'll help prevent shinsplints and knee problems.

4 **Arm cranks.** Machines that work the upper and lower body simultaneously allow you to burn more calories in the same amount of time as the legs-only version of the exercise would. But that's an added benefit enjoyed only by the fittest of the fit: trained rowers, swimmers, and cross-country skiers. Regular folks will just become tired faster from doing upper- and lower-body exercise at the same time.

5 **Magazine rack.** Great for distraction, but also a compromise to workout intensity. "If you're not sweating through what you're reading, you're not working hard enough," says Ludlow. For at least part of your workout, you should be pumping so hard that you can't focus on the words on the page.

The Best Gym for You

Choosing a gym is a lot like settling down with a woman: You don't want to make a snap decision based on a dazzling appearance. We asked Steve Morgan, who trains managers and staff for Life Fitness Academy (the education arm of the company that makes LifeCycles and other equipment), to tell us the most important criteria to consider when shopping for a gym (or a woman, for that matter).

▶**Location.** Choose a club close to either your home or your workplace, whichever makes more sense.

▶**Convenience.** Think of all your favorite excuses for skipping workouts, then choose a club that eliminates them. If you travel constantly, for example, join a club that's part of a national chain.

▶**Facilities and services.** Even if all you want from a gym is weights and tasteful lighting, you should give yourself more options. Someday you may want the pool, physical therapists, or child care, if not the Kardio Goose-Stepping class.

▶**Atmosphere.** Get a free workout pass, go when you plan to use the club, and soak it in. Don't assume you'll suddenly grow fond of pulsing techno music if you're a lifetime connoisseur of ZZ Top.

▶**People.** You can tell a lot about the club's appeal by the longevity of its employees. "It's a bad sign if none of them has been there for more than a few years," says Morgan.

▶**Upkeep.** Tour the club the way a new girlfriend would check out your apartment. Warning signs include equipment strewn about, out-of-order machines, scummy showers, and bottles of expired antibiotics.

▶**Price.** "You're not going to find significant price differences among clubs with comparable facilities and services," says Morgan. That's why price is last on our list. It's best to choose the club you want based on the other factors, then find a way to fit the cost into your budget.

Some Membership Issues to Consider

▶**"Who's using my StairMaster?"** Tour the club at the time of day when you're most likely to use it. Look carefully at the equipment you know you're going to use. If every machine is occupied on your tour, that means you'll have to wait in line for it.

Worst-case scenario: Your favorite machine is out of order. See if you can shake your salesman long enough to ask a member how long the thing has been on the fritz. Rule of thumb: The popular stuff is always fixed fast, but it's a sign of a good gym if everything else receives prompt attention, too.

▶**"How do I get out of this place?"** Before you sign up for a membership, you should know exactly how to get out of it: how many months you have to belong before you can cancel, how much notice they need. Point to any date on the calendar and ask, "If I quit then, what will I owe you?" You should hear a straight answer, to the dollar.

▶**"If I leave today, will it be cheaper tomorrow?"** The best clubs offer one set of prices for everyone, says Richard Cotton, a spokesman for the American Council on Exercise.

BY ETHAN BOLDT

Exercise Made Easy

Simplifying your workout saves time and energy—and might even leave you in better shape

It seems that anything worth doing is worth making incredibly complicated. Especially workouts. We start adding exercises to hit every muscle from every angle; we run forward, backward, and sideways; we do intervals and outervals; we crunch, reverse crunch, side crunch, and numbers crunch. And then we're so confused that we forget why we were working out in the first place.

Drop the slide rule. It's time to make exercise simple again. We found 24 ways any man can cut time, aggravation, and wasted effort from his workout without sacrificing results. In fact, by stripping down your routine, you'll enjoy it more and profit more from it—which is why you got into this racket in the first place.

1. Stick with Black, White, and Gray

Buy workout clothes in black, white, or gray. They go with everything, and you'll never again waste time looking for a T-shirt that matches your gold-and-purple Lakers shorts.

Bare Necessities: Strip your workouts of all the stuff you don't need, and it's easier to build the body you want.

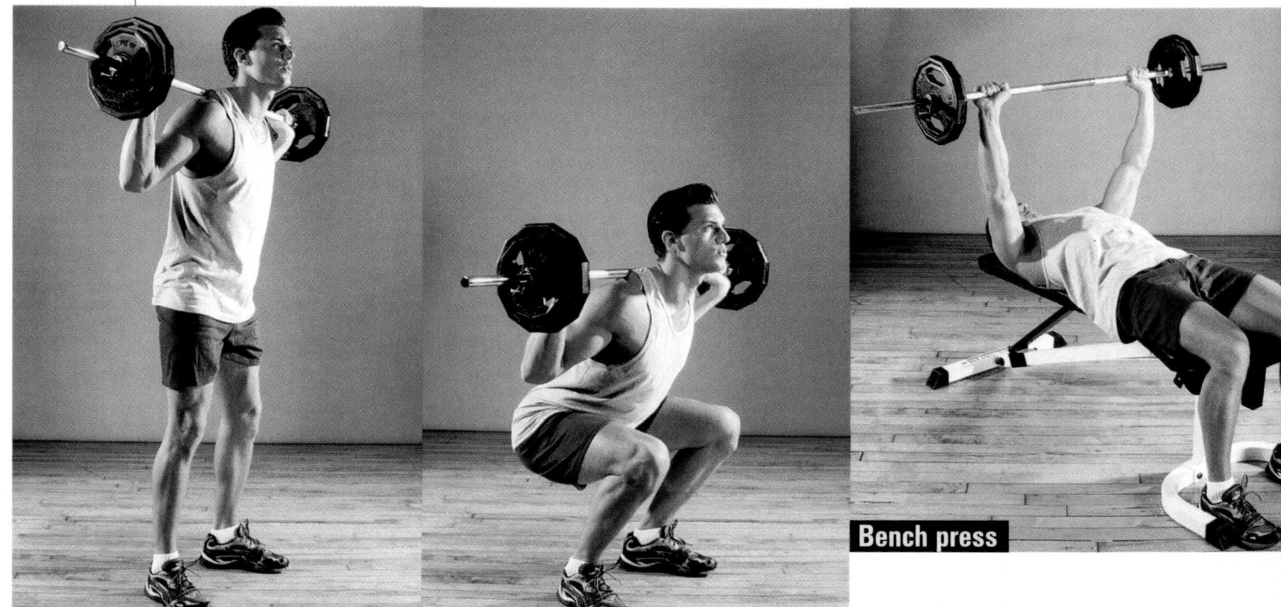
Squat

Bench press

2. The Simplest Total-Body Workout

It's three exercises: the squat, bench press, and bent-over row. These three hit all your major muscles and most of your minor ones. They also offer maximum stimulation of your most powerful muscle-building hormones.

3. Prep Yourself the Night Before

Be your own mom: Lay out your workout clothes the night before. If you work out in the morning, put 'em on and you're ready to run, ride, or lift. If you work out later in the day, pack your gym bag before you go to bed. You'll have one less thing to remember when you're rushing to work in the morning.

4. Leave the Accessories at Home

Weight lifting isn't golf. You don't need a lot of extra stuff—gloves, wrist straps, weight belt, knee wraps—to do it right. "Gloves and straps weaken grip strength, belts weaken your abdominals and lower back, and knee wraps enable you to use elasticity instead of true leg strength when you come up out of a squat," says New York City–based personal trainer and strength coach Michael Mejia, C.S.C.S.

5. But Have These Two Things

Take a water bottle and a towel, says Paul Manfre, C.S.C.S., a trainer in Dayton, Ohio. Constant trips to the water fountain waste time; and when you train without a towel, you're asking everyone else in the gym to sample your bodily fluids. It'll anger most and turn on a couple, and you want to avoid both possibilities.

6. Put Yourself on the Clock

Try to exercise at the same time each workout day. That increases the chances that you'll stick with it, says San Diego exercise physiologist William Sukala, C.S.C.S.

7. Pick the Time You Like

You may have heard that morning workouts are better since testosterone levels are higher. Forget you heard that. "Although hormonal

Bent-over row

fluctuations are important, they don't necessarily correlate to performance gains. The optimal time to work out is any time you can fit it into your schedule," says exercise scientist Greg Haff, Ph.D., of Appalachian State University in Boone, North Carolina.

8. Simplify Your Schedule

Weight lifting more than 4 days a week is too much since the single best predictor of injury is how many consecutive days you work out, says Tom Seabourne, Ph.D., C.S.C.S., a sports psychologist in Texarcana, Texas. The more you work out, the higher your injury risk. So divide your exercises into two workouts—upper body and lower body, say—and do one workout every other day. You train each muscle twice every 8 days, give yourself plenty of time to recover from each workout, and dramatically reduce your chance of injury.

9. Work Out for Only an Hour

The dropout rate is much higher when your routine lasts longer than 60 minutes, says New York City trainer Brian Pfeufer, C.S.C.S. Plus, you run the risk of breaking down your body more than you're building it up: Your body slows down its production of muscle-building hormones and cranks up the muscle-wasting hormones at about the 60-minute mark.

10. Employ Three Sets Most of the Time

For absolute beginners, doing one set of each exercise in a workout seems to be as good as doing multiple sets. But most men need three sets of an exercise to get all its benefits, says Seabourne. That's because your body has three types of muscle fibers, and it's hard to work them all in just one set. When you're doing low repetitions for strength, you need to increase to four to six sets.

11. Do One Exercise per Muscle Group (If You're Ambitious, Maybe Two)

"Unless you're a bodybuilder, there's no need to hit a muscle from every conceivable angle each time you train it," says Mejia. Work hard on one or two exercises per muscle group and you'll build plenty of muscle and have more time to show it off.

12. Conquer One Goal at a Time

Don't try to get big, strong, and cover-model lean all at the same time—you'll end up splitting the focus of your workouts and falling short of any goal, says Lyle McDonald, C.S.C.S., a trainer in Austin, Texas. Instead, pick just one of those goals, give yourself 6 to 12 weeks to achieve it, then move on to the next.

Get bigger. Stick with 6 to 12 repetitions per set, increase the weights consistently, eat lots, and cut cardiovascular exercise to a healthy minimum (30 minutes three times a week).

Simple Alternatives

Too many men go into the gym convinced that one particular piece of equipment is the key to their own personal happiness. If that station isn't available when they're ready for it, their workout is sunk. This is stupid. There's always an exercise you can do instead

If the SQUAT RACK isn't available, try the BARBELL LUNGE or LEG PRESS.

If the SHOULDER-PRESS STATION isn't available, try the DUMBBELL LATERAL RAISE ON AN INCLINE.

If the BARBELL BENCH-PRESS STATION isn't available, try the DECLINE DUMBBELL BENCH PRESS.

Get stronger. Do 1 to 5 repetitions per set, increase weights religiously, and, again, cut back on cardiovascular exercise.

Get leaner. Eat less, do more aerobic exercise and do it more intensely, and try to maintain strength (it'll be very hard to increase it) while doing sets of 8 to 15 repetitions.

13. Stay with a Program till It Stops Working

Switching from program to program too often can sidetrack your goals, Sukala says.

that's at least as good, says Shawn Dassie, C.S.C.S., who trains athletes in Sioux City, Iowa. He recommends these alternatives to popular workout stations.

If the TRICEPS-PRESSDOWN STATION isn't available, try the DECLINE BARBELL TRICEPS EXTENSION.

If the LYING LEG-CURL MACHINE isn't available, try the STANDING LEG CURL.

If DUMBBELLS FOR BICEPS CURLS aren't available, try the BARBELL PREACHER CURL.

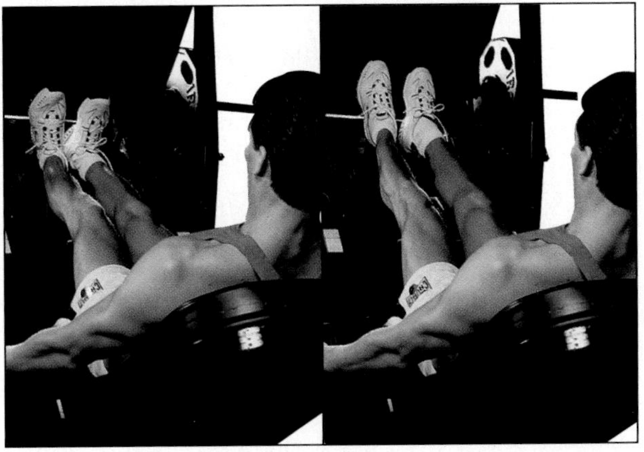

If the CALF MACHINE isn't available, try CALF RAISES ON THE LEG-PRESS MACHINE.

Resist the urge to jump on every new workout routine you see; you'll make your workouts simpler (and see better results) if you stick to one program for 6 to 12 weeks, or until it quits working.

Back-Up Plan: Put this simple twist in your routine.

14. Figure Out whether It's Working

Two benchmarks: Your waist tightens and your strength improves, says Seabourne. If you're not lifting more weight from one workout to the next, and if your belts aren't getting looser, the program isn't working. So switch already.

15. Use One Stretch—This One

Hit your hamstrings, lower back, chest, front shoulders, and biceps with this move (see above photo) from Jim Liston, C.S.C.S., a Los Angeles strength-and-conditioning coach: Lie on your back, arms straight out to your sides. Cross your left leg over your torso and try to touch your left foot to your right hand, keeping both shoulders on the floor. Keep your left knee bent slightly. Hold for 10 seconds, then switch sides. Repeat once or twice for both sides.

16. Make Your Cardio Work for You

If you're training to build the most muscle with the least fat, follow these simple rules.

▶Do aerobic exercise after—not before—your weight workout.

▶It's better to do aerobics and weights on separate days.

▶On the days you don't lift, interval aerobics are best of all. After a thorough warmup, go hard for a minute, then easy for a minute or two, and repeat for 10 to 15 minutes.

17. Stick to One Partner

Whether you're a runner, lifter, or cat burglar, having more than one partner is asking for missed, delayed, truncated, or inefficient workouts, says Mejia. Exercising with one other person will improve your adherence and motivation; trying to exercise with more than one will make you the fitness equivalent of a plane circling O'Hare.

18. Do the Workout, Then Cross It Off

Mark an X on your calendar on the days you exercise. A University of Calgary study found that exercisers who used this simple system of tracking workouts made more progress than those who didn't.

19. Keep Your Stuff Together

Throw all your dirty workout clothes into a single mesh laundry bag. At the end of the week, tie a knot in the bag and throw it into the wash. You'll always know where your favorite workout shirts are, and you won't actually have to touch your sweat socks when they're fully ripe.

20. Double Up on Shoes

Next time you're buying exercise shoes, purchase two pairs of the same kind. Alternate them and you'll cut down on visits to the shoe store (as well as foot odor).

Write on them, too. Worn-out shoes are a leading cause of running injuries. To protect yourself, write an "expiration date" on your shoes as soon as you buy them. This will save you the hassle of tracking their mileage as well as the stress of wondering whether they're shot yet.

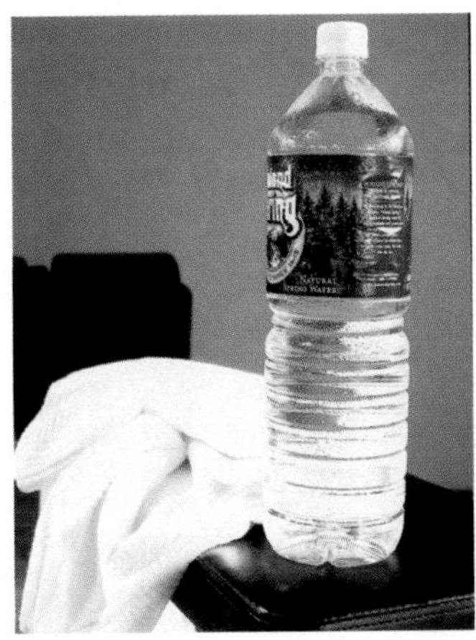

Because shoes should last about 500 miles, simply divide 500 by your average weekly mileage to determine how many weeks your shoes should last. One exception: If you're heavier or your ankles roll too far in or out, you may go through shoes faster—in as few as 350 miles.

21. Follow These Two Simple Eating Rules

Finding time to exercise can be tough, especially when you have to adjust your workout to your eating schedule. Here's an easy-to-remember guide to pre- and post-exercise nutrition.

1. Don't eat for an hour before you work out. If you feel that you need to have something before you exercise, grab a sports drink 5 minutes before your workout and sip on it throughout the session.

2. Eat lots of carbohydrates and some protein as soon as you can after your workout. The carbs help replace energy stores needed for your next workout; the protein repairs your muscle.

22. Stop Counting Grams of Fat . . .

"If you're exercising a lot and you're happy with your current weight, you probably don't have to worry much about fat intake. Total calories are more important, so just make sure you aren't gorging," says nutrition researcher Rachel Brown, Ph.D., of the University of Otago in New Zealand. In a recent study, Brown found that the most active men actually eat more fat than the least active guys. We like studies like that.

. . . Unless you quit exercising. If you have to lay off from exercise, drop the chalupas as well.

23. You Need Water, So Drink

"Start the day with a liter bottle of water. Finish it off by the end of the day. Along with other beverages like milk and juice, that should keep you hydrated," says Pam Legowski, R.D., a researcher at Purdue University in West Lafayette, Indiana. Alcohol, soda, and coffee don't count. Alcohol leaves you dehydrated, and caffeinated drinks are a break-even proposition: drink, whiz, drink, whiz.

24. Finally, Ignore All Advice

If you're improving from one workout to the next—getting stronger and more muscular—don't be thrown off course by the loud, strange advice from the hulks in the gym. Stick to what's working for you. And come to us if you need anything.

BY ADAM CAMPBELL, C.S.C.S

You *Can* Take It with You

Use that battered old piece of Samsonite to build a body like Samson's

You don't have to lose your body because you're away from your gym. Pack a few simple workout tools in your suitcase before you hit the road, and you'll be able to throw yourself a magnificent sweat-fest without leaving your room, says Michael Mejia, C.S.C.S., a personal trainer and strength coach in New York City who designed this hotel-compatible workout program.

You don't even need to travel to use this routine. It'll work in any confined space, whether it's your house or the Big House. (You never know when those creative tax deductions will catch up with you.)

Warmup

Warm up for 5 minutes. Two options:

Jump rope. If you're a novice jumper, do

as many jumps as you can, then swing the rope alongside you as you hop up and down. Keep at it until you're warm (or until you've tripped on the rope and face-planted on the floor). If the ceiling in your room isn't high enough, try a stairwell landing.

Jumping jacks. Just like in gym class. Start slowly, and build up speed as your body loosens up.

How to Train on the Road

▶Do 8 to 12 repetitions of each exercise. Perform the exercises in a circuit—one after the other with little or no rest in between. At the end of each circuit, rest for 2 minutes, then start the next one. Work up to three circuits.

▶The exercises have three levels: beginner, intermediate, and advanced. When you can do three circuits of 12 repetitions of any exercise, move up to the next level.

▶Do this workout two or three times a week, with at least one day between workouts. You can take a brisk walk or run on your days off.

▶These exercises all employ your body weight for resistance. You can't beat the convenience, but producing results can become a problem once your body grows accustomed to the exercises. So as you get better at them, slow down your movements. That will increase the length of time your muscles are under tension, which will lead to greater muscle gains.

▶You can also make the workout harder—and give yourself a better cardiovascular boost—by jumping rope or doing jumping jacks during the 2 minutes between circuits.

1 WIDE-ARM PUSHUP

Beginner: Place your hands about 5 inches beyond shoulder-width apart. Take 2 full sec-

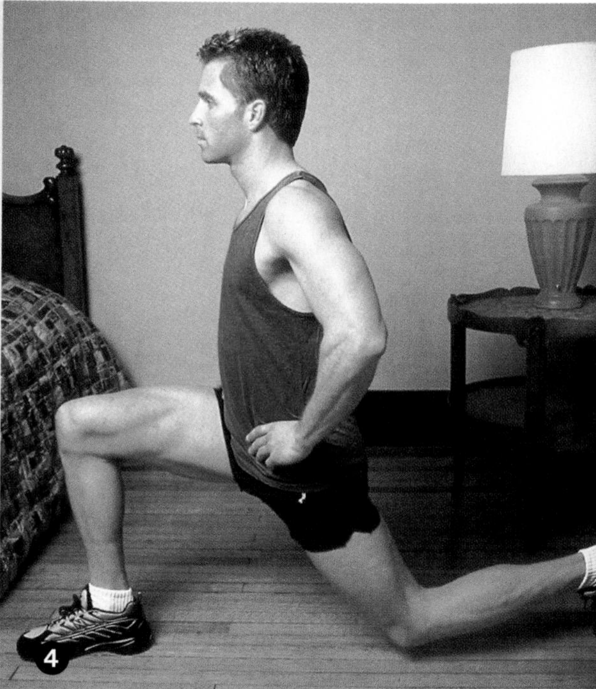

onds to lower yourself, pause a second, then push back up in 1 second.
Intermediate: Same as above, but take 4 seconds to lower yourself.
Advanced: Put your feet on a chair or bed.

❷ WALL SQUAT (see photo on page 39)

Beginner: Lean against a wall with your feet about 2 feet away from it, shoulder-width apart. Bend your knees slightly and hold for 10 seconds. Bend deeper and hold for 10 seconds. Continue until you've hit five different positions, the last position as low as you can go.
Intermediate: Hold each position for 15 to 20 seconds.
Advanced: Hold each position for 30 seconds.

❸ CHINUP

Beginner: Set a chinup bar in a door frame. Stand on a chair, grasp the bar with a shoulder-width, underhand grip, and pull yourself up. You can push with your legs, but try to make your upper body do most of the work. Take 6 to 10 seconds to lower yourself.
Intermediate: Do regular chinups without the chair.
Advanced: Same as above, but hold for 1 second at the top, and take 4 seconds to lower.

❹ REVERSE LUNGE

Beginner: Stand with your feet together, and step backward with your left foot, lowering your body until your right knee is bent 90 degrees and your left knee nearly touches the floor. Pause, then return to the starting position. Finish all the repetitions with your left leg, then repeat the entire set with your right leg.

Intermediate/Advanced: Take 2 full seconds to lower your body, pause for 2 seconds, then push yourself back to the starting position.

5 REVERSE PUSHUP

Beginner: Place the chinup bar in a doorway at waist level. Lie under the bar and grasp it with an underhand grip, your hands shoulder-width apart. Keep your body straight and pull your chest to the bar.
Intermediate: Change to an overhand grip, hands wider than shoulder-width apart.
Advanced: Same as intermediate, but put your feet up on a chair.

6 BRIDGE

Beginner/Intermediate: Lie facedown on the floor, then bring your body up and balance on your forearms and toes, forming a straight line. Pull in your abdominal muscles, trying to bring your belly button back to your spine. Work up to holding the position for 30 seconds.

Advanced: Get into pushup position, with your weight on your hands and toes. Slowly lift your left hand and right foot off the floor until they're in a straight line with your torso. Hold for 1 second, carefully lower your arm and leg, and repeat on the other side. Try for five or six repetitions on each side.

7 CHAIR DIP (see photo on page 42)

Beginner: Rest your hands on a chair seat, with your legs out in front. Lower your body until your upper arms are parallel to the floor.

Pack It Up

- ▶Leather jump rope ($10)
- ▶Doorway chinup bar ($20)
- ▶Ultimate Fastdraw water bottle ($10)
- ▶Amphipod Active Sport Pocket ($15)
- ▶Shirt
- ▶Shorts
- ▶Socks
- ▶Running shoes

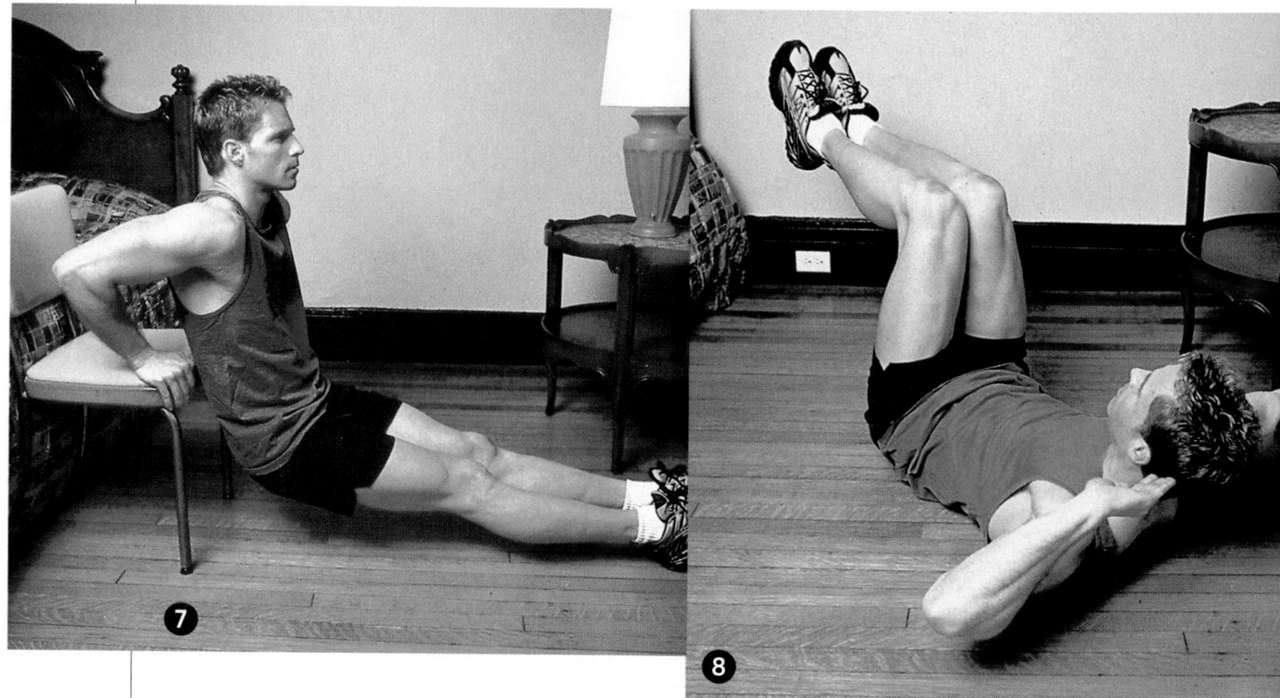

Intermediate: Put your feet up on another chair.
Advanced: Take 3 seconds to lower your body, pause for 1 second, then take 3 seconds to push back up to the starting position.

PEAK performance

Deflate, Stay Pumped

A post-workout cooldown can be like great sex after sitting through a chick flick: You remember the fantastic finish, not the tedium that led to it. A researcher at Springfield College in Massachusetts put students through two stationary-bike workouts: 15 minutes with no cooldown, and 15 minutes plus a 5-minute cooldown. Most students said they'd rather repeat the longer session, which felt easier. So a cooldown is not only better for your muscles but also a way to trick yourself into staying motivated for your next workout. "If the last thing you do is perceived as pleasant, you're more likely to do it again," says the study author, clinical psychologist Britt Brewer, Ph.D.

8 CRUNCH

Beginner: Lie flat on your back with your feet up in the air and your knees bent. Lift your head and shoulders, then slowly return to the starting position.
Intermediate: Place your feet flat on the floor and pull your body up into a full situp.
Advanced: Do full situps, but pause halfway up for 1 second. Then pause halfway down for 1 second.

Got an exercise question? Go to the fitness message board at www.menshealth.com. Michael Mejia and our other certified trainers are there to help you out.

Trainer's Forum

with MICHAEL MEJIA

IRREGULAR GUY

Q I work sporadic and sometimes long hours, so it's tough to follow a regular workout program. Because of this, I never seem to make any progress getting in shape. It's discouraging. Any suggestions?

Z. B., SPOKANE, WASHINGTON

A The only way to make an exercise program deliver is to make a committed effort to stick to it. For starters, you can't let your schedule beat you. No matter how busy you are, you have to make time for your workouts.

Next, stop thinking of exercise as a time-consuming albatross that's going to wreck your entire day. As long as you're doing some form of strenuous exercise at least three times per week, you should see improvement. Shoot for 5- to 10-minute miniworkouts spread out over the course of the day. Crank out a few sets of pushups and crunches before work in the morning. Do 15 minutes of intense cardio exercise at lunch. And instead of lying on the couch cruising 57 channels at night, get down on the floor and stretch for 10 minutes or so.

The key is progression. Log your workouts and try to do a little more each time. Believe it or not, doing one extra rep or shaving 5 seconds off your best time can add up to big improvements over the long haul.

TOUGH TALK

"If you want to be the best CEO of a company, you're going to have to really put your head to it and go at it harder than anyone else does. It relates to sports also. The hard trainers are the guys who are making it to the top."

—MARTY NOTHSTEIN, WORLD-CHAMPION CYCLIST

SMART SHOPPER

Get the Best Deal on Your Home Gym

When Internet shopping, look for free shipping. If you're just buying weights, you probably won't find free shipping. But you can still cut costs by buying a lot at once.

Never buy a machine you haven't tried out first. Price isn't everything. If you're buying an aerobic or weight machine, you have to make sure that you like it and that it fits your body. Even if you ultimately buy the machine on the Internet, try it out at a local fitness or sporting-goods store first.

Get to know your local Play It Again manager. Used sports and exercise equipment is now a billion-dollar-a-year business. Stores like Play It Again Sports sell great stuff, often in near-new condition. The catch is that you never know when it's coming in. Make sure the manager of the local store knows what you're looking for.

CONTINUED

PLATEAU PUNCH

Q When I started working out, I initially lost a lot of weight. Now I seem to have stopped progressing. What should I do?

D. P., SCRANTON, PENNSYLVANIA

A Whenever you go from no exercise to regular exercise, you're going to notice fast improvements. Inevitably, though, your body becomes accustomed to it and stops responding—this is the plateau you've no doubt heard about. In order to get your metabolism back into fat-burning mode, you're going to have to shake things up a bit.

To most people interested in burning fat, this usually means upping the amount of cardio they do. My opinion? Big mistake. Too much cardiovascular exercise can cause muscle wasting. Muscle is highly active metabolic tissue—that is, it uses lots of energy. So the more muscle you have, the more calories you burn each day, both during exercise and at rest. Therefore, my recommendation is to focus more heavily on strength training to increase your metabolic rate.

Compound large-muscle-group exercises like squats, deadlifts, bench presses, and rows are the best way to build the calorie-burning muscle you'll need to blast through any plateau. They not only release fat-fighting hormones such as growth hormone and testosterone but also help keep your metabolism elevated longer than a typical aerobic workout would.

TOUGH TALK

"If you're depressed and depression is making you gain weight, get it treated. What makes you fat isn't what you eat—it's what's eating you."

—MARC C. DAVIS, *MEN'S HEALTH* BELLY-OFF CLUB MEMBER, ON LOSING 168 POUNDS

AT THE GYM

Who Works Here, Anyway?

You don't need a Ph.D. in exercise science to work the front desk, but people giving advice at a health club should have credentials.

Training: Checking certification is the only way to weed out the dumbest of the dumbbell brigade. Best bets: a degree in exercise science, plus a training certification from the National Strength and Conditioning Association, American College of Sports Medicine, or American Council on Exercise. He'd better not have a belly, either.

▶ Early in the conversation, a trainer should ask about your goals, exercise experience, health history, and physical limitations.

▶ Ideally, a trainer will spend at least a half-hour with you before he starts designing a program, says Miklos Horvath, C.S.C.S., fitness director of the Healthplex Sports Club in Springfield, Pennsylvania.

▶ Make sure he gives you a written program so you can do it without his help.

Nutrition: Anyone offering nutrition advice should have "R.D." after his or her name. Leave if he tries to push supplements.

Massage: Even the masseuses should be able to produce some proof of training, no matter how cute they are.

Let Your Shorts Hide Your Shortcomings

5 Ways to Look Better at the Gym

Beer guts, stubby legs, second heads. It's hard hiding our body problems—especially at the gym, where we wear next to nothing. Fortunately, fashion can help.

PROBLEM 1:
You're short.

Biggest mistake: A black-and-red striped T-shirt with black shorts.
Solution: Long pants and solid-colored shirts in lighter shades. "An absence of distracting colors and patterns takes the focus off your body, allowing you to appear taller," says Brian Boyé, *Men's Health* fashion director. Avoid horizontal stripes—they'll make you look stocky.

PROBLEM 2:
You're very tall.

Biggest mistake: A tank top and short shorts. You'll be all body and no clothes.
Solution: Horizontal stripes. Best bet: a multicolored, long-sleeved rugby shirt. It'll emphasize the width of your body, not the height, says Boyé. For the lower body, stick with long pants.

PROBLEM 3:
You have skinny legs.

Biggest mistake: Baggy Bermudas.
Solution: Cotton shorts that end midthigh. Shorts that are too long or too short emphasize your toothpicks.

PROBLEM 4:
You have narrow shoulders.

Biggest mistake: A tank top.
Solution: A light-colored, short-sleeved T-shirt with sleeves that extend in one piece to the neckline will enhance shoulder width. Baseball shirts will create the illusion that your shoulders are bigger than they actually are. Dark shorts or long pants also help, says Boyé. "They narrow the hips and broaden the shoulders."

PROBLEM 5:
You have a beer belly.

Biggest mistake: A white, tight warmup suit—unless you're singing "Stayin' Alive."
Solution: Dark colors. They're slimming. For shirts, stick with black, dark blue, and deep shades of gray in lightweight materials that wick moisture. Choose shorts two shades lighter than your shirt; the lighter hue will draw people's attention down and away from your gut. Shorts with white vertical side stripes will make you look even leaner.

—LISA JONES AND ANDREW TABER

BUILD

PART THREE

MUSCLE

We'll state the obvious: Build muscle and you'll look better, be stronger, live healthier, and have better sex. Luckily, the basic science of muscle growth isn't all that complicated. Make your muscles work harder and they'll come back bigger and stronger.

You can work those muscles in a number of ways. And we've got a bunch of them right here.

In fact, we're going to show you so many ways to keep your muscles guessing that they'll never get bored. And neither will you.

MH • QUIZ

How Fit Are You?

If you're like a lot of guys, your definition of fitness revolves around an elusive flat gut and an ability to play an hour of lunchtime ball without keeling over. Well, as much as we hate to say it, you need more than that.

Do you already have what you need? Take this quiz to find out. Then turn the page and get to work.

1. I can touch my toes.
   ☐ Yes ☐ No

2. I have balanced strength.
   ☐ Yes ☐ No

3. I can do more than 27 pushups in 1 minute.
   ☐ Yes ☐ No

4. My resting heart rate is below 60.
   ☐ Yes ☐ No

5. I can walk 2 miles in 28 minutes.
   ☐ Yes ☐ No

6. I can stand on one foot for 10 seconds.
   ☐ Yes ☐ No

7. I can kick Jack LaLanne's butt.
   ☐ How would I know?

Extra Credit: I'm a sex-twice-a-week guy.
   ☐ Yes ☐ No

WHAT YOUR ANSWERS SAY ABOUT YOU

1. Sit on the floor with your left leg straight in front of you and your right leg bent, with the foot tucked against your left thigh so that your legs make a figure 4. Reach your left arm toward your toes, as far as you can. If you're between 20 and 41 years old and you can touch your toes with your fingertips, you have average flexibility. You can reach your wrist to your toes? Good going, Gumby. Once you're over 41, just touching your ankle means you have average flexibility. Reaching to your toes is really good.

If your muscles are as tight as J Lo's buns, try stretching for 10 minutes a day. First warm up your muscles by walking or jogging slowly for about 10 minutes. Then stretch to the point where you feel a slight tug in your muscles, holding the position for 30 seconds. (For specific stretches, see Stretch Your Assets on page 50.)

2. We don't mean one-armed handstands on a two-by-four. We mean balanced strength in opposing muscle groups, such as your biceps and triceps, or hamstrings and quads. With uneven strength, you may wind up placing a greater load on the weaker muscle. The result? You'll get hurt.

Most men overdo pushing exercises like bench presses and squats, so it's rare to find a guy with balanced muscular strength. Your biceps and triceps should have a 1:1 strength ratio. That means if you can curl a 50-pound barbell 10 times, you should be able to do triceps pushdowns with 50 pounds for 10 repetitions—no fewer, no more.

As for your legs, your quads and hamstrings should have a 3:2 ratio. If you can do 10 leg curls with 65 pounds, you should be able to do exactly 10 leg presses with 100 pounds. If you have uneven strength, customize your workout with weight-lifting exercises that work both opposing muscle groups.

3. The key here is to be able to do more than 27 pushups *with good form.* Good form means your back and legs are straight and your chest lowers to within 6 inches of the floor. If you can't make it past the magic number, you need to build up your triceps, advises New York City–based personal trainer and strength coach Michael Mejia, C.S.C.S. Incorporate dips and close-grip bench presses into your workouts and your pushup performance will improve noticeably. Stronger triceps can also be a bonus in the bedroom. You knew that.

Another good test is the number of pullups you can do. Ten or 11 is not bad. Twelve and above is excellent.

Or test the situps you can do in 2 minutes. More than 60? Good going. Seventy or more is even better.

4. Your heart will beat a fixed number of times before it shuts down. So you don't blow your quota by age 50, you need to keep your resting heart rate below 60 beats per minute, says Harvard Medical School cardiologist Thomas Graboys, M.D.

Check your heart rate in the morning, before you roll out of bed. Find your pulse, count the beats for 15 seconds, then multiply that number by four.

Over time, you can lower your resting heart rate by doing at least four 40-minute aerobic workouts a week. To maintain an effective workout pace, use a heart-rate monitor or keep varying your intensity. For example, run, bike, or row slowly for 3 minutes, go all out for 1 minute, then return to a slower pace, and so on.

5. According to Swedish researchers, a fit 40-year-old man should be able to walk 2 miles in under 30 minutes. If you can cover that ground in less than 28 minutes, you're in excellent shape.

6. Scaling rock walls or skiing fresh powder, you'll need more than brawn to prevent a dangerous spill. Such feats also require exceptional balance. To test yours, simply count how long you can stand on one foot. If you flail about and wobble in less than 10 seconds, try adding yoga or tai chi to your workout routine.

7. LaLanne exercises for 2 hours each day. He weight trains, performs rigorous floor exercises, and does a strenuous water workout, pushing each of his 640 muscles to its limit.

To see if you can keep up with him, try the Hindu jump, a series of exercises he invented: (1) Squat deeply with your feet shoulder-width apart and your butt as close to the floor as possible. Then jump as high you can. (2) Dip your body into a lunge position. Alternate right and left. (3) March in place, lifting each knee chest-high.

Do each move for 30 seconds before moving on to the next. Jack can do six sets. Can you?

Extra Credit: The average guy has sex 1.5 times a week. Fit guys have great sex and more of it. In one study, men who did aerobic exercise reported increased sex drive. They also had 30 percent more sex and 26 percent more orgasms, says study author James R. White, Ph.D., professor emeritus at the University of California, San Diego.

Another study found a strong correlation between a man's physical fitness and his sexual satisfaction.

—MICKIE BARG

BY RICHARD LALIBERTE

Stretch

Stay injury-free and

Few of us look at an example of physical perfection like, say, the model on the cover of this book and think, "I'll bet *he* could reach past his toes." Our appreciation of conditioning generally doesn't stretch much beyond his abs and biceps.

That's understandable. It's also unfortunate, because flexibility is extremely important—especially for men. "In my experience, men's muscles tend to be much tighter than women's," says William D. Bandy, Ph.D., P.T., professor of physical therapy at the University of Central Arkansas in Conway. For active men in particular, that can cause problems. For example:

- ▶Stiff muscles that are subjected to sudden elongation during exercise or sports can more easily become torn or strained.
- ▶Muscle tightness can cause pain elsewhere in the body. Tight calves, for example, can cause knee pain, shinsplints, and foot pain. Tense muscle at various points in the lower back can cause pain to radiate throughout the entire torso.
- ▶Lack of flexibility can cause muscular imbalances. A tight hamstring, for example, can make your thighs work harder at keeping your body properly aligned, causing knee pain.

Beyond that, muscle stiffness makes you slow down, move more carefully, and act more tentatively—it's the first way a young man starts to feel like an old one. "Some tightness results from a loss of elasticity with age, but for most people, it's simply because they're inactive," says Michael Kaplan, M.D., Ph.D., director of the Rehabili-

Your Assets

get more from your muscles

tation Team in Catonsville, Maryland. "We're not talking about an unavoidable situation," he says. "People who work at it can stay flexible well into old age."

Requirements for Resilience

"You can be very strong and very fit and still not be flexible," Dr. Kaplan says. The good news? Flexibility is the easiest fitness element to develop. As with other types of training, improvement in flexibility depends on subjecting muscles to more than they're accustomed to, by working them through a range of motion in a controlled and systematic way. But you don't need to add a second workout to what you already do. You merely need 10 extra minutes or so. Follow these guidelines.

Soften up. When muscles are cold, they're stiffer. Light exercise before stretching warms them and makes them more pliable, improving the stretch and reducing the risk of muscle strain. "You shouldn't exercise so much in a warmup that you fatigue yourself before your workout," says Bryant Stamford, Ph.D., director of the health-promotion center at the University of Louisville School of Education. He recommends walking or slowly jogging for 10 minutes or so. "You should just be verging on a light sweat," he says. If the weather is hot and you're already sweating, you can shorten your warmup exercise to about 5 minutes (although going the full 10 minutes won't hurt).

Stretch, don't strain. Extend the muscle far enough to make a difference, but not so far that you cause its fibers to tear. Stretch until

(continued on page 54)

Seven Stretches to Remember

There are plenty of useful stretches, as any yoga course will teach. But a basic overall stretching program need only hit several major muscle groups, particularly in the lower body, where the vast majority of flexibility-related problems occur. Here are some good basic moves that hit all the important areas.

Shoulder stretch

Lie on your back on the floor and point your toes. Extend your arms straight above your face, interlocking your fingers with your palms pointing toward the ceiling.

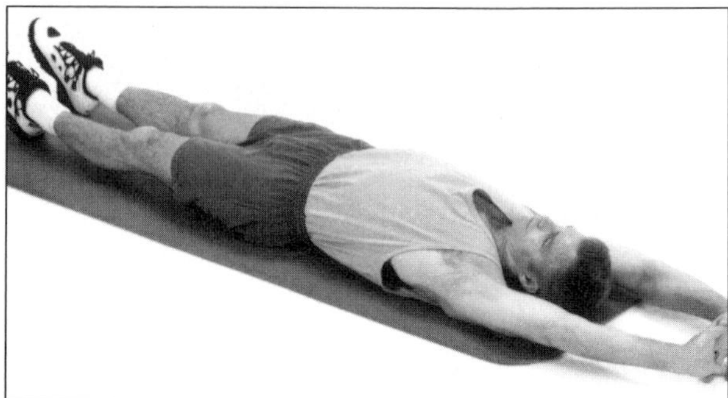

Keeping your arms straight, slowly lower your hands until they rest on the floor behind the crown of your head. Hold.

Hip stretch

Lie on your back with your legs straight. Lace your hands behind your right upper thigh, pull your right knee toward your chest, and hold. Return to the starting position and repeat with your left leg.

Lower-back stretch

Get on your hands and knees, with your hands directly under your shoulders.

Lean back onto your heels, feeling the stretch along your back.

Hamstring stretch

Sit on the edge of a bench or bed with your right leg extended on the bench. Rest your right hand on your right knee, then slowly slide your fingers to your toes, reaching as far as is comfortable. Hold. Repeat on the left side. (This position takes stress off the lower back, unlike similar exercises in which you sit on the floor.)

Groin stretch

Sit on the floor with your legs bent frog-style, the soles of your feet pressed together. Gently push your knees toward the floor with your elbows or hands. Hold.

Calf stretch

Stand on a step with the heel of your right foot extending over the edge.

Lower your right heel below the step until you feel a tug. Hold, then repeat with your left heel.

Thigh stretch

Stand touching a wall or chair for support. Bending your right knee, grab your right foot with your left hand and pull your foot up so that your heel presses against your buttocks. Hold, and repeat with your left leg.

you feel a slight tug—don't push beyond that point.

Put muscles on hold. Hold each stretch for 30 seconds. In studies, Bandy has found that the length of time you hold a stretch has a direct bearing on improved flexibility. Holding for 15 seconds is no better than not stretching at all. Holding for 30 seconds has significant benefit, with measurable weekly improvements. Holding for 60 seconds, however, provides no greater benefit than 30 seconds.

Banish bouncing. Stretches should be slow and steady, not fast and jerky. Some athletes such as gymnasts do use bounce stretches, but only because their bodies already are extremely elastic. Bounce stretches pose a particular potential for injury because when you lengthen a muscle, electrical impulses involuntarily signal it to snap back in a contraction. "The body actively resists overstretching," Bandy says. Stretching too far too fast puts excessive strain on muscles; it's the difference between bending a tree branch slowly and giving it a hard snap. Slow, steady stretches over time make muscles adapt to ever-greater lengthening.

Philosophies of Flex

Here in the Western world, we don't get too excited about flexibility, unless it has to do with the God-given talents of Katarina Witt. In the East, however, flexibility is practically a religion. You can benefit from two of the best-known Eastern mind-and-movement disciplines without subscribing to their spiritual and philosophical tenets.

▶**Yoga.** Its image is that of incense-burning mystics in flowing robes, but not all yoga is about contemplating the universe. Practicing it involves moving your body through a range of poses that not only increase flexibility but also build strength, balance, speed, and endurance. Traditional yoga emphasizes breathing, with poses held for sustained periods, which allows plenty of time to, well, contemplate the universe. However, one form of yoga, ashtanga (also known as power yoga), keeps you moving fluidly through poses without pausing, providing an intense workout.

▶**Tai chi.** The grace and control of tai chi initially was inspired by animal movements. It's a kind of slow-motion calisthenics in which you're supposed to be relaxed yet fully aware of your body as it moves through a variety of positions. Tai chi is categorized as a martial art, although there's nothing explosive or aggressive about it. Rather, the discipline extols quiet, inner strength. As with yoga, balance and breathing are important, and its benefits include increased flexibility, muscle tone—and maybe even wisdom.

It's tough to learn yoga or tai chi by looking at pictures or reading descriptions. The best form of instruction is to get lessons from somebody whose moves you can follow and whose coaching can ensure good technique. Look in the Yellow Pages under *Yoga*, *Martial arts*, or *Karate*, or check with the local YMCA.

BY ETHAN BOLDT

8 ESSENTIAL READING

MUSCLE in a Minute

In the lost and wasted moments of the day, build muscles that show

You have time to exercise. It's the prep work that's the problem. Gather your gear, drive to the gym, navigate the reception desk and locker room, warm up, cool down, stretch, shower, dress, and drive home—you invest more time accommodating exercise than actually working out. And we didn't even factor in all the time spent posing in the locker room.

We've found plenty of exercises you can do without all that wasted time. These moves take only moments to pump you up or calm you down, and they contribute to your overall strength, flexibility, posture, and muscle.

Best of all, they fit into the pockets of time hidden throughout the day: when you're between tasks at work, walking the dog, getting

ready for bed. On the busiest day of your life, you'll still have time to squeeze all of them in.

6:15 A.M.: Wake Up and Smell the Abs

You wake up in the morning starving and dehydrated. That's the downside. The upside is that your abs are about as visible as they're going to be all day. So take advantage: Do these two abdominal exercises as soon as you wake up—hey, you don't even have to get out of bed for the first one. You'll strengthen the muscles that help you maintain good posture throughout the day, says Jim Liston, C.S.C.S., a Los Angeles strength-and-conditioning coach.

Lying vacuum. Lie on your back in bed and try to suck your belly button all the way back to your spine. While you're at it, try to tighten up the muscles on the sides of your midsection, too. Hold for 10 seconds while you take shallow breaths. Try it three times.

Bridge (see photo on page 55). Get out of bed and lie facedown on the floor (assuming the floor is carpeted; if not, lie on a mat or rug). Prop yourself up so your weight is on your toes, forearms, and hands. Your body should form a straight line from head to heels. Don't let your chest or stomach sag toward the floor. You have to tighten all your muscles to hold this position, with your abs and the muscles between your shoulders doing the hardest work. Again, hold for 10 seconds while breathing, and do three repetitions.

6:29 A.M.: Dry Your Back, Save Your Shoulders

The next time you get out of the shower and towel off, add this easy, two-part stretch. It will help combat the tightness that develops in your shoulders when you hunch over a keyboard all day, says Darren Steeves, C.S.C.S., a trainer in Halifax, Nova Scotia.

Towel stretch. Grab the ends of the towel with your right hand behind your head and your left hand at the middle of your back. Gently pull down with your left hand until you feel a good stretch in your right shoulder and triceps. Hold for 15 to 30 seconds.

Then pull up with your right hand until you feel a stretch in your left shoulder, and hold that for 15 to 30 seconds.

Repeat two or three times, slowly going from one stretch to the other. Reverse hand positions and repeat two or three more times.

7:15 A.M.: Walk the Dog, Bulletproof Your Body

Your body has muscles that move it and muscles that stabilize it as it moves. "Your stabilizing muscles get weakest fastest, and that sets you up for debilitating injuries," says physical therapist Mike Clark, C.S.C.S., a trainer in Phoenix. So when your dog is on the leash, you should work on your stabilizers.

On the way to his favorite bush, do a set of walking lunges for 20 feet or so. After he does his dirty work, do another set on the way back. You'll work the stabilizing muscles in your calves, inner and outer thighs, and midsection.

7:45 A.M.: Take a Stance, Protect Your Knees

Thanks to the ab and shoulder exercises you've already done, you're so invigorated that you're actually running ahead of schedule. You can use those free minutes to develop your leg muscles.

The two stances on the next page come from the world of martial arts; fighters use them to build strength and stamina in their lower bodies. These two are particularly beneficial to the muscles surrounding your knees, increasing their stability, according to Adrian Crook, conditioning and flexibility consultant for the Detroit Lions.

Horse stance
Hold for up to 60 seconds, then shift to the bow-and-arrow stance.

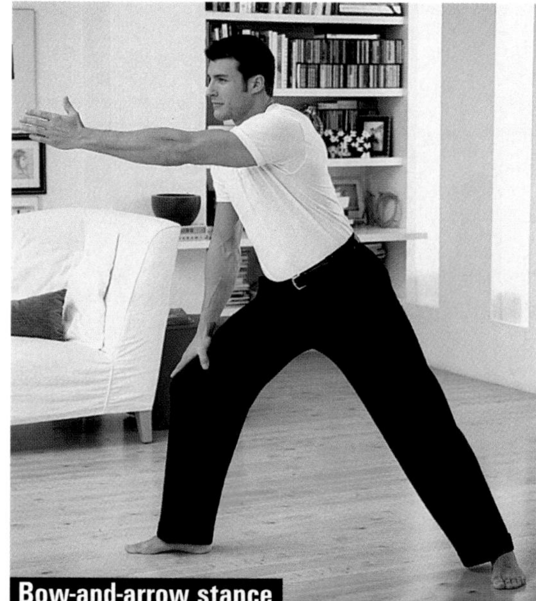
Bow-and-arrow stance
Hold for up to 60 seconds, return to the horse stance for 60 seconds, then repeat the bow-and-arrow stance in the opposite direction for 60 seconds.

9:45 A.M.: Turn Pugnacious, K.O. Your Assignments

It's still too early, your brain is still foggy, and if the first six cups of coffee aren't helping, why put all your faith in a seventh? So leave your office, walk out behind the building, and start kicking some ass.

Figuratively, that is. A quick shadowboxing routine will give you a shot of adrenaline and raise your body temperature a bit, opening blood vessels and allowing more oxygen into your brain. But if you're going to do it, you may as well do it right, suggests Nick Delury, who trains amateur and professional boxers at the Boxing Connection and Fitness Center in Yonkers, New York. You'll avoid injury and scare anyone who discovers you.

Put up your dukes. First, put up your fists, keep your elbows down, and get up on the balls of your feet. As you bounce back and forth, shifting your weight and developing a rhythm, breathe in through your nose and out through your mouth.

Work the jab. If you're right-handed, jab with your left. Make sure your knuckles are parallel to the floor at the end of each punch. Go slowly—you can injure an elbow by flinging punches at full velocity with cold muscles.

Develop combinations. Try two jabs with your left, then a straight right hand, then a left hook, then a right uppercut. Or any variation on that theme. "It's like lotto—look

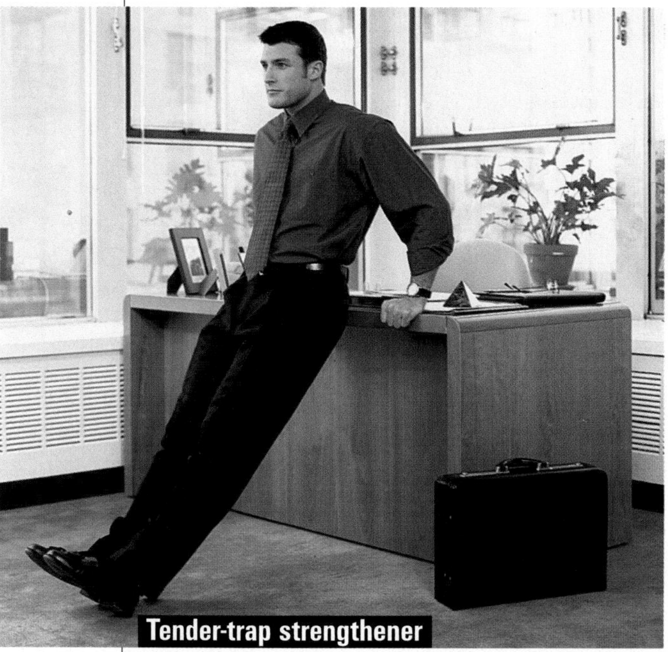

Tender-trap strengthener

1. Get out of your chair. Turn your back to your desk, rest your hands on the edge of it, and bend your elbows a bit (shoot for a 120-degree angle, if you want to be really technical). Your heels should be on the floor.

2. Without bending your elbows any more, lower your butt toward the floor, then lift yourself back to the original position. This should feel like a bench dip, except your elbows stay in the same position and your body moves only 4 to 5 inches. That makes your lower traps do most of the work.

how many combinations of those four numbers you can pick," suggests Delury.

11:57 A.M.: Dip at Your Desk, Build Your Back

It's 3 minutes before you're due to meet a client for lunch. You'd like to present yourself as a confident, square-shouldered guy, but your back isn't cooperating. The problem is with the lower portion of your trapezius muscle, in the middle of your back. Its job is to depress your shoulder blades, or hold them down. But hunching your shoulders all day leaves your lower trapezius as weak and inflexible as a rubber band that's always stretched but never allowed to return to its original length.

For a quick fix, Liston suggests the maneuver pictured above.

6:45 P.M.: Walk the Dog (Again), Unleash Your Hip Flexors

This time when you cruise the block, make use of a nearby fire hydrant (preferably not one he's just liquidated) to stretch out your hip flexors. These muscles, which sit on the front of your pelvis, have been shortened and tightened from a full day of sitting.

Hip-flexor stretch. Plant your left foot on the hydrant, then lean toward it, bending your left leg while keeping your right leg straight. Feel the stretch on the front of your right hip. Hold for 30 seconds, then switch legs.

10:45 P.M.: Fall Asleep with a Wave of Your Hands

At the end of the day, some guys wind down faster than a street vendor's Rolex; others need some time to relax. If you're in the second group, try this easy exercise from the ancient discipline of tai chi, suggests Linda Morrissey, an instructor at Nyack Kung Fu/T'ai Chi Academy in New York. You'll get so much relaxation you just may need adult diapers.

Waving hands like clouds. First thing: Make sure the blinds are closed. Okay. Now stand with your feet shoulder-width apart, head up and eyes forward. Take a deep breath. Raise your left arm to chest height, palm down, as if resting it on your own personal cloud. Support the bottom of the cloud with your right hand, which should be palm up.

As you slowly turn to your left, twisting at the waist, lower your left arm to release the cloud, and raise your right arm to chest height. Exhale as you do this.

Then inhale and turn slowly to your right, lowering your right arm and raising your left. Repeat six to nine times. Each repetition should last as long as you need to take a deep breath and exhale.

If that doesn't work, simply turn to your wife, ask her how her day was, and exhale slowly. You should be asleep within 5 minutes.

PEAK performance

Personalize It

When you're on tight deadlines, consider signing up with a personal trainer—an exercise expert who can help you get impressive results fast. Personal trainers don't give away their time, but their rates aren't necessarily stratospheric, either. Most charge between $30 and $200 for a 50-minute session. The rate may include the use of a local gym or health club, or the trainer may work with you at home.

The advantage of working with a personal trainer is that you get personalized attention, plus you're able to work at your own pace. Here's what experts suggest you do before making the hire.

Cast a wide network. **You can always peruse the Yellow Pages, but a better way to find a good trainer is to ask your friends and co-workers if they can recommend anyone. Or ask around at the health club.**

Look for longevity. **Ask prospective trainers how long they've been in business and what their experience is. You're looking for seasoned pros, not beginners trying to break in to a new profession.**

Ask about credentials. **The most reputable programs that certify trainers are the American College of Sports Medicine, the American Council on Exercise, and the National Strength and Conditioning Association. Other good programs include the Cooper Institute for Aerobics Research, the National Academy of Sports Medicine, and the Aerobics and Fitness Association of America.**

Request references. **Good trainers have satisfied customers and won't hesitate to put you in touch with them. Ask to speak to three, at least one of whom should be a guy whose fitness level and goals are similar to yours.**

Take a trial run. **Before signing up for a long-term program, arrange a 1-month trial period. How well you get along with this person will really determine whether you stick with the program or drop out after 2 weeks. If it's not a good match, move on.**

BY LOU SCHULER

ABS for Anyone

If *Men's Health* editors can get them, anyone can. Here's how they did it

If you walked into the offices of *Men's Health,* you'd notice some strange things. First, of course, the odor. Second, the fact that few of our guys look like our cover models. All of us are a bit different from the ideal we put forward. And, of course, so are you.

So we thought, "If we can tell our readers how to lose their bellies and build abs, shouldn't we do these things ourselves?" Seven editors agreed to give it a try. Here is a story of seven men and their search for abdominal perfection—or at least less of the messy fat that covers their abs.

The Flat Man: Tom McGrath

37 years old, 5 foot 10

Vital stats at the beginning:

▶32-inch waist
▶11.5 percent body fat
▶145 pounds

The battle for a bulge

Vital stats at the end:

▶31.5-inch waist
▶8.5 percent body fat
▶145 pounds

The problem:

▶Tom is a dedicated runner. "I was about as chiseled as a small peasant child," he says.

The solutions:

▶In addition to his normal 25 miles of running per week, Tom began doing the following ab workout every third day: hip lifts, clams, oblique crunches, bridge extensions, and back extensions. (For a program you can do, see page 66.)
▶He also cranked out 60 pushups every morning.

The results:

▶Besides the impressive drop in body fat—from 11.5 percent to 8.5 percent—he finally found his abdominal muscles. "My abs really pop when I laugh," Tom says. "So now I laugh a lot when my shirt is off." So do the rest of us.

The Big Man: Ted Spiker

32 years old, 6 foot 2

Vital stats at the beginning:

▶37-inch waist
▶22.8 percent body fat
▶222 pounds

One-third of body fat—gone!

Vital stats at the end:

▶36-inch waist
▶15 percent body fat
▶204 pounds

The problems:

▶Ted carries weight in his hips, butt, and thighs. It makes him a wicked low-post player, but finding pants that fit isn't easy.
▶A doctor once told him he had an "extra gland" in his chest. That physician no longer practices.
▶Two-hour commute; twin boys.

The solutions:

▶New York City–based personal trainer and strength coach Michael Mejia, C.S.C.S., put Ted on a four-times-a-week weight-lifting program, with four sessions of cardiovascular exercise (see workout on page 62 for details).
▶Reading, Massachusetts, nutritionist Elizabeth Ward, R.D., recommended two strategies to curb our big man's huge appetite: drinking 1% instead of fat-free milk to satiate him longer, and measuring 1 cup of the foods he tends to overeat—like cereal and ice cream—then waiting 20 minutes before having more.

The results:

▶Ted had the most eye-opening results of the group, losing almost 8 percentage points of fat in 8 weeks, or about one-third of his total body fat. "I lost more weight doing mostly weight lifting than I did 2 years ago when I ran 5 days a week for 3 months," Ted says.
▶He remained addicted to ice cream. In fact, he ate it every day—and still lost 18 pounds. The only catch was that he ate just 1 cup of low-fat ice cream after dinner—and resisted any other sweets throughout the day.

Belly Off

If you're serious about losing fat, this is the program for you. One *Men's Health* contributing editor, Ted Spiker, used it to ditch more than a third of his body fat in 8 weeks. Here's what to do.

- Lift four times a week, doing each workout twice.
- Two times a week, do 20 to 30 minutes of steady, medium-intensity cardiovascular exercise after weight workouts. Increase the cardio sessions by 5 minutes every 2 weeks.
- Two times a week, on days you don't lift, do interval workouts: Warm up for 5 minutes, then go really hard for 30 seconds. Ease off and go easy for 1½ to 2 minutes, then repeat for a total of 10 to 12 intervals. Cool down for 5 minutes.
- In the upper-body workout, do the exercises in pairs as supersets—one right after the other, no rest. Rest for 30 to 60 seconds between supersets, and do each superset three times.

Upper-Body Workout

EXERCISE		REPETITIONS
Pair 1:	**Dumbbell bench press**	8–10
	Cable row	10–12
Pair 2:	**Lat pulldown**	10–12
	Dumbbell shoulder press	10–12
Pair 3:	**Dip**	8–10
	Upright row	10–12
Pair 4:	**Reverse crunch**	12–15
	Back extension	10–12

- In the lower-body workout (shown), do all five leg exercises, plus the clams, as one giant set—no rest between exercises. Rest for 1½ to 2 minutes after the ordeal, and repeat twice more.

Squat

Leg extension

Stepup

Lower-Body Workout

EXERCISE	REPETITIONS
Squat	10–12
Leg extension	12–15
Stepup	10–12 (each leg)
Leg curl	10–12
Standing calf raise	10–12
Clam	12–15

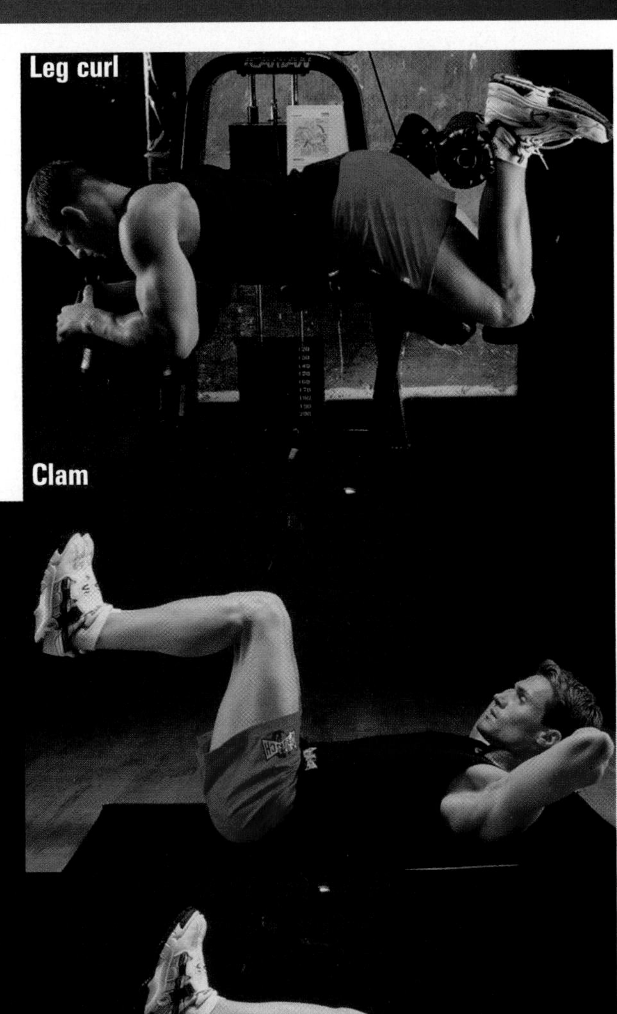

Leg curl

Clam

Standing calf raise

The Skinny Guy: Peter Moore

44 years old, 5 foot 11

Vital stats at the beginning:

▶$31^1/_4$-inch waist
▶15.3 percent body fat
▶150 pounds

Vital stats at the end:

▶31-inch waist
▶14.8 percent body fat
▶153 pounds

He'll settle for a one-pack.

The problems:

▶Peter has one of the most stressful jobs at the magazine. And he runs, and runs, to fight stress. Combine high stress and extended aerobics, and you generate too much cortisol—a hormone that destroys muscle and causes fat to be stored in the midsection.

▶Peter consumes too few calories to create muscle mass.

The solutions:

▶For the midsection, Peter did three sets each of slant-board reverse crunches, back extensions, oblique crunches, and cable crunches.

▶For more overall muscularity, he added three sets of decline pushups (hands on the floor, feet up on a bench) and three sets of pullups.

▶He worked more fat and carbohydrates into his lean diet—cream in the coffee, cheeseburgers at Wendy's, more pasta with olive oil.

The results:

▶Three new pounds of muscle, which his wife enjoyed rubbing. And his 8-year-old began ramming his head into dad's steely abs.

The Former Athlete: Jeff Csatari

39 years old, 5 foot 9

Vital stats at the beginning:

▶36.5-inch waist
▶13.8 percent body fat
▶175 pounds

Vital stats at the end:

▶34.5-inch waist
▶12.6 percent body fat
▶167 pounds

The problems:

▶Like most former small-college football players gone to seed, Jeff has a belly.

▶He also has a weakness for sweets, pizza, and pasta.

▶Launching *Men's Health*'s teen spin-off magazine, *MH-18*, and trying to spend time with his family (he has two little girls) leaves little time for working out.

The solutions:

▶Mejia put Jeff on a three-times-a-week weight-lifting program, alternating upper-body and lower-body workouts. Jeff did three sets of each exercise, with 30 seconds' rest between sets. His upper-body workout consisted of the bench press, cable row, lat pulldown, dumbbell shoulder press, dip, upright row, re-

Two inches off his waist.

verse crunch, and back extension. For his lower body, he did the barbell squat, leg extension, stepup, leg curl, standing calf raise, and abdominal crunch.

▶"I'd rather have you eat a steak than all that pasta," Ward told Jeff. She also suggested he substitute bran cereal and high-fiber, sweet-tasting alternatives such as dried fruits for the cookies and cakes he likes with his morning coffee.

▶At summer barbecues, Jeff followed Ward's advice to start off with a tall glass of ice water and then sip one following any alcoholic beverage he drinks, to cut down on liquid calories.

The results:

▶Chest, arm, and leg muscles, in hibernation since college, returned (but so did a rotator-cuff injury).

▶Thanks to a 2-inch drop in his waist size, 5-year-old daughter Katelyn now sings "I see London, I see France, I see Daddy's underpants" at inopportune times.

The Genetic Mistake: Joe Kita

42 years old, 6 feet

Vital stats at the beginning:

▶33-inch waist
▶11 percent body fat
▶165 pounds

Vital stats at the end:

▶33-inch waist
▶10.2 percent body fat
▶165 pounds

Okay, so his turned out crooked.

The problem:

▶Like most cardio-only guys, Joe is very lean but has little upper-body muscle. The only way to see his abs was to build them first.

The solution:

▶Mejia put Joe on an advanced ab-building program with these five exercises done twice weekly: hanging leg raise, hip lift, oblique crunch, cable crunch, and back extension.

The result:

▶A noticeable six-pack began to emerge after just 4 weeks. "Oddly, my abs turned out crooked," Joe laments. It's a structural anomaly he'll just have to live with.

The Marathon Man: Warren Greene

28 years old, 5 foot 8

At long last, abs.

Vital stats at the beginning:

▶32-inch waist
▶6.6 percent body fat
▶148 pounds

Vital stats at the end:

▶32¾-inch waist
▶3.8 percent body fat
▶150 pounds

The problem:

▶Warren did crunches for years and has never developed any visible abs—this despite annual Boston Marathon runs and virtually no body fat.

The solution:

▶Mejia started Warren with one set of each of these ab exercises on a Swiss ball: jackknife, rotational crunch, weighted crunch, and bridge (held for 30 seconds). Warren quickly worked up to three sets.

The result:

▶Of the four guys trying to build abs, he got the most visible results—after spending just 20 minutes twice a week to exercise them.

Abs On

We'd like to tell you it's easy to get abs the size of French rolls. Unfortunately, we have seven editors who'd swear it isn't true. But a few of our guys did end up with sixish-packs, so we also know it can be done in 8 weeks. All it takes is the right exercises . . . and the sheer panic that comes with knowing you're going to be photographed with your shirt off. Here are the exercises. They should take about 15 minutes; do them twice a week. The panic we'll leave to you.

EXERCISE	REPETITIONS
Hanging leg raise	6–10
Swiss-ball jackknife	6–8
Oblique crunch	10–12 (each side)
Cable crunch	8–12
Swiss-ball bridge	Hold for 15–30 sec

Do three sets. You can do all the sets of a particular exercise—resting for 30 to 60 seconds between sets—before moving on to the next exercise. Or do all five exercises in a circuit without rest between them, for a total of three circuits, resting for 1 to 2 minutes in between.

Hanging leg raise

Swiss-ball jackknife

Oblique crunch

Cable crunch

Swiss-ball bridge

The Beginner:
Hugh O'Neill

48 years old, 5 foot 11

Vital stats at the beginning:
▶38-inch waist
▶24.6 percent body fat
▶185 pounds

Vital stats at the end:
▶36-inch waist
▶24.2 percent body fat
▶177 pounds

The problems:
▶Hugh had never lifted weights in his life, although he ran 15 to 20 miles a week.
▶Following a high-carbohydrate, mostly vegetarian diet to curb his high cholesterol hadn't done his physique any favors. He's 25 percent fat, despite being in decent cardiovascular condition.
▶Hugh drinks juice and wine to the tune of 600 calories a day. No water, either.

The solutions:
▶A basic beginner's program: one set each of eight exercises—10 to 12 repetitions of the upper-body exercises, 12 to 15 repetitions of the lower-body moves. After 4 weeks, Hugh started doing three sets of each exercise.
▶Ward had him add chicken to his pasta-and-vegetable dinners to increase his protein intake.
▶He cut way, way back on the juice and alcohol, and added 32 ounces of water daily.

At least he stopped snoring!

The results:
▶Hugh's strength increased rapidly, and by the end of the 8 weeks he was doing biceps curls and shoulder presses with 25-pound dumbbells.
▶He felt that his posture improved and his arms got bigger.
▶The weirdest result: Hugh stopped snoring. We're expecting a thank-you note from Mrs. O'Neill any time now.

BY ADAM CAMPBELL, C.S.C.S.

Home-Grown MUSCLE

Build the perfect home gym—and the perfect body—on any budget

You can build as much muscle in your spare bedroom as you can in a high-priced health club, and on the following pages we're going to show you how to do it. We found the best home-workout equipment on the market, then put together three great home gyms for men on three different budgets—from money-is-no-object to money-is-a-very-big-object.

And we didn't stop there: We got strength coach Craig Ballantyne, C.S.C.S., of Canada's McMaster University, to design a full-body workout program for each home gym. So if you're looking for a way to get back in shape without waiting in lines or listening to other people's music, set up one of these home gyms and start your program. The next pool of sweat you lie in will be all your own.

Note: The products and prices mentioned were accurate at the time this publication went to press. They may be subject to change; check with the manufacturer.

The $100 Gym: Big Muscle on a Small Budget

These are the bare essentials: flat bench, barbell, weight plates, jump rope. It may not seem like much, but it's the no-nonsense prison-yard equipment that'll make you look like John Coffey in *The Green Mile*. Well, maybe not that big. But you can look better than Tom Hanks, at least, if you devote yourself to these workout basics. Added bonus: Once you outgrow this stuff, you've shown that you can stick to a program, which should help convince your wife that you really need the more expensive stuff.

▶**Flat bench.** It wasn't fun, but after combing dozens of yard sales, we found a $50 bench that was in one piece and wide enough to fit a grown man. If you go this route, make sure the bench is at least 10 inches wide, feels sturdy, and doesn't wobble.

▶**110 pounds of weights.** The barbell is smaller than you'll find in your local gym, and the weights probably aren't the same, but your muscles won't know the difference. And the price couldn't be better: $50 at www.newyorkbarbells.com.

▶**Leather speed rope.** We chose this $10 rope from www.titleboxing.com because (1) it's tangle-free; (2) the weighted handles can be removed, allowing you to vary your workout; and (3) we like leather.

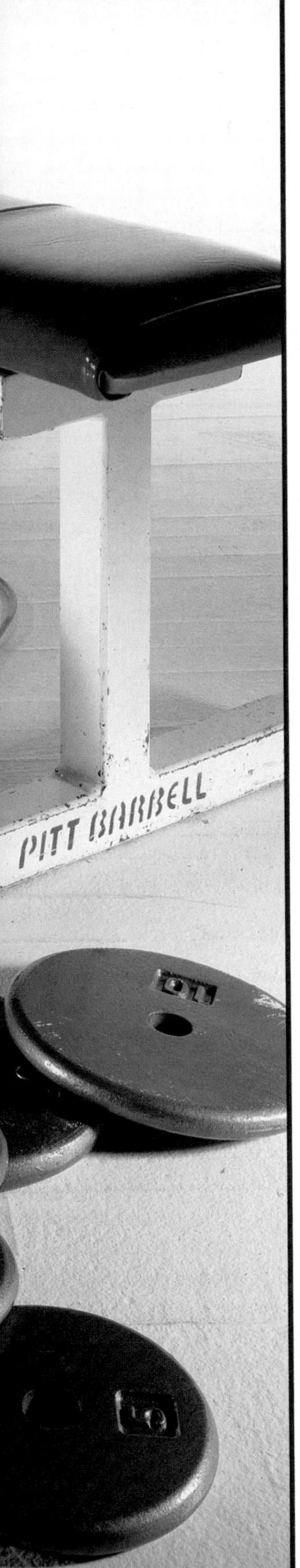

The $100 Workout (Beginner Level)

Do one set of 10 repetitions of each exercise twice a week, and add one or two warmup sets of the exercises marked with an asterisk (*). Increase the weight you use each week. When you can't increase weight any more, bump up the repetitions to 12 to 15 per set, then add more sets. When you can do three sets of 15 bench presses or bent-over rows with all the weights in your set, buy more weights.

Step-back lunge*
Bent-over row*

Bench press*
Biceps curl

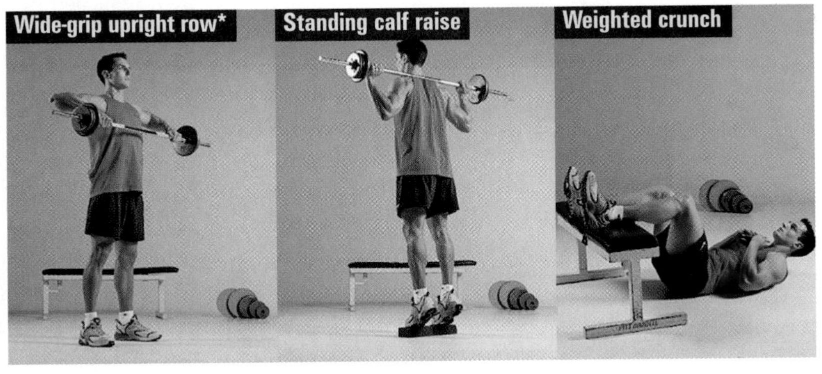
Wide-grip upright row*
Standing calf raise
Weighted crunch

The $1,000 Gym: Maximum Power, Medium Price

Gyms used to be places where it was okay to grunt and sweat and occasionally let a half-ton of iron slip from your chalked fingers and fall to the floor. Do that in a health club nowadays and 90-pound aerobics instructors will taunt you through their headset microphones. But for about a grand, you can create your own heaving haven.

▶**Body Solid power rack.** We liked this $279 power rack mostly because, for the price and quality, we couldn't find anything that could beat it. It allows you to do heavy bench presses and squats without a spotter (remember to set the safety bars). Order it at www.fitnessfactory.com.

▶**Plate-load lat attachment.** While you're logged on to fitnessfactory.com, drop $239 on this. It comes with a high- and low-pulley system that lets you do pulldowns, triceps extensions, and cable curls.

▶**Flat/incline/decline bench.** This $219 bench allows you to hit body parts at multiple angles to maximize your muscle. It's also available at fitnessfactory.com.

▶**Weight set.** At $120 on www.newyorkbarbells.com, this 7-foot Olympic barbell and 300-pound weight set costs less than the introductory offer at the average gym.

▶**EZ-curl bar.** Because EZ-curl bars are excellent for isolating the biceps and building great guns, we had to have it. Plus, fitnessfactory.com offered it for only $24.

▶**DuraBall.** This Swiss ball is antiburst tested for up to 1,000 pounds. Get it for $40, from www.paulchekseminars.com.

▶**Performance Traveler trainer.** Okay, we cheated a little: We included a $100 stationary trainer in our $1,000 budget, but not the bike. This one from www.performancebike.com folds for convenient storage, sets up easily, and with seven levels of magnetic resistance, provides a great workout.

▶**T-bar platform and Lat Blaster.** We really like this combo from the Fitness Factory Web site. Connect one end of an Olympic barbell to the T-bar platform and the other end to the Lat Blaster, add weight, and lift. Spend just $90 and a few minutes a week, and you'll have a back wide enough to show movies on.

The $1,000 Workout (Advanced Level)

This workout isn't for just anybody. But if you've left enough sweat in the weight room to fill the neighbor's pool, try this push/pull split routine. The benefit: balanced muscle, to prevent injury and provide maximum power. And you'll look good coming and going. Do three sets of 6 to 10 repetitions of each exercise. For exercises marked with an asterisk (*), do one or two warmup sets of 8 to 10 with a lighter weight before tackling your heavy sets. Do each workout twice a week.

Workout A (Push)

Wide-stance squat*
Barbell lunge*
Incline press*

Lying triceps extension
Swiss-ball crunch

Workout B (Pull)

Deadlift*
T-bar row*
Lat pulldown

Shrug
Biceps curl

The $10,000 Gym: A Setup So Sweet You Could Sell Memberships

One of the joys of achieving some success in life is that you can start having things your way. Want to work out at 3:00 in the morning while listening to atonal jazz? Of course not—nobody does. But wouldn't it be cool to have, in your own home, workout gear that performs as well as—and looks better than—the equipment you find in health clubs?

▶**Vectra On-Line 1600.** This impressed us because you can release a stabilizing mechanism to make exercising on it feel more like using a barbell than like working out on a conventional weight machine. Doing so gives you the muscle-building qualities of the former with the comfort and safety of the latter. If you can spare $3,625, call (800) 283-2872 for a dealer.

▶**Vectra vertical dumbbell racks.** If you're going to spend 10 grand, everything may as well match. That's why we added these $750 ($250 each) dumbbell racks, also by Vectra.

▶**Cap barbell SDR Hex dumbbells.** These have contour grips, which makes them easier to hold on to than standard grips. Plus, the dumbbell heads are rubber-coated to protect your hardwood floors in case you drop them. Which, after paying $2,625 ($1.25 a pound; 5 to 100 pounds in 5-pound increments), you probably won't want to do. Find a dealer by calling (800) 225-0505.

▶**StairMaster StepMill 5000 PT.** Four revolving 6-inch steps, a hand-grip heart-rate monitor . . . the only thing missing is a couple of gym bunnies working out next to you. But if you can handle the $2,350 price tag at www.stairmaster.com, why not spring for the bunnies, too?

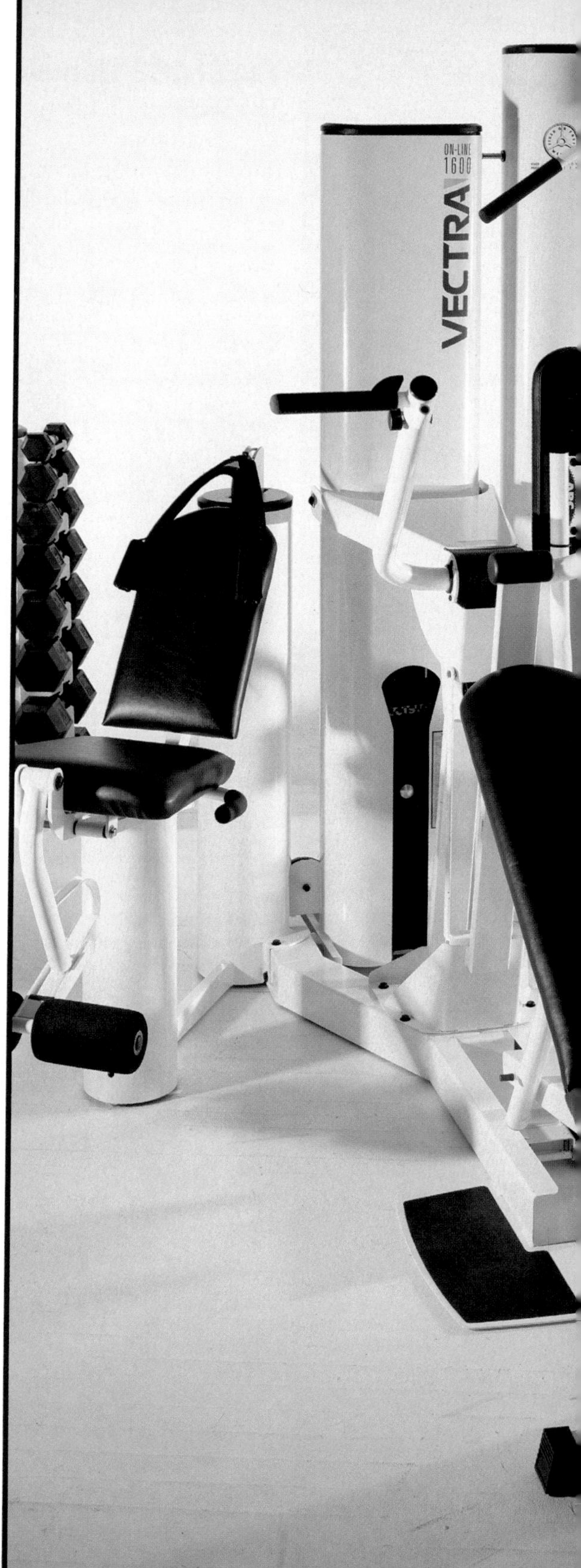

The $10,000 Workout (Intermediate Level)

If you can afford this gym, you're probably older and wiser than most of us. So here's a routine for men who don't move quite as well as they used to. Do one to three sets of 8 to 15 repetitions of each exercise. If you want to do more sets, do three to five sets of the first five exercises on one day, and three to five sets of the last four exercises the next day.

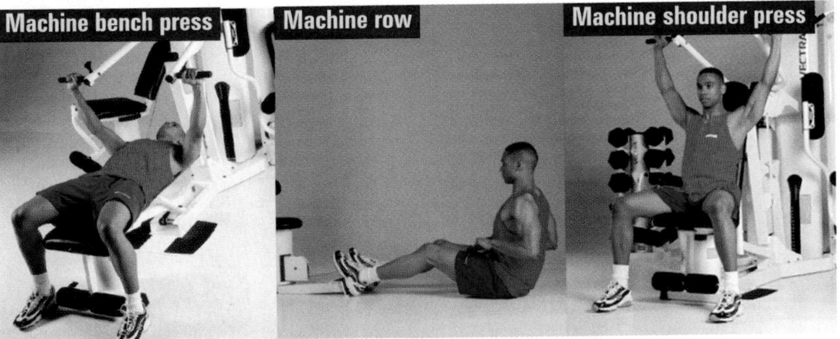

BY LOU SCHULER

Look GREAT Naked

Need to look beddable by 7:00 P.M.? Start inflating your muscles at 6:00 P.M. with this workout

There's always that moment, after the post-workout shower, when you can't help but notice how godlike you've suddenly become. "If only Charlize could see me now," you think. But then, what would she be doing in the men's locker room?

With the right workout, you can be your date's personal Adonis, says exercise scientist Tim Ziegenfuss, Ph.D., C.S.C.S., of Kent State University in Ohio. "The positive effects of a workout normally last 2 to 3 hours," he notes.

A good pre-date workout will force blood away from internal organs and into your muscles. You may also enjoy a temporary surge in testosterone (a noted wood preservative).

"Grab these, will ya? My arm's getting tired."

The Workout

Do one to three sets of 8 to 15 repetitions of each of these exercises, using lighter weights than usual and trying for a few more repetitions.

BENCH PRESS (to produce a tugging at the buttonholes). Lie on your back on a flat bench. Grab a bar with an overhand grip and hold it over your chin, at arm's length. Slowly lower the bar to your chest. Pause, then push it back up until your arms are straight.
Alternatives: dumbbell bench press, incline bench press

SQUAT (for the rear view). With a bar resting on your upper trapezius muscles, slowly lower your body as if you were sitting back onto a chair, keeping your back in its natural alignment. When your thighs are parallel to the floor, pause, then stand up.
Alternatives: leg press, leg-extension/leg-curl combo

SEATED ROW (helps you stand straight and tall). At a seated-row station, grab the bar with an overhand grip, your arms extended in front of you. Sit up straight and pull your shoulders back. Pull the bar to your abdomen. Pause, then slowly return to the starting position.
Alternatives: bent-over dumbbell row, machine row

BICEPS CURL (for when you offer her your arm). Grab an EZ-curl bar with an underhand grip. Stand with your arms extended down so the bar rests against your thighs. Keep your upper arms tucked against your sides. Curl the bar as high as you can without letting your upper arms move forward. Pause, then return to the starting position.
Alternative: dumbbell biceps curl (any variation)

TRICEPS PRESSDOWN (to make your arms look big). Attach a straight bar to the high pulley of a cable station. Pull the bar down until your elbows are bent 90 degrees. Stand straight, with your upper arms tucked in. Push the bar down until your arms are straight, while keeping the rest of your body still. Keep your upper arms against your sides. Pause, then slowly allow the bar to rise until your elbows are again bent 90 degrees.
Alternatives: bench dip or parallel-bar dip, dumbbell triceps extension (any variation)

Make Dinner Serve You

The wrong menu selection can negate your entire workout. "A high-fat meal can make you tired and sluggish. So can a meal really high in carbohydrates but lacking protein," says Tim Ziegenfuss, whose name means "flaming sheets" in Flemish. And excess salt on anything will make you retain water and take the edges off your pumped-up muscles.

The perfect post-workout/precoital dinner is a piece of grilled chicken or fish with vegetables (broccoli is best), along with a mixed-green salad with an olive oil–based dressing.

And have a glass of wine. "Alcohol causes fluid shifts and dilates blood vessels close to the skin," Ziegenfuss says. This can make you look even leaner by pumping more blood into your muscles and pulling water away from underneath your skin.

Dessert? Have them wrap it up to go. It'll taste better in bed. Pretty much everything does.

Trainer's Forum

with MICHAEL MEJIA

SET POINTS

Q What's the difference between a superset, compound set, triset, and giant set? Should I be doing any of them?

K. Y., BROKEN ARROW, OKLAHOMA

A A superset refers to exercising two opposing muscle groups consecutively, without any rest. So, you might do a set of bench presses followed by a set of cable rows.

A compound set exercises the same muscle group in two consecutive sets, without rest. You might do a set of machine military presses immediately followed by a set of dumbbell front raises.

As the name suggests, a triset refers to performing three consecutive exercises for the same muscle group, with no rest between them. For example, you could start with a set of shoulder presses, move right into a set of upright rows, then finish with a set of lateral raises.

A giant set involves doing *more* than three exercises for the same muscle group. You might go from squats to leg presses to lunges, and finish with leg extensions.

All are excellent ways to increase the intensity of your workouts. They can also reduce your training time dramatically.

Whether or not you should use these techniques depends largely on your goals. Supersets work equally well in strength programs (which use heavier weights) and hypertrophy programs (which use lighter weights). Trisets and giant sets are better suited to lighter-weight workouts because they improve muscular endurance and growth rather than strength. Supersets are fine for beginning lifters, but the other two could lead to injury if you skimp on technique as your muscles get tired.

TOUGH TALK

"The results of a recent survey revealed that only 37 percent of high school students get regular vigorous exercise, and of that group 26 percent considered filling out the survey to be vigorous exercise."

—COMEDIAN DENNIS MILLER

TRAINING

Secrets of the *Men's Health* Gym

Our fitness director, Lou Schuler, knows that every job has its perks. Even the guy riding the garbage truck scores an occasional talking bass. Lou? He gets to talk to the smartest trainers in the world. Here, he shares some of the best tips he's heard.

▶**Set a record every workout.** "The Guinness folks aren't going to call when you curl 65 pounds five times. But if you've never done it before, it's your personal record."

▶**Know your body.** "Recently, on the Internet, I found a workout program that was brilliant in every respect—except I couldn't do it. It required squats three times a week, and my knees aren't up to that. So I found a different workout. The lesson: Don't do what the other guys do; do what works for your body."

▶**Don't confuse pain with productivity.** "A good new workout will often create soreness, but that soreness should be in the belly of the muscle, not in the elbow, knee, hip, shoulder, or lower-back joints. If you feel equal soreness on both sides of your body, you've done something right. If it's on one side but not the other, and it restricts movement, you're injured."

▶**Never do a garbage set.** "Every set should have a purpose. It's either a warmup (preparing your muscles for harder work to follow), a work set (increasing strength or muscle mass), or a back-off set (a higher-repetition set meant to more deeply exhaust muscle fibers). Some extremely advanced workouts are based on pure volume (5 sets of 5, 10 sets of 10), and in those cases the volume is intended to create a specific effect. But if you don't know what a set is supposed to accomplish, don't bother with it."

COMEBACK QUARTERBACK

Q I haven't played sports since college, but now I want to play touch football on weekends. What's the *least* I can do to get myself in shape?

T. R., AQUASCO, MARYLAND

A The first thing you need to do is analyze the specific demands of the activity. Football is an anaerobic sport, meaning it relies on short, repetitive bursts of maximal or near-maximal energy. Unfortunately, that means those 5-mile jaunts you do on the treadmill every other day will be little help in preparing you to play. You need to increase your training intensity with sprints, preferably ones that involve quick changes in direction.

After a thorough warmup, try running all-out for 6 to 8 seconds, throwing in some quick changes of direction. Then rest by simulating a 30- to 45-second walk back to the huddle. Repeat this drill 10 to 15 times, three times a week for 2 weeks, then add 5 more sprints for the next 2 weeks. In a month's time, you should have the wind to run with anyone on your block.

Sprinting this way is pretty strenuous work, so you'll need to improve your flexibility to reduce your likelihood of injury. Be sure to include stretches for your hamstrings, quadriceps, hip flexors, and calves both before and, especially, after you train. And do all running drills outside on a grass field to ease the strain on your hips, knees, and ankles.

Take Your Workout on Vacation

10 Ways to Lose Fat and Gain Muscle without Even Trying

Worried about going away on vacation and forfeiting all the progress you've made in your quest for lean muscle? Fear not. There are lots of ways you can burn calories just having fun. And isn't fun the whole point?

1 *Playing in the water (with a ball or Frisbee)*

Muscles worked: All major muscle groups—shoulders and abs in particular.

Calories burned: 1 hour of thrashing = 570 calories.

2 *Souvenir shopping*

Muscles worked: Legs and arms (all that bag-toting).

Calories burned: 1 hour spent wandering = 200 to 300 calories.

For a real workout, buy heavy stuff like, say, cases of the local microbrew. Or find stores on hills.

3 *Vacation sex*

Muscles worked: Shoulders, chest, pelvis, legs, and abs.

Calories burned: Nice and slow for 1 hour = 79 calories; in the groove for 1 hour = 103 calories; full steam ahead for 1 hour = 119 calories.

If you turn an hour into an all-nighter, you'll burn even more. Do the math.

4 *Beach walking with partner*

Muscles worked: All the muscles of the legs and torso.

Calories burned: 1-hour walk = 300 to 400 calories.

If you walk in soft sand, you'll burn more calories and your leg muscles will work harder than when walking on the hard stuff by the water. Vacationing in Rio? The soft sand is where all those thong-clad Brazilian women lie in the sun anyway. Pretend you're looking for exotic shells.

5 *Tennis*

Muscles worked: All major muscle groups, especially shoulders (one more than the other), trunk, and legs.

Calories burned: 1-hour game of singles = 635 calories; doubles = 470.

An all-over workout that's great for agility and coordination. Stop-start in nature, but if you're equally matched with your opponent, you'll get a good workout.

6 Playing video games

Muscles worked: Fingers, thumbs, and forearms.

Calories burned: Not many more than your resting rate of calorie expenditure (resting rates account for 65 to 75 percent of all calories burned). Good for hand/eye coordination, reaction times, stress relief, and feeling superior to teenagers.

7 Horse/camel riding

Muscles worked: Thighs (especially inner thighs), stomach, back, and shoulders.

Calories burned: 1-hour ride at a trot = 300 to 500 calories.

Good news if you're planning a trip to Morocco: A camel may have the edge on a horse when it comes to giving a more vigorous ride. It will also take more of your balance and coordination.

8 Scuba diving

Muscles worked: All major muscle groups, at a low level.

Calories burned: 1-hour dive = 600 calories.

Great way to get away from it all and relieve stress.

9 A night out dancing

Muscles worked: All muscle groups to varying degrees, depending on your style—or lack of it.

Calories burned: 1 hour of dancing = 300 to 600 calories.

If you dance in a nightclub, much of the energy you expend may well be offset by the copious amounts of alcohol you consume. Oh well.

10 Inline skating

Muscles worked: Legs, trunk, and shoulders.

Especially good for the buttocks.

Calories burned: hour of skating = 550 calories.

It's a great calorie burner, good for coordination, agility, and balance. If you can stay upright.

Note: The number of calories you burn depends on several factors, including the intensity of the activity, your body mass, and your metabolism. For each minute of any given activity, a very fit person can burn more than twice as many calories as a sedentary person.

—JON LEWIS

The Complete Ian King Workouts

The King of

When my wife fell and broke her leg 10 days before our baby was born, neither of us had any idea how flabby I'd get.

Oh, my wife had a rough time, too. For 6 weeks, she left her wheelchair only to sleep and give birth. So props to her. But let's talk about me.

I had to take on both sets of parental duties, and for weeks on end the only exercise I managed was burping a 7-pound baby. I didn't gain any weight; in fact, I dropped 5 pounds. I also lost strength, muscle tone, and energy. When I finally returned to the gym, it was as if I was starting all over again.

I wanted to get back into the workout habit, but I didn't really know where to begin.

I didn't get mad, though. I got Ian.

That is, I asked the smartest fitness people I know how to install Lou, Version 2.0, and the advice I kept getting was to call Ian King, C.S.C.S. He's an Australian strength coach who has trained Olympic and professional athletes on four continents in the past 2 decades. (He trained athletes who won gold and silver medals at the 2000 Sydney Games.)

King's workouts looked like none I'd ever seen before. Besides taking less time—30 to 40 minutes, on average, three times a week—they were also more challenging to my balance and coordination, and more focused on flexibility and abdominal strength.

My first thought was "Damn! So that's what my abs look like." And my second thought was "I'll bet if *Men's Health* readers tried this, they'd look better, feel better, stick with the program longer, and give me more job security than ever before."

So I dialed up Australia and asked King to design an entire series of workouts for MH—workouts to take you through 6 months of building more muscle than you ever thought possible. And, after checking currency exchange rates, he agreed, creating a six-phase program.

1. An 8-week program to get you back into the exercise habit and start building muscle

All Workouts

It's simple. It works. It's the plan your body has been waiting for. Introducing a revolutionary new workout program

BY LOU SCHULER

2. A more aggressive muscle-building routine (Trust me: You'll want to master the previous phase before you tackle this one)

3. A focus on pure strength

4. Increasing chest size

5. Bulking up your arms

6. Developing abdominal muscles that ripple like desert sand

Each of the workouts is different, but all six of them are based on the following principles.

Continuity is more important than volume. King believes that almost everyone who lifts weights overdoes it—too many sets in a workout, too many workouts in a week, too many weeks of workouts without a break. "The goal of training is to get stronger or bigger or leaner from week to week, and the greatest challenge is the law of diminishing returns," he says.

You'll do three workouts a week for 3 weeks, take a week off, and then move on to a different workout. The idea is to keep you coming back for more—we don't want you getting hurt because you should've been doing less.

Fitness starts with middle management. Most workout routines finish with abdominal exercises, but King likes to start with abs. "If you always work them last, you always get an inferior training effect," says King, who believes the abs are too important for strength, posture, and overall quality of life to exercise when your body is tired.

In the first phase, you'll do four abdominal exercises and always start your workouts with one of them. However, in some of the other phases you'll do your ab exercises later in the routine, which brings us to another of King's principles . . .

Variety is the key to progress. You probably have a pattern to your workouts: You always do bench presses on Monday, and you always do them first in the workout. When King designed this program, one of his main goals was to shake up these habits, for one simple reason: The only way you can make your

Pull Here

If you want bigger muscles, you have to give 'em a stretch

Most men stretch only when they want a better view of the yoga class. But that's not enough to avoid injury. "Bones have an optimal gap between them. Any form of training shortens and tightens the connective tissue and reduces that gap," says Ian King. Eventually, you pay the price with chronic, nagging injuries, particularly in your back and shoulders.

The solution, says King, is to spend at least 25 percent of your exercise time stretching. In other words, if you're in the gym for 40 minutes, he recommends that you spend 10 minutes stretching.

Start with these eight moves. King suggests stretching your weaker or tighter side first, then your stronger or looser side.

muscle fibers grow is to surprise them with new stimuli. There are big surprises—and bigger muscles—ahead.

Each month, you'll change the exercises, the order of the exercises, and the system of sets and repetitions. The most important moves—squats, deadlifts, bench presses, shoulder presses, pullups, and lat pulldowns—show up most months, but you'll do them differently each time. And, as a consequence, you'll see better results than you ever thought possible.

Strength begins at the bottom. That is, in your feet and ankles. The first 8 weeks of this program include one-legged squats and deadlifts that require you to develop the tiny muscles that help with balance. You probably won't even use weights on these exercises—moving your own body up and down while standing on one leg will be challenging enough.

The balance you'll develop will help you later in the program, when you start in on the two-legged exercises. That's when you'll see that developing the smallest muscles first can lead to the biggest gains later.

But enough with the explanations. You won't believe any of this until you try it yourself. So let's get to work.

The Heart Part

A plan of attack for your most important muscle

Cardiovascular exercise is an important adjunct to Ian King's workouts. But it's not the main event. Your goal is not to improve your 10-K time but to burn a few extra calories and get your body used to working at an elevated heart rate, improving the efficiency of your heart and lungs.

King recommends three aerobic sessions per week, after weight workouts or on separate days.

▶**How long:** 20 to 40 minutes per session.

▶**How hard:** 60 to 90 percent of your maximum heart rate. You can estimate your maximum by subtracting your age from 220.

▶**Extra credit:** If your main goal is weight reduction, or if you haven't exercised since the second Reagan administration, you can add three more cardio sessions a week, for a total of six. But King suggests that the extra sessions be short and easy—a brisk 20-minute walk after lunch on the days you don't lift, for example.

Get Back in Shape Phase 1

Here's your workout and training log for the first 8 weeks of our program

WEEKS 1 TO 3

The Beginner Routine. If you're just starting out or you haven't exercised in a while, you can expect to increase your strength quickly in the first 3 weeks.

Do one set of 15 to 20 repetitions of each exercise. Rest as little as possible between exercises. When you can complete 20 repetitions with a particular weight, increase it the next workout, but only enough that you can still do 15 repetitions.

The Advanced Routine. Do one set of 10 to 15 repetitions of each exercise. Rest as little as possible between exercises. When you hit 15 repetitions with a weight, increase it a little the next workout, but make sure you can do at least 10 with the heavier weight.

WEEK 4

Take a week off.

WEEKS 5 TO 7

You'll start to see more results in weeks 5 to 7: a tighter waist, bigger muscles (especially in your upper body), and more endurance.

The exercises are now divided into two workouts, A and B. If you work out Monday, Wednesday, and Friday, you'll do workout A on Monday and Friday, workout B on Wednesday. The next week, do the opposite: workout B on Monday and Friday, workout A on Wednesday. Do each workout five times (the last workout will be in week 8 if you train three times a week).

You'll also see that each workout is divided into two four-exercise circuits. Do all the exercises in one circuit without stopping, take a short rest, then repeat or move to the next circuit.

Use the first circuit as a warmup. Use about 70 percent of the weight you'll use in the second and third circuits. For example, if you want to do bench presses with 40-pound dumbbells, use 25- or 30-pound dumbbells in the first circuit, then 40s in the second and third circuits.

The Beginner Routine: Do 12 to 15 repetitions of each exercise. When you can complete 15, increase the weight slightly next time. Do each circuit one or two times in week 5, two times in week 6, and two or three times in week 7.

The Advanced Routine: Do 8 to 12 repetitions of each exercise. Do each circuit two or three times.

WEEK 8

Take all or part of the week off. Then move on to Phase 2, a rapid muscle-building workout.

THE EXERCISES

Lower the weight (or your body) for 3 seconds, pause for a second, then take 2 seconds to lift the weight or your body back to the starting position.

Shoulder press works shoulders and triceps

1. Grab a pair of dumbbells and sit holding them just outside your shoulders, with your arms bent and your palms facing forward.

2. Push the weights straight overhead. Pause, then slowly lower.

Triceps extension

1. Grab a pair of dumbbells with an overhand grip and sit at the end of a bench with your back straight. Hold the dumbbells behind your head, with your elbows bent and your forearms perpendicular to floor.

2. Straighten your arms up over your head, palms facing one another. Keep your upper arms still throughout. Pause before lowering again.

Biceps curl

1. Grab a pair of dumbbells with an overhand grip and sit, letting your arms hang straight down from your shoulders. Keep your back straight and your upper arms tucked against your sides.

2. Curl the weights upward, rotating your palms until they're facing straight up. Curl as high as you can without moving your upper arms forward. Pause, then slowly return to the starting position.

Shrug works trapezius (upper back)

1. Grab a pair of dumbbells with an overhand grip and hold them at your sides, with your arms extended and your palms toward your thighs.

2. Shrug your shoulders. Pause, then lower.

Bench press works chest, triceps, and front shoulders

1. Grab a pair of dumbbells with an overhand grip. Lie on your back on a flat bench with your feet on the floor. Hold the weights over your chin at arm's length.

2. Slowly lower the weights to your chest. Pause, then push the weights back up until your arms are straight and the weights are over your chin again.

Pullover works latissimus (middle back) and chest

1. Grab a pair of dumbbells with an overhand grip and lie on your back on a bench. Hold the dumbbells directly above your chest, with your arms slightly bent and your palms facing each other.

2. Lower the dumbbells behind your head until they line up with the back of your head. Do not change the angle of your elbows throughout the lift. Pause, then return to the starting position.

One-leg deadlift
works thighs, gluteals, and lower back

1. Stand with your feet hip-width apart. Bend your dominant leg so your lower leg is parallel to the floor.

2. Bend your nondominant leg to slowly lower your body as far as you can without rounding your back. When you can't lower yourself any farther or your dominant leg is almost touching the floor, pause and then return to the starting position. Finish the set, then repeat with your other leg.

ADVANCED VERSION: Hold dumbbells.

Static lunge works thighs and gluteals

1. Stand with your nondominant foot about 2 feet in front of your body and your dominant foot about 2 feet behind you. Lace your fingers behind your ears.

2. Lower your body until your front knee is bent 90 degrees. Your lower front leg should be perpendicular to the floor. Your back knee should bend and almost touch the floor. Press your front foot into the floor and push your body back to the starting position. Repeat with your other leg.

ADVANCED VERSION: Hold barbell across shoulders.

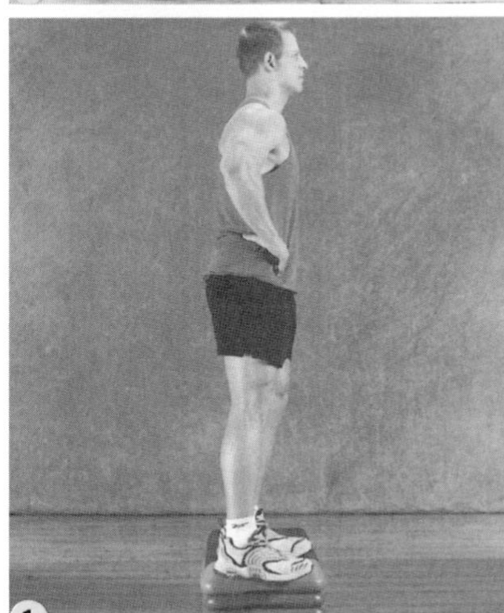

One-leg partial squat works quadriceps (front thighs)

1. Stand on a 6- to 12-inch-high block, with your left foot on the edge and your right foot hanging off the side. Your knees should be slightly bent.

2. Without rounding your back, bend your left leg to slowly lower your body until your right foot is almost touching the ground. Pause, then return to the starting position. Finish the set, then repeat with your other leg.

ADVANCED VERSION: Hold dumbbells.

Standing calf raise

1. Stand on a 6- to 12-inch-high block with the balls of your feet on the edge and your heels hanging off the side as low as possible.

2. Lift your heels as high as you can. Pause, then lower.

ADVANCED VERSION: Hold dumbbells.

Lying dumbbell row

works trapezius (upper back) and rear shoulders

1. Set a bench on blocks so that it is about a foot off the floor. Grab a pair of dumbbells and lie facedown. Let your arms hang straight down from your shoulders and turn your palms so your thumbs face each other.

2. Lift your upper arms as high as you can by bending your elbows and squeezing your shoulder blades together. At the top of the move, your upper arms should be perpendicular to your body. Your forearms should point toward the floor. Pause, then slowly lower to the starting position.

Hip/thigh extension

works gluteals, hamstrings (rear thighs), and lower back

1. Set a bench on blocks so that it is about a foot off the floor. Place your body so that your abdomen rests on the bench but your lower body from the hips down is completely off of it. Keep your legs together and, without bending them, lower them to the floor by bending at your waist.

2. Pause, then lift your hips and thighs as high as you can. Slowly lower, and return to the starting position.

Bridge works abdominals and lower back (suck in abs as you hold this position)

1. Lie facedown on the floor in a pushup position but with your weight resting on your elbows and toes. Your body should form a straight line from your shoulders to your ankles. Keep your back flat throughout the exercise. Pull your abdominal muscles in, trying to bring your belly button back to your spine. Hold, then relax.

Oblique crunch works abdominals, emphasizing oblique muscles on sides of waist

1. Lie on your back on the floor with your hands behind your ears. With your knees bent and your feet together, turn your hips and legs to the right so that your right leg rests on the floor.

2. Raise your head and shoulders and crunch toward your left hip. Pause, then slowly return to the starting position. Repeat with your knees pointed in the opposite direction.

Lying vacuum works abdominals

1. Lie on your back with your legs bent and your feet flat on the floor, about hip-width apart. Place your hands on your abs. Try to make your abdomen as thin as possible by pulling in your abdominals and exhaling completely. Breathe while holding in your abdominals. Hold for 10 seconds, then relax.

ADVANCED VERSION: See next page.

Lying vacuum

ADVANCED VERSION: Alternate legs as you hold in abdominals.

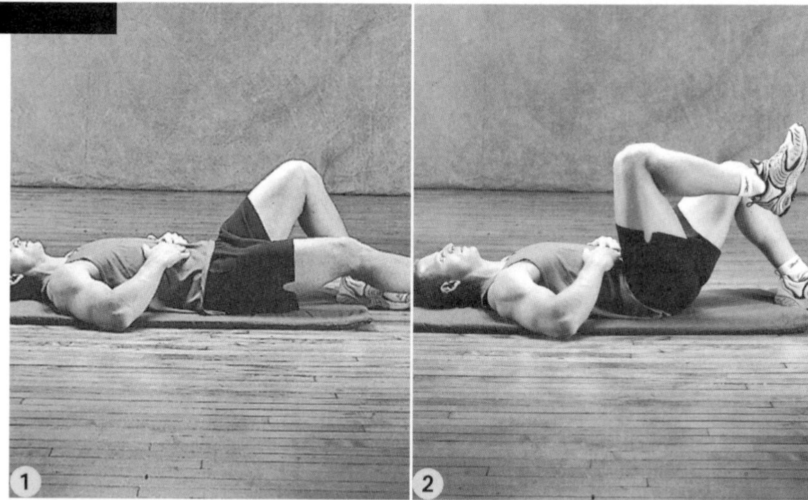

Slow curlup works abdominals

1. Lie on your back with your knees bent and your feet flat on the floor, about hip-width apart. Hold your arms at your sides, slightly off the ground and with your palms facing down.

2. Slowly lift your torso to a sitting position while keeping your arms parallel to the floor.

ADVANCED VERSION: Place your fingers behind your ears throughout the whole movement.

PHASE 1: Weeks 1–3

	WEEK 1						WEEK 2						WEEK 3					
	MON		WED		FRI		MON		WED		FRI		MON		WED		FRI	
	WEIGHT	REPS	WEIGHT	REPS	WEIGHT	REPS	WEIGHT	REPS	WEIGHT	REPS	WEIGHT	REPS	WEIGHT	REPS	WEIGHT	REPS	WEIGHT	REPS
Lying vacuum*																		
Static lunge																		
Lying dumbbell row																		
Bench press																		
Slow curlup†																		
One-leg partial squat																		
Pullover																		
Shoulder press																		
Oblique crunch																		
One-leg deadlift																		
Biceps curl																		
Triceps extension																		
Bridge‡																		
Standing calf raise																		
Hip/thigh extension																		
Shrug																		

* If you're doing the beginner version of the exercise, hold for 5 to 10 seconds for 10 to 15 repetitions. If you're doing the advanced version, use the same repetition speed you use for the other exercises.

† If you're doing the beginner version of the exercise, try to take a full 5 seconds to lower yourself. In the advanced version, take 5 seconds to raise your body and 5 seconds to lower. A set should take 60 to 100 seconds.

‡ Beginners should hold the position 5 seconds at a time, rest on the knees for a second, then continue the set. Advanced exercisers should hold for 10 seconds, rest for 1 second, then continue for 60 to 100 seconds.

PHASE 1: Weeks 5–7

		WEEK 1						WEEK 2						WEEK 3					
	Workout A	MON		WED		FRI		MON		WED		FRI		MON		WED		FRI	
		WEIGHT	REPS	WEIGHT	REPS	WEIGHT	REPS	WEIGHT	REPS	WEIGHT	REPS	WEIGHT	REPS	WEIGHT	REPS	WEIGHT	REPS	WEIGHT	REPS
CIRCUIT 1	Lying vacuum*																		
	One-leg partial squat																		
	Lying dumbbell row																		
	Shrug																		
CIRCUIT 2	Oblique crunch																		
	Static lunge																		
	Pullover																		
	Biceps curl																		
	Workout B	MON		WED		FRI		MON		WED		FRI		MON		WED		FRI	
CIRCUIT 1	Slow curlup†																		
	One-leg deadlift																		
	Bench press																		
	Hip/thigh extension																		
CIRCUIT 2	Bridge																		
	Standing calf raise																		
	Shoulder press																		
	Triceps extension																		

* If you're doing the beginner version of the exercise, hold for 5 to 10 seconds for 10 to 15 repetitions. If you're doing the advanced version, use the same repetition speed you use for the other exercises.

† If you're doing the beginner version of the exercise, try to take a full 5 seconds to lower yourself. In the advanced version, take 5 seconds to raise your body and 5 seconds to lower. A set should take 60 to 100 seconds.

Bigger, Badder, Better Phase 2

You've probably noticed that men's clothes have gotten a bit tighter. Oh, you can still find the relaxed-fit stuff over on the back wall. But the cool-looking shirts and pants in the front of the store are designed to hug your body like a new girlfriend.

This muscle-building routine will transform your triple-pleated body into this year's flat-front model. Three weeks from now, you can spring-clean the baggy stuff out of your closet.

WHICH WORKOUT TO CHOOSE

If you've done squats and deadlifts and can do more than five chinups in consecutive sets, you're ready for the Advanced workout. If not, stick with the Beginner program.

FREQUENCY

Do each workout once a week for 3 weeks, then rest a week.

WARMUPS AND WORK SETS

On your heaviest exercises, you'll start with one or two warmup sets, then progress to work sets. Here's how to use King's system.

1. Decide how much weight you're going to use for the first work set of your first exercise. It should be tough, but you should finish all the repetitions with strength to spare. As an example, we'll say you're doing workout C and using 135 pounds for your first work set of bench presses.

2. Choose a weight that's about 40 percent of the 135 pounds: 55 pounds. That's your first warmup weight. Do 10 repetitions.

3. For your second warmup, use a weight that's about 70 percent of your first work set. So 95 pounds would work. (You don't have to whip out the calculator here; these are ballpark figures.)

4. Do your first work set with the 135 pounds. Do your second work set with a little more weight—155 pounds, say. You should complete all the repetitions in this set, too, but it should feel closer to an all-out effort.

STRIP SETS

A strip set is three consecutive sets of the same exercise, using less weight on each set and taking no rest in between.

THE EXERCISES

Take 3 seconds to lower the weight, pause for 1 second, then lift the weight in 1 second. Rest for 2 minutes between sets (no rest within a strip set).

Increase the weights in each set of each exercise each workout (again, strip sets are the exception). Caution: The heavier the weight you use, the more you need a spotter.

Underhand lat pulldown works back and biceps

1. Grab the bar with a shoulder-width underhand grip.

2. Pull the bar down to your chest. Pause, then slowly return to the starting position.

1

2

Weighted chinup

1. Grab the chinup bar with a shoulder-width, underhand grip. Pull your chin up above the bar as high as you can. Pause, then slowly return to the starting position.

1

Overhand lat pulldown works back and biceps

1. Grab the bar with an overhand grip that's just beyond shoulder-width.

2. Pull the bar down to your chest. Pause, then slowly return to the starting position.

1

2

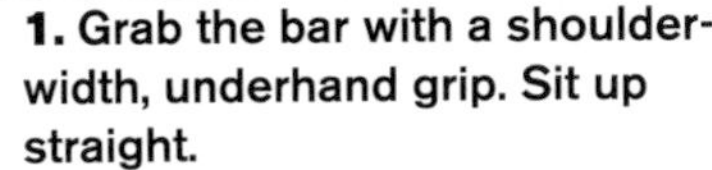

Underhand seated row works back and biceps

1. Grab the bar with a shoulder-width, underhand grip. Sit up straight.

2. Pull the bar to your abdomen. Pause, then slowly return to the starting position.

Overhand seated row works back and biceps

1. Grab the bar with an overhand grip that's just beyond shoulder-width. Sit up straight.

2. Pull the bar to your abdomen. Pause, then slowly return to the starting position.

Biceps curl

1. Grab an EZ-curl bar with an underhand grip. Hold the bar at arm's length against the fronts of your thighs, with your back straight and your knees slightly flexed. Keep your upper arms tucked against your sides.

2. Curl the bar as high as you can without moving your upper arms forward. Pause, then slowly return to the starting position.

Wrist-to-knee situp works abdominals

1. Lie on your back with your hips and knees bent 90 degrees, your lower legs parallel to the floor, and your hands touching your ears or forehead.

2. Raise your head and shoulders off the floor as you simultaneously bring your left knee toward your chest. Rotate at the waist so your right elbow or wrist touches your knee. Pause, then slowly return to the starting position. Repeat on the other side, left elbow or wrist to right knee.

1

2

Squat works quadriceps, hamstrings, and gluteals

1. Set a bar on a squat rack and step under it so the bar rests across your upper back. Grab the bar with an overhand grip. Lift the bar off the rack and step back. Set your feet shoulder-width apart.

2. Slowly lower your body until your thighs are parallel to the floor. Keep your knees even with or behind your toes. Pause, then slowly return to the starting position.

1

2

Deadlift works hamstrings, gluteals, and lower back

1. Load the barbell and roll it against your shins. Grab the bar with an overhand grip, your hands just beyond shoulder-width. Squat and pull your shoulders back.

2. Stand with the bar, thrusting your hips forward. Pause, then slowly lower the bar to the floor, keeping it as close to your body as possible.

1

2

Wide-grip stiff-legged deadlift

works lower back, gluteals, and hamstrings

1. Grab the barbell with an overhand grip that's about twice shoulder-width. Stand holding the bar at arm's length so it rests against the fronts of your thighs. Your feet should be shoulder-width apart and your knees slightly bent.

2. Slowly lower the bar to just below your knees. Don't change the angle of your knees. Keep your head and chest up and your lower back arched. Lift your torso back to the starting position, keeping the bar as close to your body as possible.

Dynamic lunge works gluteals, quadriceps, and hamstrings

1. Stand with a barbell across your shoulders.

2. Step forward with your nondominant leg (your left if you're right-handed) and lower your body until your front knee is bent 90 degrees and your rear knee nearly touches the floor. Your front lower leg should be perpendicular to the floor, and your torso should remain upright. Push yourself back up to the starting position as quickly as you can, and repeat with your dominant leg.

Hip lift works abdominals

1. Lie on your back with your arms along your sides or at 90-degree angles from your body, and your legs in the air, perpendicular to the floor.

2. Raise your hips off the floor as high as you can while keeping your legs vertical. Keep your head still. Hold as long as you can (3 to 5 seconds is ideal), then return to the starting position.

Bench press works chest, triceps, and front shoulders

1. Lie on your back on a flat bench with your feet on the floor. Grab the bar with an overhand grip, your hands just beyond shoulder-width apart, and lift it off the uprights. Hold it at arm's length.

2. Slowly lower the bar to your chest. Keep your butt on the bench and avoid arching your back beyond its natural position. Pause, then push the bar back up.

1

2

Wide-grip bench press works chest and triceps

1. Lie on your back on the flat bench with your feet on the floor. Grab the bar with an overhand grip, your hands a bit farther apart than for the regular bench press, and lift the bar off the uprights. Hold it over your chin at arm's length.

2. Slowly lower the bar to your chest. Keep your butt on the bench and avoid arching your back beyond its natural position. Pause, then push the bar back up.

1

2

Shoulder press works shoulders and triceps

1. Grab a barbell with an overhand grip, your hands just beyond shoulder-width apart. Holding the barbell at shoulder level, stand with your feet shoulder-width apart and your knees slightly bent.

2. Push the weight straight overhead, leaning your head back slightly but keeping your torso upright. Pause, then slowly lower the bar to the starting position.

1

2

Upright row works shoulders and upper back

1. Grab a barbell with an overhand grip, your hands just less than shoulder-width apart. Hold the bar at arm's length against the fronts of your thighs.

2. Lift the bar straight up along your body until your upper arms are parallel to the floor. Pause, then slowly lower the bar to the starting position.

Triceps pressdown

1. Attach a straight bar to the high pulley of a cable station. Grab the bar with a shoulder-width, overhand grip, and pull it down until your elbows are bent 90 degrees. Stand straight with your upper arms tucked against your sides. Your feet should be hip-width apart, and your knees should be slightly bent.

2. Push the bar down until your arms are straight, keeping the rest of your body in the starting position. Keep your upper arms at your sides. Pause, then slowly allow the bar to rise until your elbows are again bent 90 degrees.

Twisting situp works abdominals

1. Lie on your back on the floor, with your knees bent and your feet flat on the floor. Touch your ears with your hands.

2. Lift your torso off the floor while twisting at the waist so your right elbow touches your left knee. Keep your feet on the floor. Pause, then slowly return to the starting position. Repeat to the other side, touching your left elbow to your right knee.

PHASE 2: Workout-A Training Log

	REPETITIONS		WEEK 1		WEEK 2		WEEK 3	
	BEGINNER	ADVANCED	WEIGHT	REPS	WEIGHT	REPS	WEIGHT	REPS
Underhand lat pulldown								
Warmup set 1	10 at 40%	10 at 40%						
Warmup set 2	8 at 70%	10 at 40%						
Work set 1	6	5						
Work set 2*	6	5						
Overhand lat pulldown								
Work set 1	10–12	8–10						
Work set 2†	15–20	10–12						
Underhand seated row								
Warmup set 1	10 at 40%	10 at 40%						
Warmup set 2	8 at 70%	8 at 70%						
Work set 1	6	5						
Work set 2*	6	5						
Overhand seated row								
Work set 1	10–12	8–10						
Work set 2†	15–20	10–12						
Biceps curl‡								
Warmup set	10 at 60%	10 at 60%						
Work set 1	10	6						
Work set 2	10	8						
Work set 3	10	10						
Wrist-to-knee situp								
Work set 1	10–20	10–20						
Work set 2	10–20	10–20						

* Use slightly more weight on the second work set. If you can, do weighted chinups instead of pulldowns. Use a weighted belt when necessary.

† Use slightly less weight on the second work set.

‡ Strip sets: Drop 5 to 10 pounds per set, and continue with as little rest as possible.

PHASE 2: Workout-B Training Log

	REPETITIONS		WEEK 1		WEEK 2		WEEK 3	
	BEGINNER	ADVANCED	WEIGHT	REPS	WEIGHT	REPS	WEIGHT	REPS
Squat								
Warmup set 1	10 at 40%	10 at 40%						
Warmup set 2	8 at 70%	10 at 40%						
Work set 1	6	5						
Work set 2*	6	5						
Deadlift								
Warmup set 1	10 at 40%	10 at 40%						
Warmup set 2	8 at 70%	8 at 70%						
Work set 1	6	5						
Work set 2*	6	5						
Wide-grip stiff-legged deadlift								
Warmup set	6 at 60%	6 at 60%						
Work set	10–12	8–10						
Dynamic lunge								
Warmup set	6 at 60%	6 at 60%						
Work set	10–12†	8–10†						
Hip lift								
Work set 1	10–15	10–15						
Work set 2	10–15	10–15						

* Use slightly more weight on the second work set.
†Each leg.

PHASE 2: Workout-C Training Log

	REPETITIONS		WEEK 1		WEEK 2		WEEK 3	
	BEGINNER	ADVANCED	WEIGHT	REPS	WEIGHT	REPS	WEIGHT	REPS
Bench press								
Warmup set 1	10 at 40%	10 at 40%						
Warmup set 2	8 at 70%	8 at 70%						
Work set 1	6	5						
Work set 2*	6	5						
Wide-grip bench press								
Work set 1	10–12	8–10						
Work set 2†	15–20	12–15						
Shoulder press								
Warmup set 1	10 at 40%	10 at 40%						
Warmup set 2	8 at 70%	8 at 70%						
Work set 1	6	5						
Work set 2*	6	5						
Upright row								
Work set 1	10–12	8–10						
Work set 2†	15–20	12–15						
Triceps pressdown‡								
Warmup set	10 at 60%	10 at 60%						
Work set 1	10	6						
Work set 2	10	8						
Work set 3	10	10						
Twisting situp								
Work set 1	10–20	10–20						
Work set 2	10–20	10–20						

* Use slightly more weight on the second work set.

† Use slightly less weight on the second work set.

‡ Strip sets: Drop 5 to 10 pounds per set, and continue with as little rest as possible.

Strong Stuff

Phase 3

Extra strength" is a great sales pitch for aspirin. You swallow the same little pill and get twice the payoff. Similarly, you can add strength gains to a workout without adding time, says King. In this phase of his workout program, you'll do just four exercises in 45 minutes, but you'll see tremendous strength gains that you can parlay into a size upgrade in next month's phase.

WHICH WORKOUT TO CHOOSE

You'll see that we have two different repetition schemes, one for beginners and one for advanced lifters. If you've done squats and deadlifts in the past and can do more than five pullups in consecutive sets, you're ready for the Advanced workout. If not, stick with the Beginner program.

FREQUENCY

Do each workout (A, B, and C) once a week for 3 weeks, then rest a week.

WARMUPS AND WORK SETS

For most exercises, you'll start with two or three warmup sets (identified as such on your training log), then progress to work sets. Here's how to use King's system.

1. Decide how much weight you're going to use for the first work set of your first exercise—155 pounds, say.

2. Choose a weight that's about 30 percent of that (say, 45 pounds) and do 10 repetitions.

3. For your second warmup, do eight repetitions with a weight that's about 60 percent of your first work-set weight (90 or 95 pounds).

4. For your third warmup, do six repetitions with about 80 percent of your first work-set weight (115 pounds).

5. Do your first work set, then increase the weight slightly for subsequent sets.

THE EXERCISES

Take 2 seconds to lower the weight, pause for 1 second, then lift the weight in 1 second.

Rest for 2 to 3 minutes between sets. There are two exceptions.

1. For abdominal exercises, try to rest just 1 minute between sets.

2. For Advanced-program sets marked "N" (for negative, or eccentric, repetitions), choose a weight that's about 20 percent heavier than you can lift once. Have a spotter or training partner put the bar in the starting position. Then lower it for 5 seconds and have the spotter help you lift it back to the starting position.

You should increase the weights for each set of each exercise every time you do the workout. Caution: The heavier the weight you use, the more you need a spotter.

Bench press works chest, triceps, and front shoulders

1. Lie on your back on a flat bench with your feet on the floor. Grab the bar with an overhand grip, your hands just beyond shoulder-width, and lift it off the uprights. Hold it over your chin at arm's length. Your wrists should be straight, with the bar resting on your lower palms.

2. Slowly lower the bar to your chest. Pause, then push the bar back up until your arms are straight and the bar is over your chin again. Throughout, keep your butt on the bench and don't arch your back beyond its natural position.

1

2

Parallel-grip seated row works back and biceps

1. Grab the parallel-grip handle of a seated-row station so your palms face each other. Sit up straight and pull your shoulders back.

2. Pull the handle to your abdomen. Pause, then slowly return to the starting position.

1

2

Close-grip bench press works triceps and chest

1. Lie on your back on a flat bench with your feet on the floor. Grab the bar with an overhand grip, your hands a bit narrower than shoulder-width apart. Lift the bar off the uprights and hold it over your chest at arm's length.

2. Slowly lower the bar to your chest. Pause, then push the bar back up until your arms are straight and the bar is over your chin again. Throughout, keep your butt on the bench and avoid arching your back beyond its natural position.

1

2

1

2

Decline knee-up works abdominals

1. Lie on a slant board with your hips lower than your head. Grab the bar behind your head for support. Bend your hips and knees 90 degrees. If you need more of a challenge, hold a medicine ball between your knees.

2. Pull your hips up toward your chest as if you were emptying a bucket of water resting on your pelvis. Keep your hips and knees at 90-degree angles. Pause, then slowly lower your hips to the starting position.

1

2

Squat works quadriceps, hamstrings, and gluteals

1. Set a bar on a squat rack and step under it so the bar rests across your upper back. Grab the bar with an overhand grip. Lift the bar off the rack and step back. Set your feet shoulder-width apart.

2. Slowly lower your body until your thighs are parallel to the floor. Keep your knees even with or behind your toes. Pause, then slowly return to the starting position.

1

2

Deadlift works hamstrings, gluteals, and lower back

1. Load the barbell and roll it against your shins. Grab the bar with an overhand grip, your hands just beyond shoulder-width. Squat down, focus your eyes straight ahead, and pull your shoulders back.

2. Stand with the bar, thrusting your hips forward and keeping your shoulders pulled back. Pause, then slowly lower the bar to the floor, keeping it as close to your body as possible. When you bring the bar down past your knees, squat down, rather than bending forward at the waist.

Seated calf raise

1. Position yourself in a seated-calf-raise station so the pad lies comfortably across your thighs, just above your knees. Set the balls of your feet on the lifting platform. Release the locking mechanism (it's a little different on each brand of machine) and lower your heels as far as you can.

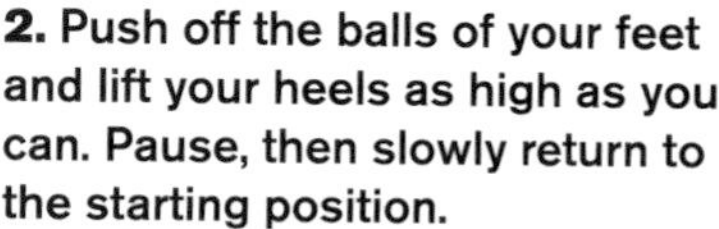

2. Push off the balls of your feet and lift your heels as high as you can. Pause, then slowly return to the starting position.

Side raise on bench works obliques

1. Position two benches so you can lie on your hip on one and lock your feet under the other. Your body should be perpendicular to the bench your hip rests on.

2. Lower your torso as far as you can, then lift it as high as you can. Pause, then repeat, finishing all your repetitions on one side before switching to the other.

Overhand lat pulldown works back and biceps

1. Grab the bar with an overhand grip that's just beyond shoulder-width.

2. Pull the bar down to your chest. Pause, then slowly return to the starting position.

Weighted pullup works back and biceps

1. Hang from the chinup bar using an overhand grip that's just beyond shoulder-width. Cross your feet behind you. If you need more resistance (especially on the negative repetitions), use a weighted belt. Pull yourself up as high as you can—your chin should go over the bar. Pause, then slowly lower yourself to the starting position.

Shoulder press works shoulders and triceps

1. Grab a barbell with an overhand grip, your hands just beyond shoulder-width apart. Stand and hold the barbell at shoulder level.

2. Push the barbell straight overhead, leaning your head back slightly to allow the bar to clear your chin. Pause, then slowly lower the bar to the starting position.

Preacher curl works biceps

1. Grab an EZ-curl bar with an underhand, shoulder-width grip. As you sit on the preacher-bench seat, the top of the sloping pad should reach your armpits. Rest your upper arms on the pad and hold the bar at arm's length.

2. Curl the bar upward until your elbows are bent about 90 degrees. Pause, then slowly return to the starting position.

Weighted situp works abdominals

1. Lie on your back holding a weight plate or dumbbell across your upper chest, your knees bent and your feet flat on the floor.

2. Curl your torso upward until your upper body is perpendicular to the floor. Slowly lower your torso to the floor.

PHASE 3: Workout-A Training Log

	REPETITIONS		WEEK 1		WEEK 2		WEEK 3	
	BEGINNER	ADVANCED	WEIGHT	REPS	WEIGHT	REPS	WEIGHT	REPS
Bench press								
Warmup set 1	10 at 30%	10 at 30%						
Warmup set 2	8 at 60%	8 at 60%						
Warmup set 3	6 at 80%	6 at 80%						
Work set 1	4	4						
Work set 2	4	3						
Work set 3	8–10	2						
Work set 4	15–20	4 (N)*						
Work set 5	—	10–15						
Parallel-grip seated row								
Warmup set 1	10 at 30%	10 at 30%						
Warmup set 2	8 at 60%	8 at 60%						
Warmup set 3	6 at 80%	6 at 80%						
Work set 1	4	4						
Work set 2	4	3						
Work set 3	8–10	2						
Work set 4	15–20	4 (N)*						
Work set 5	—	10–15						
Close-grip bench press								
Warmup set 1	10 at 40%	10 at 40%						
Warmup set 2	8 at 70%	8 at 70%						
Work set 1	6	4–5						
Work set 2†	6	4–5						
Decline knee-up								
Work set 1	10–20	10–20						
Work set 2	10–20	10–20						

* Increase weights for the sets of three and two repetitions. Then use 20 percent more weight than you can lift for the set of four negative, or eccentric, repetitions. Have a spotter help you lift the weight, then lower it for 5 seconds.

† Use slightly more weight for the second work set.

PHASE 3: Workout-B Training Log

	REPETITIONS		WEEK 1		WEEK 2		WEEK 3	
	BEGINNER	ADVANCED	WEIGHT	REPS	WEIGHT	REPS	WEIGHT	REPS
Squat								
Warmup set 1	10 at 30%	10 at 30%						
Warmup set 2	8 at 60%	8 at 60%						
Warmup set 3	6 at 80%	6 at 80%						
Work set 1	4	4						
Work set 2	4†	3						
Work set 3	8–10	2						
Work set 4	15–20	4*						
Work set 5	—	8–10						
Deadlift								
Warmup set 1	10 at 30%	10 at 30%						
Warmup set 2	8 at 60%	8 at 60%						
Warmup set 3	6 at 80%	6 at 80%						
Work set 1	4	4						
Work set 2	4	3						
Work set 3	8–10	2						
Work set 4	15–20	4*						
Work set 5	—	8–10						
Seated calf raise								
Warmup set	15 at 60%	15 at 60%						
Work set 1	15	12–15						
Work set 2†	15	12–15						
Side raise on bench								
Work set 1	10–15§	10–15§						
Work set 2	10–15	10–15						

* Increase weights for the sets of three and two repetitions, then decrease the weight for the second set of four (you should still use more weight than you did for the first set of four).

† Use slightly more weight than you did for the first set.

§ Each side.

PHASE 3: Workout-C Training Log

	REPETITIONS		WEEK 1		WEEK 2		WEEK 3	
	BEGINNER	ADVANCED	WEIGHT	REPS	WEIGHT	REPS	WEIGHT	REPS
Overhand lat pulldown								
Warmup set 1	10 at 30%	10 at 30%						
Warmup set 2	8 at 60%	8 at 60%						
Warmup set 3	6 at 80%	6 at 80%						
Work set 1	4	4ll						
Work set 2	4†	3ll						
Work set 3	8–10	2ll						
Work set 4	15–20	4 (N) *ll						
Work set 5	—	10–15						
Shoulder press								
Warmup set 1	10 at 30%	10 at 30%						
Warmup set 2	8 at 60%	8 at 60%						
Warmup set 3	6 at 80%	6 at 80%						
Work set 1	4	4						
Work set 2	4†	3						
Work set 3	8–10	2						
Work set 4	15–20	4 (N) *						
Work set 5	—	10–15						
Preacher curl								
Warmup set 1	10 at 40%	10 at 40%						
Warmup set 2	8 at 70%	8 at 70%						
Work set 1	6	4–5						
Work set 2†	6	4–5						
Weighted situp								
Work set 1	10–20	10–20						
Work set 2†	10–20	10–20						

* Increase weights for the sets of three and two repetitions, then decrease the weight for the second set of four (you should still use more weight than you did for the first set of four).

† Use slightly more weight for the second work set.

ll Do weighted pullups instead of overhand lat pulldowns.

Torque Your Torso Phase 4

Men can be pretty predictable. The more our workouts focus on our pectoral muscles, the more we like them. So for Phase 4, we asked King to give us a pec-centric program. He obliged with a 3-week program of three intense 45-minute workouts a week. It provides a balance between front and back exercises so when your chest starts to swell, you'll have a back strong enough to hold it up.

WHICH WORKOUT TO CHOOSE

If you've done squats and deadlifts in the past and can do more than five chinups in consecutive sets, you're ready for the Advanced workout. If not, stick with the Beginner program. Either way, you'll see great gains.

FREQUENCY

Do each workout once a week (Monday, Wednesday, and Friday) for 3 weeks, then rest a week.

WARMUPS AND WORK SETS

For most exercises, you'll start with one, two, or three warmup sets (they're identified as such on your training log), then progress to work sets. Here's how.

1. Decide how much weight you're going to use for the first work set of your first exercise. It should be tough, but you should finish all the repetitions with strength to spare. Let's say you're doing workout A and want to use 155 pounds for your first work set of bench presses.

2. Choose a weight that's about 30 percent of that—say, 45 pounds (just the Olympic bar, in other words). That's your first warmup weight. Do 10 repetitions. Use the same speed you'll use during your work sets.

3. For your second warmup, use a weight that's about 60 percent of your first work set. So 95 pounds would work. (You don't have to whip out the calculator here; these are ballpark figures.)

4. For your third warmup, use about 80 percent of your first work-set weight, or about 115 pounds.

5. Do your first work set with the 155 pounds. Do your second work set with a little more weight—175 pounds, say. You should complete all the repetitions in this set, too, but it should feel closer to an all-out effort. Then continue, if the exercise calls for more sets.

STRIP SETS

A strip set is three consecutive sets of the same exercise, using less weight on each set and taking no rest in between.

THE EXERCISES

Take 2 seconds to lower the weight, pause for 1 second, then lift the weight in 1 second.

Rest for 2 to 3 minutes between sets (1 minute between abdominal sets; no rest within a strip set).

You should increase the weights for each set of each exercise each time you do the workout (except for strip sets).

Bench press works chest, triceps, and front shoulders

1. Lie on your back on a flat bench with your feet on the floor. Grab the bar with an overhand grip, your hands just beyond shoulder-width, and lift it off the uprights. Hold it over your chin at arm's length.

2. Slowly lower the bar to your chest. Pause, then push the bar back up until your arms are straight and the bar is over your chin again.

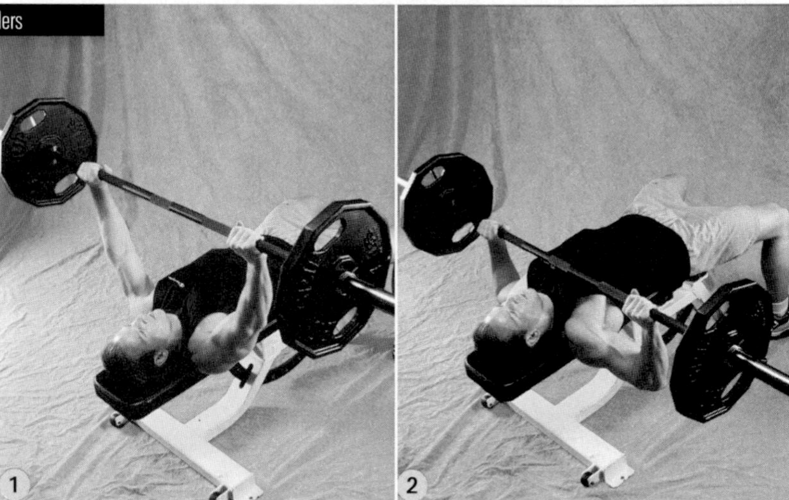

Wide-grip bench press works chest and triceps

1. Grab the bar with your hands a bit farther apart than for the regular bench press.

2. Slowly lower the bar to your chest. Pause, then push the bar back up.

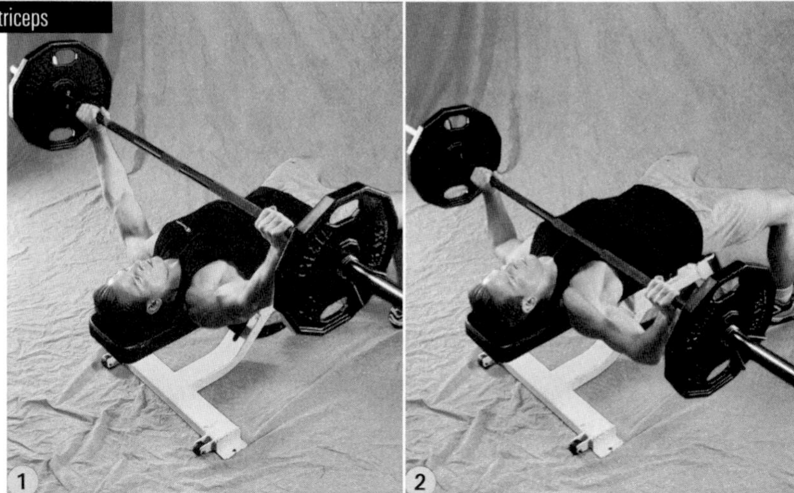

Wide-grip bench press with legs up works chest and front shoulders

1. Lie on your back on a flat bench with your hips bent 90 degrees and your feet in the air, ankles crossed. Grab the bar with an overhand grip, your hands a bit farther apart than for the regular bench press.

2. Slowly lower the bar to your chest. Pause, then push the bar back up.

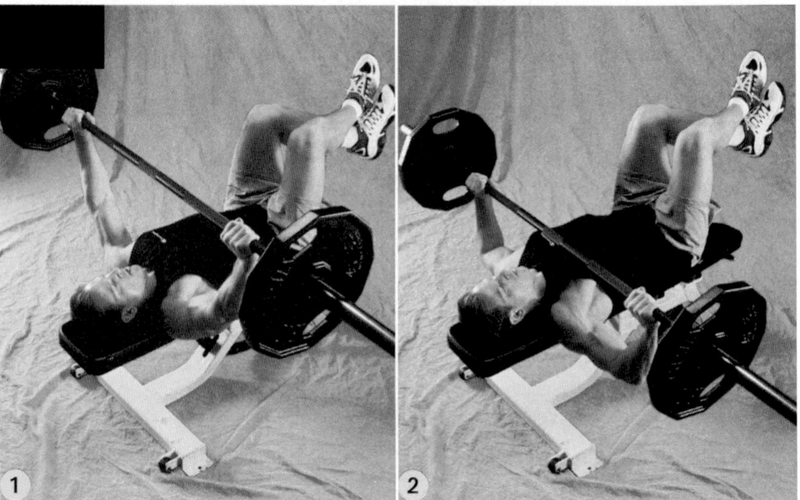

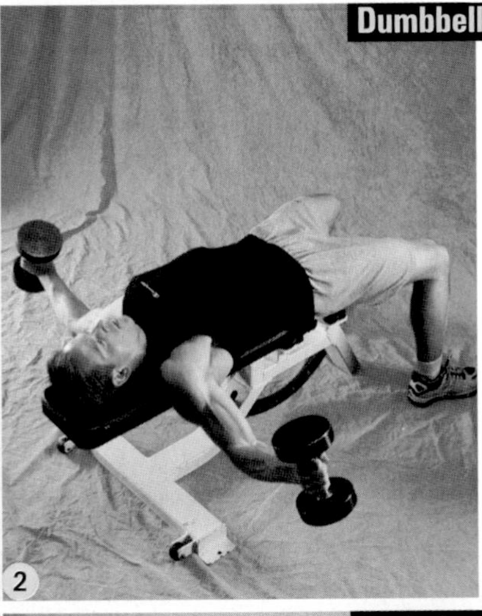

Dumbbell fly works chest

1. Grab a pair of dumbbells and lie on your back on a flat bench, your feet on the floor. Hold the dumbbells over your chest with your elbows slightly bent and your thumbs turned toward each other.

2. Slowly lower the weights until your upper arms are parallel to the floor. Pause, then lift the weights back to the starting position.

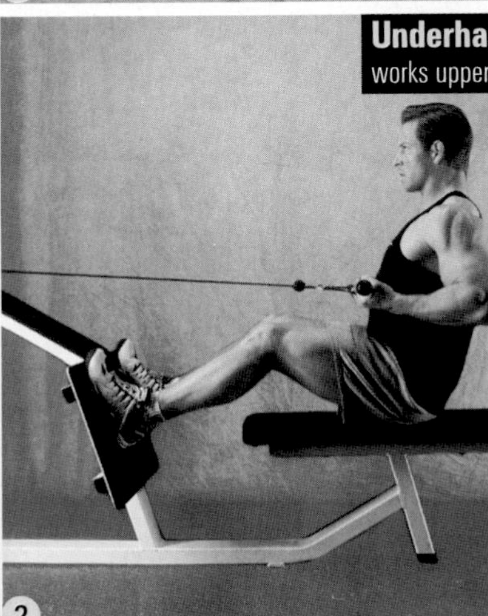

Underhand-grip seated row works upper and middle back and biceps

1. Attach a straight bar to the cable of a seated-row station and grab the bar with an underhand, shoulder-width grip. Sit up straight and pull your shoulders back.

2. Pull the bar to your abdomen. Pause, then slowly return to the starting position.

Hanging knee raise works abdominals

1. Hang from a pullup bar, using your hands or elbow supports like the ones shown. Bend your knees slightly.

2. Lift your knees up to your chest. Pause, then slowly lower your legs.

Wide-grip deadlift works hamstrings, gluteals, and back

1. Load the barbell and roll it against your shins. Grab the bar with an overhand grip, your hands a few inches beyond shoulder-width apart. Squat down, focus your eyes straight ahead, and pull your shoulders back.

2. Stand with the bar, thrusting your hips forward and keeping your shoulders pulled back. Pause, then slowly lower the bar to the floor, keeping it as close to your body as possible.

1

2

Front squat works quadriceps and gluteals

1. Set a bar on a squat rack and step under it so the bar sits just above the front part of your deltoid muscles. Support the bar by grabbing it underhand just outside your shoulders—the bar should rest on your fingers, not your palms. Hold your upper arms parallel to the floor. Lift the bar off the rack and step back. Set your feet shoulder-width apart, and keep your knees slightly bent, your back straight, and your eyes focused straight ahead.

2. Slowly squat down until your thighs are parallel to the floor. Stand back up to the starting position.

1

2

Stiff-legged deadlift works hamstrings, gluteals, and back

1. Grab the bar with an overhand grip that's just beyond shoulder-width. Stand with the bar resting on the fronts of your thighs. Your feet should be shoulder-width apart and your knees slightly bent.

2. Slowly bend at the waist as you lower the bar to just below your knees. Don't change the angle of your knees. Keep your head and chest up and your lower back arched. Lift your torso back to the starting position, keeping the bar as close to your body as possible.

1

2

Stepup works quadriceps, hamstrings, and gluteals

1. Set the barbell in a squat rack and step under it so it rests across your upper trapezius muscles. Lift the bar off the rack and move over to a step or bench that's 6 to 12 inches high. Lift your right foot and place it firmly on the bench.

2. Push down with your right heel, and step up onto the bench so you're standing on it with both feet. Step down with your left foot first, then your right. Finish the set with your right leg, then do the same number of repetitions starting with your left foot.

Calf raise on leg-press machine

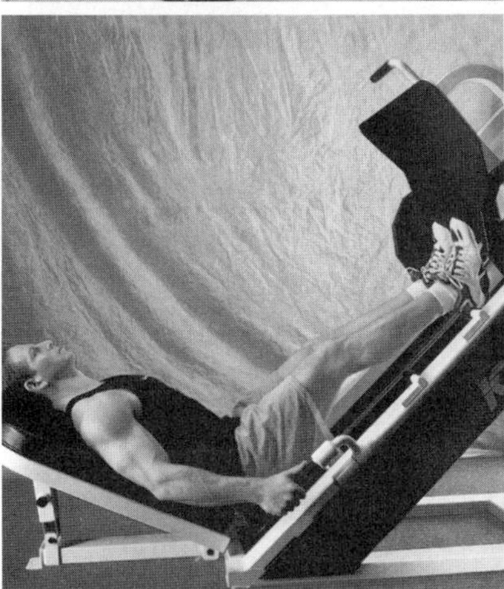

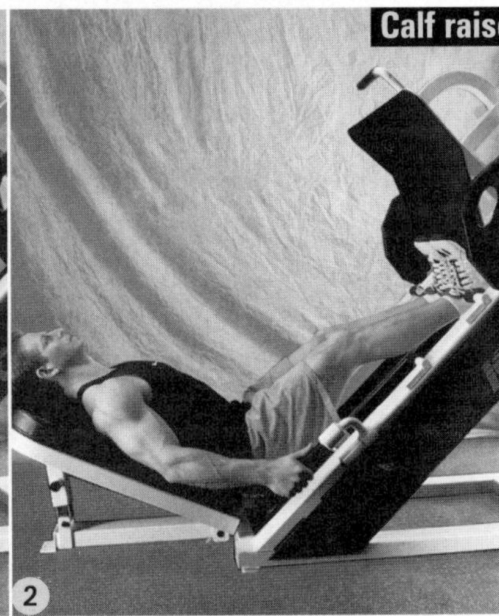

1. Position yourself in the leg-press station with your feet shoulder-width apart and your legs fully extended.

2. Lower the weight as far as you can, then push off the balls of your feet and raise it as high as you can. Pause, then lower the weight again.

Russian twist works obliques

1. Sit on a mat with your knees bent 90 degrees and your feet flat on the floor. Either clasp your hands together or grab a weight plate or dumbbell and extend your arms in front of your chest. Lean back so your body is at a 45-degree angle to the floor.

2. Rotate at the waist, swinging your arms as far as you can to the right and then to the left. That's one repetition.

Shoulder press works shoulders and triceps

1. Grab a pair of dumbbells and sit holding them just outside your shoulders, with your arms bent and your palms facing forward.

2. Push the weights straight up. Pause, then slowly lower the weights to the starting position.

1

2

Dip works chest, front shoulders, and triceps

1. Grab the parallel dip bars and lift yourself so your arms are fully extended.

2. Bend your elbows and slowly lower your body until your upper arms are parallel to the floor. Pause, then push yourself back up to the starting position.

1

2

BEGINNER VERSION: Bench dip

1. Sit on the side of a bench. Place your palms (fingers forward) on the bench, beside your hips. Your legs should be straight out in front of you, heels on the floor. Straighten your arms and move your torso forward so your butt and back are just in front of the bench.

2. Bend your elbows to a 90-degree angle, lowering your butt toward the floor. Pause, then raise yourself to the starting position.

Close-grip bench press works triceps and chest

1. Grab the bar with your hands a bit narrower than shoulder-width apart.

2. Slowly lower it to your chest. Pause, then push the bar back up.

Neutral-grip lat pulldown
works upper back and biceps

1. Attach the parallel-grip handle to the lat-pulldown cable. Grab the handle with an overhand grip so your palms face each other. Sit and position your knees under the pad.

2. Pull the handle down to your chest. Pause, then slowly return to the starting position.

ADVANCED VERSION: Neutral-grip pullup

1. Hang from the parallel chinup bars using an overhand grip with your palms facing each other. Cross your feet behind you.

2. Pull yourself up as high as you can—your chin should go over the bars. Pause, then slowly lower yourself to the starting position.

(continued)

Reverse-grip biceps curl works biceps and forearms

1. Grab an EZ-curl bar with an overhand, shoulder-width grip. Stand with your feet shoulder-width apart, your knees slightly bent, and your back straight. Hold the bar at arm's length in front of your thighs.

2. Curl the bar upward as high as you can without moving your upper arms—they should stay tucked against your sides. Pause, then slowly return to the starting position.

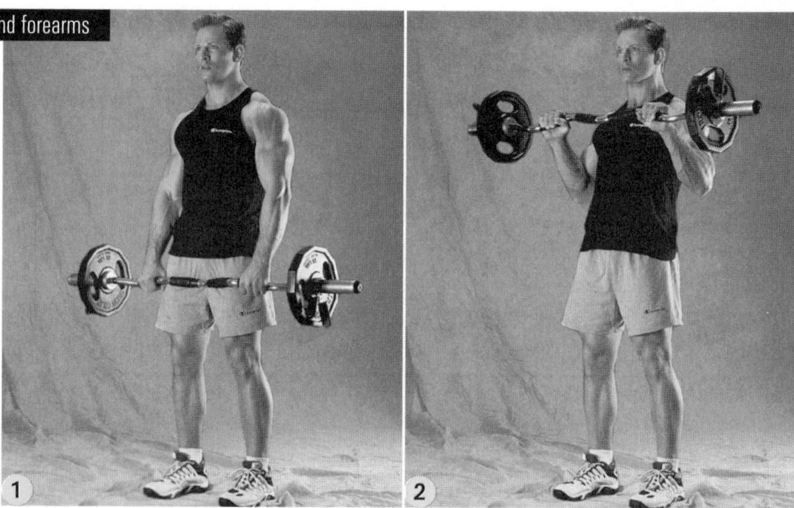

Bar rollout works abdominals

1. Load a barbell with a 10-pound plate on each side and affix collars. (Make sure they're on tight.) Get down on your knees and grab the bar with an overhand, shoulder-width grip. Your shoulders should be over the barbell to start.

2. Slowly roll the bar forward, extending your body as far as you can. Use your abdominal muscles to roll the bar back to your knees.

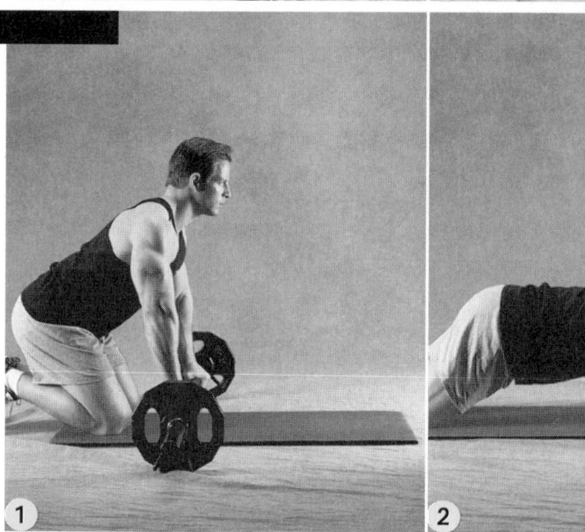

PHASE 4: Workout-A Training Log

	REPETITIONS		WEEK 1		WEEK 2		WEEK 3	
	BEGINNER	ADVANCED	WEIGHT	REPS	WEIGHT	REPS	WEIGHT	REPS
Bench press								
Warmup set 1	10 at 30%	10 at 30%						
Warmup set 2	8 at 60%	8 at 60%						
Warmup set 3	6 at 80%	6 at 80%						
Work set 1	5–6	4–5						
Work set 2	5–6†	4–5						
Wide-grip bench press								
Work set 1	8–10	6–8						
Work set 2	8–10‡	6–8						
Wide-grip bench press with legs up								
Work set 1	15–20	12–15						
Dumbbell fly*								
Warmup	6 at 60%	6 at 60%						
Work set 1	10	6						
Work set 2	10	8						
Work set 3	10	10						
Underhand-grip seated row								
Warmup set 1	10 at 30%	10 at 30%						
Warmup set 2	8 at 60%	8 at 60%						
Warmup set 3	6 at 80%	6 at 80%						
Work set 1	6–8	5–6						
Work set 2	6–8†	5–6						
Hanging knee raise								
Work set 1	5–15	5–15						
Work set 2	5–15	5–15						

* Strip sets: Use less weight for each set, and change weights as quickly as possible between sets.
† Use slightly more weight than you did for the first work set.
‡ Try to use the same weight for both sets.

PHASE 4: Workout-B Training Log

	REPETITIONS		WEEK 1		WEEK 2		WEEK 3	
	BEGINNER	ADVANCED	WEIGHT	REPS	WEIGHT	REPS	WEIGHT	REPS
Wide-grip deadlift								
Warmup set 1	10 at 30%	10 at 30%						
Warmup set 2	8 at 60%	8 at 60%						
Warmup set 3	6 at 80%	6 at 80%						
Work set 1	6	5						
Work set 2†	6	5						
Work set 3	—	10						
Front squat								
Warmup set 1	10 at 30%	10 at 30%						
Warmup set 2	8 at 60%	8 at 60%						
Warmup set 3	6 at 80%	6 at 80%						
Work set 1	6	5						
Work set 2†	6	5						
Work set 3	—	10						
Stiff-legged deadlift								
Warmup set	8 at 60%	6 at 60%						
Work set	8	6						
Stepup								
Warmup set	8 at 60%	8 at 60%						
Work set	8	6						
Calf raise on leg-press machine+								
Warmup set	15 at 60%	15 at 60%						
Work set 1	15–20	12–15						
Work set 2	15–20	12–15						
Russian twist								
Work set 1	15–20	15–20						
Work set 2	15–20	15–20						

† Use slightly more weight than you did for the first work set.
‡ Try to use the same weight for both sets.
+ You can substitute the donkey calf raise, if your gym has that machine.

PHASE 4: Workout-C Training Log

	REPETITIONS		WEEK 1		WEEK 2		WEEK 3	
	BEGINNER	ADVANCED	WEIGHT	REPS	WEIGHT	REPS	WEIGHT	REPS
Shoulder press								
Warmup set 1	10 at 30%	10 at 30%						
Warmup set 2	8 at 60%	8 at 60%						
Warmup set 3	6 at 80%	6 at 80%						
Work set 1	5–6	4–5						
Work set 2†	5–6	4–5						
Dip or bench dip								
Warmup set++	6	6						
Work set 1§	8–10	6–8						
Work set 2	8–10	6–8						
Close-grip bench press								
Work set	15–20	12–15						
Neutral-grip pullup or lat pulldown								
Warmup set 1	10 at 30%	10 at 30%						
Warmup set 2	8 at 60%	8 at 60%						
Warmup set 3	6 at 80%	6 at 80%						
Work set 1	6–8	5–6						
Work set 2†	6–8	5–6						
Reverse-grip biceps curl								
Warmup set 1	10 at 40%	10 at 40%						
Warmup set 2	8 at 70%	8 at 70%						
Work set 1	8–10	6–8						
Work set 2†	8–10	6–8						
Bar rollout								
Work set 1	10–20	10–20						
Work set 2	10–20	10–20						

† Use slightly more weight than you did for the first work set.

++ Use bench dips for the warmup, even if you're going to do standard dips in your work sets.

§ If you need to, use a weighted belt to add resistance on the dips. Try to stay at the same weight for both work sets.

Arm Services

Phase 5

If the standard-issue arm exercises worked, we'd all have guns worthy of registration with the ATF. No such luck. That's why we asked King for arm exercises and techniques you haven't tried before, for results you've never seen before. Try them for just nine workouts, and you won't come up short in short sleeves.

WHICH WORKOUT TO CHOOSE

Choose Advanced if you can do consecutive sets of six or more pullups.

FREQUENCY

Do each workout once a week for 3 weeks, then rest a week.

WARMUPS AND WORK SETS

For most exercises, you'll start with one, two, or three warmup sets (they're identified as such on your training log), then progress to work sets. Here's how.

1. Decide how much weight you're going to use for the first work set of your first exercise. It should be tough, but you should be able to finish all the repetitions with strength to spare.

2. Now use the designated percentage of that weight (30, 40, 60, 70, 80, or 100 percent) for the warmup set or sets. You don't have to whip out the calculator to make sure you get the exact percentage; these are ballpark figures to make sure you warm up appropriately for each exercise.

SUPERSETS AND TRISETS

A superset is consecutive sets of two exercises, performed without rest. A triset is consecutive sets of three different exercises, with no rest in between.

STRIP SETS

A strip set is three consecutive sets of the same exercise, using less weight on each set and taking no rest in between.

21s

Do seven repetitions in the first half of the range of motion—half as far as you would normally push or pull the weight. The next seven are the full range of motion, and the last seven are the second half of the motion.

THE EXERCISES

Take 3 seconds to lower the weight, pause for 1 second, then lift the weight in 1 second. Rest for 1 minute between sets (except within supersets, trisets, or strip sets).

You should increase the weights for each set of each exercise each time you do the workout (except for strip sets). Caution: The heavier the weight you use, the more you need a spotter.

1

2

Wrist curl works forearm flexors

1. Grab a bar with an underhand grip and kneel next to a bench with your forearms lying across the pad and your hands hanging off the side.

2. Curl your hands toward your forearms as far as you can. Pause, then slowly lower the bar to the starting position.

1

2

Reverse wrist curl works forearm extensors

1. Grab a bar with an overhand grip and kneel next to a bench with your forearms lying across the pad and your hands hanging off the side.

2. Curl your hands toward your forearms as far as you can. Pause, then slowly lower the bar to the starting position.

1

2

Incline dumbbell curl works biceps

1. Set an incline bench to a 45-degree angle. Grab a pair of dumbbells and sit with your back against the pad. Let your arms hang straight down from your shoulders and turn your palms forward.

2. Moving only from the elbows, curl the weights as high as you can. Pause, then slowly lower the weights.

Seated hammer curl works biceps

1. Set an incline bench to a right-degree angle. Grab a pair of dumbbells and sit with your back against the pad. Let your arms hang straight down from your shoulders and turn your palms toward each other.

2. Moving only from the elbows, curl the weights as high as you can. Pause, then slowly lower them.

Zottman curl works biceps and forearms

1. Start with your arms hanging straight down and your palms facing forward.

2. At the top of the curl, rotate your wrists so your palms continue facing forward. Slowly lower the weights with your hands in that position, then turn your palms back to the starting position to start the next repetition.

Lying triceps extension

1. Grab an EZ-curl bar with an overhand grip, your palms angled toward each other. Lie on a flat bench and hold the bar with straight arms over your head.

2. Moving only from the elbows, slowly lower the bar back beyond your forehead. Pause, then lift the bar to the starting position.

1

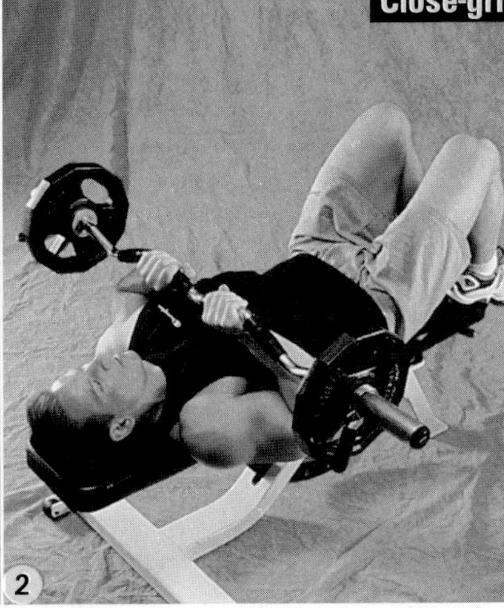
2

Close-grip bench press works triceps and chest

1. Grab the EZ-curl bar with your hands a bit narrower than shoulder-width apart.

2. Slowly lower the bar to your chest. Pause, then push the bar back up.

1

2

Dip (advanced) works chest, front shoulders, and triceps

1. Grab the parallel dip bars and lift yourself so your arms are fully extended.

2. Bend your elbows and slowly lower your body until your upper arms are parallel to the floor. Pause, then push yourself back up to the starting position.

BEGINNER VERSION: Bench dip

1. Sit on the side of a bench. Place your palms (fingers forward) on the bench, beside your hips. Your legs should be straight out in front of you, heels on the floor. Straighten your arms and move your torso forward so your butt and back are just in front of the bench.

2. Bend your elbows to a 90-degree angle, lowering your butt toward the floor. Pause, then raise yourself to the starting position.

(continued)

Squat works quadriceps, hamstrings, and gluteals

1. Set a bar on a squat rack and step under it so the bar rests across your upper back. Grab the bar with an overhand grip. Lift the bar off the rack and step back. Set your feet shoulder-width apart.

2. Slowly lower your body until your thighs are parallel to the floor. Keep your knees even with or behind your toes. Pause, then slowly return to the starting position.

Swiss-ball reverse crunch works abdominals

1. Lie on your back on a Swiss ball and reach behind you to grab a sturdy bar or rack. Bend your hips and knees 90 degrees.

2. Using only your abdominal muscles, pull your hips up toward your rib cage. Pause, then slowly lower your hips.

Wide-grip seated row works upper back

1. Grab the bar with a wide overhand grip.

2. Pull the bar toward your torso. Pause, then slowly return to the starting position.

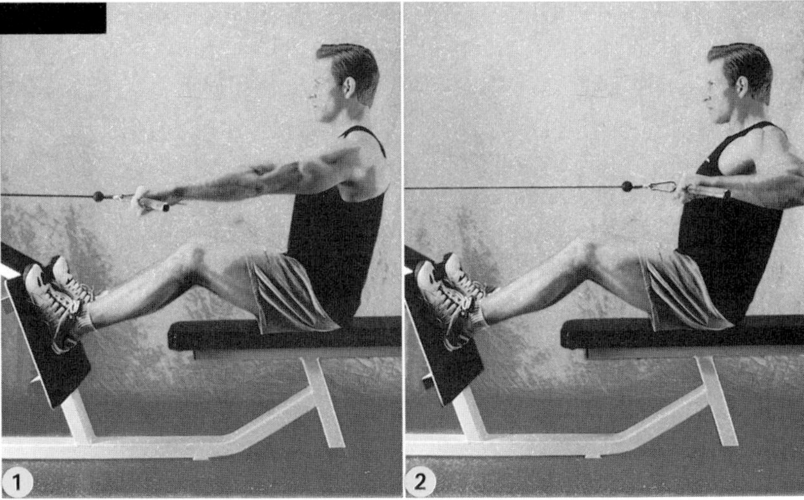

Wide-grip incline bench press works chest and triceps

1. Lie on your back on a bench set at a low incline and grab the bar with a wide overhand grip. Lift the bar so it's over your eyes.

2. Slowly lower the weight to your chest. Pause, then push the bar back up over your eyes.

Wide-grip lat pulldown works upper back

1. Grab the pulldown bar with a wide overhand grip.

2. Pull the bar down to your chest. Pause, then slowly return to the starting position.

ADVANCED VERSION: Wide-grip pullup

1. Grab a chinup bar with a wide overhand grip and hang with your knees bent and your ankles crossed behind you.

2. Pull yourself up until your chin is over the bar. Pause, then slowly lower yourself.

(continued)

Shoulder press (works shoulders and triceps)

1. Grab a pair of dumbbells and sit holding them just outside your shoulders, with your arms bent and your palms facing each other.

2. Push the weights straight overhead. Pause, then slowly lower.

Standing calf raise

1. Stand on a 6- to 12-inch block with the balls of your feet on the edge and your heels hanging off the side as low as possible.

2. Lift your heels as high as you can. Pause, then lower.

ADVANCED VERSION: Hold dumbbells.

Swiss-ball side crunch works obliques

1. Lie on your side on a Swiss ball, with the sides of your feet resting on the floor and your hands behind your ears.

2. Raise your upper torso until you feel a squeeze in your obliques. Pause, then slowly lower. Finish your repetitions and repeat on your other side.

Preacher curl works biceps

1. Grab an EZ-curl bar with an underhand, shoulder-width grip. As you sit on the preacher-bench seat, the top of the sloping pad should reach your armpits. Rest your upper arms on the pad and hold the bar at arm's length.

2. Curl the bar upward until your elbows are bent about 90 degrees. Pause, then slowly return to the starting position.

Rope triceps extension

1. Attach a rope to the high-cable pulley and grab it so your palms face each other. Start with your elbows bent 90 degrees and your upper arms against your sides.

2. Straighten your arms, allowing your hands to pull the rope handles outward at the bottom. Pause, then slowly return to the starting position.

Wide-grip biceps curl

1. Grab an EZ-curl bar with an underhand grip, your hands as far apart as is comfortable. Hold the bar down at arm's length in front of you.

2. Bend at the elbows and curl the bar as high as you can without moving your elbows forward or back. Pause, then slowly lower the bar.

Overhead triceps extension

1. Grab the EZ-curl bar with a shoulder-width, overhand grip. Hold the bar at arm's length over your head.

2. Keeping your upper arms still, lower the bar behind your head. Pause, then straighten your arms.

Deadlift works hamstrings, gluteals, and lower back

1. Load the barbell and roll it against your shins. Grab the bar with an overhand grip, your hands just beyond shoulder-width. Squat and pull your shoulders back.

2. Stand with the bar, thrusting your hips forward. Pause, then slowly lower the bar to the floor, keeping it as close to your body as possible.

Swiss-ball situp works abdominals

1. Lie on your back on the ball, with your feet flat on the floor. Lower your head as far as you can. Hold your hands behind your ears.

2. Use your abdominal muscles to pull your torso to a sitting position. Pause, then slowly lower yourself.

PHASE 5: Workout-A Training Log

		Repetitions		Week 1		Week 2		Week 3	
		Beginner	Advanced	Weight	Reps	Weight	Reps	Weight	Reps
FOREARM SUPERSET	**Wrist curl**								
	Warmup set	20 at 60%	15 at 60%						
	Work set	20	15						
	Reverse wrist curl								
	Warmup set	20 at 60%	15 at 60%						
	Work set	20	15						
BICEPS TRISET	**Incline dumbbell curl**								
	Warmup set	10 at 60%	10 at 60%						
	Work set	10	10						
	Seated hammer curl								
	Warmup set	10 at 60%	10 at 60%						
	Work set	10	10						
	Zottman curl								
	Warmup set	10 at 60%	10 at 60%						
	Work set	10	10						
TRICEPS TRISET	**Lying triceps extension**								
	Warmup set	10 at 60%	10 at 60%						
	Work set	10	10						
	Close-grip bench press								
	Warmup set	10 at 60%	10 at 60%						
	Work set	10	10						
	Dip or bench dip								
	Warmup set	10 at 60%	10 at 60%						
	Work set	10	10						
	Squat								
	Warmup set 1	10 at 40%	10 at 30%						
	Warmup set 2	8 at 70%	8 at 70%						
	Warmup set 3	—	6 at 80%						
	Work set 1	8–10	6–8						
	Work set 2*	8–10	6–8						
	Swiss-ball reverse crunch								
	Work set 1	5–15	5–15						
	Work set 2	5–15	5–15						

* Use slightly more weight than you did for the first work set.

PHASE 5: Workout-B Training Log

		REPETITIONS		WEEK 1		WEEK 2		WEEK 3	
		BEGINNER	ADVANCED	WEIGHT	REPS	WEIGHT	REPS	WEIGHT	REPS
SUPERSET 1	**Wide-grip seated row**								
	Warmup set 1	10 at 40%	10 at 40%						
	Warmup set 2	8 at 70%	8 at 70%						
	Work set 1	8–10	6–8						
	Work set 2*	8–10	6–8						
	Wide-grip incline bench press								
	Warmup set 1	10 at 40%	10 at 40%						
	Warmup set 2	8 at 70%	8 at 70%						
	Work set 1	8–10	8–10						
	Work set 2	8–10	8–10						
SUPERSET 2	**Wide-grip lat pulldown or pullup**								
	Warmup set 1	10 at 40%	10 at 40%‡						
	Warmup set 2	8 at 70%	8 at 70%						
	Work set 1	8–10	8–10						
	Work set 2*	8–10	8–10						
	Shoulder press								
	Warmup set 1	10 at 40%	10 at 40%						
	Warmup set 2	8 at 70%	8 at 70%						
	Work set 1	8–10	8–10						
	Work set 2*	8–10	8–10						
	Standing calf raise+								
	Warmup set	15 at 60%	12 at 60%						
	Work set 1	15	12						
	Work set 2	15	12						
	Work set 3	15	12						
	Swiss-ball side crunch								
	Work set 1	10–20†	10–20†						
	Work set 2	10–20†	10–20†						

* Use slightly more weight than you did for the first work set.

† Each side.

‡ Use wide-grip lat pulldowns for warmup sets. Use a weighted belt if you need more resistance for your work sets.

+ Strip sets: Use less weight for each set, and change weights as quickly as possible between sets.

PHASE 5: Workout-C Training Log

		REPETITIONS		WEEK 1		WEEK 2		WEEK 3	
		BEGINNER	ADVANCED	WEIGHT	REPS	WEIGHT	REPS	WEIGHT	REPS
SUPERSET 1	**Preacher curl**								
	Warmup set	10 at 100%	10 at 100%						
	Work set	21s	21s						
	Rope triceps extension								
	Warmup set	10 at 100%	10 at 100%						
	Work set	21s	21s						
SUPERSET 2	**Wide-grip biceps curl†**								
	Warmup set	10 at 60%	10 at 60%						
	Work set 1	10	10						
	Work set 2	10	10						
	Work set 3	10	10						
	Overhead triceps extension†								
	Warmup set	10 at 60%	10 at 60%						
	Work set 1	10	10						
	Work set 2	10	10						
	Work set 3	10	10						
	Deadlift								
	Warmup set 1	10 at 40%	10 at 40%						
	Warmup set 2	8 at 70%	8 at 70%						
	Warmup set 3	—	6 at 80%						
	Work set 1	8–10	8–10						
	Work set 2*	8–10	8–10						
	Swiss-ball situp								
	Work set 1	10–20	10–20						
	Work set 2	10–20	10–20						

* Use slightly more weight than you did for the first work set.

† Strip sets: Use less weight for each set, and change weights as quickly as possible between sets.

Cutting Class Phase 6

When the thought of a day at the beach keeps you up at night—and your fears have nothing to do with shark attacks or melanoma—it's time to skim the fat once and for all. Try King's 3-week total-body potboiler. And use sunscreen.

WHICH WORKOUT TO CHOOSE

Choose Advanced if you can do consecutive sets of eight or more pullups. If not, stick with the Beginner program. Either way, you'll see great gains.

FREQUENCY

Do each workout (A, B, and C) once a week for 3 weeks, then rest a week.

TECHNIQUE

In week 1, do just one circuit (one set of each exercise). Do two circuits in week 2 and three in week 3.

REST

Don't rest until you get to the end of a circuit; then rest 2 minutes.

THE EXERCISES

You'll do the same five abdominal exercises each workout without resting between exercises. But each routine has a different focus:

Control: On each repetition, take 3 seconds to lift your body, pause, then lower for 3 seconds.

Power: Use light weights and lift your body as fast as you can, then lower in 1 second (no pause). Then lift the weight again as quickly as you can. Even though you're using the weights explosively in this phase, maintain control over them. Always keep a firm grip on the weight plate or dumbbell. You should increase the weights for each exercise each time you do the workout.

Endurance: Take 2 seconds to raise your body and 1 second to lower it (no pause).

AEROBIC STATIONS

You'll do these in between the exercises that follow the ab routine. Start with 30 seconds of any continuous-motion exercise you choose. You can jog around an indoor track, if your gym has one; hop on any piece of cardiovascular equipment to which you have access; or do something as simple as jumping jacks or shadowboxing. Add 15 seconds to your aerobic stations each workout so by the ninth workout you do 2½ minutes of aerobics after each exercise.

Reverse crunch works lower abdominals

1. Lie on your back with your knees bent, your feet off the floor, and your hands behind your ears.

2. Lift your hips up and in toward your rib cage; then lower them.

Power: Hold a light dumbbell or medicine ball between your ankles.

Situp works abdominals

1. Lie on your back with your knees bent, your feet flat on the floor, and your hands at your sides (beginner) or behind your ears (advanced).

2. Lift your torso to an upright position, then lower it.

Power: Hold a light weight on your chest with both hands.

Cycling twist works obliques

1. Sit with your knees bent, your arms extended forward, and your hands together in front of your chest. Lean back so your torso is at a 45-degree angle to the floor. Lift your feet and twist your torso to the right as you lift your left knee toward your chest.

2. Then twist to the left as you lower your left knee and raise your right knee in a cycling motion.

Power: Try the anchored Russian twist. Anchor your feet (on a situp board, for example) and hold a light weight in your hands while you twist your torso, as above. Don't cycle your legs.

Toe touch works abdominals

1. Lie on your back with your legs and arms extended toward the ceiling.

2. Slowly lift your head and shoulders as you reach as high as you can with your fingers; then lie back down.

Power: Hold a weight plate across your chest. Lift your head and shoulders off the floor without reaching with your hands.

Modified V-sit works abdominals

1. Lie on your back with your heels off the floor and your hands at your sides.

2. Lift your torso into an upright position as you bend your knees and pull them up to your chest; then return to the starting position.

Power: Hold a light weight across your chest with both hands.

Jump squat works entire lower body

1. Hold a barbell across the back of your shoulders and stand with your feet shoulder-width apart. Sit back into a squat.

2. Jump up. Land with your knees bent to absorb the impact. Pause, reset your body, and repeat.

Pullup

1. Grab the chinup bar with an overhand grip, hands a bit wider than shoulder-width apart. Hang with your arms fully extended, your knees bent, and your ankles crossed behind you. Pull yourself up until your chin crosses the bar, pause, then slowly lower yourself.

Overhand lat pulldown works back and biceps

1. Grab the bar with an overhand grip that's just beyond shoulder-width.

2. Pull the bar down to your chest. Pause, then slowly return to the starting position.

Underhand lat pulldown works back and biceps

1. Grab the bar with an underhand grip that's just less than shoulder-width.

2. Pull the bar down to your chest. Pause, then slowly return to the starting position.

Jump shrug works trapezius and calves

1. Grab a pair of dumbbells and hold them at your sides with your arms extended and your palms toward your thighs. Set your feet shoulder-width apart, and bend your knees slightly.

2. Bend your knees a bit farther, then jump as high as you can, simultaneously shrugging your shoulders and pulling your toes upward, toward your shins. Land with your knees bent to absorb the impact. Pause, reset your body, and repeat.

Shoulder press works shoulders and triceps

1. Grab a pair of dumbbells and sit on a bench. Hold the dumbbells at the sides of your shoulders, with your arms bent and your palms facing each other.

2. Push the weights straight overhead. Pause, then slowly lower them.

Walking lunge works entire lower body

1. Grab a pair of dumbbells and stand with your feet hip-width apart, at one end of your house or gym.

2. Lunge forward with your right leg, bending the knee 90 degrees. Your left knee should also bend and almost touch the floor. Stand and bring your left foot up next to your right, then repeat with the left leg lunging forward. That's one repetition. Continue until you've completed half your repetitions in this direction. Turn and do the same number of walking lunges back to your starting point.

Dip (advanced) works chest, front shoulders, and triceps

1. Grab the parallel bars and lift yourself so your arms are fully extended.

2. Bend your elbows until your upper arms are parallel to the floor. Pause, then push yourself back to the starting position.

BEGINNER VERSION: Bench dip

1. Sit on the side of a bench, your palms on the bench, beside your hips. Your legs should be straight out in front of you, heels on the floor. Straighten your arms so your butt rises up. Bend your arms 90 degrees as you lower your butt toward the floor. Pause, then push back to the starting position.

Windmill lunge works entire lower body

1. Stand with your feet hip-width apart, and hold a pair of dumbbells at your sides. Lunge forward with your right leg until your right knee is bent 90 degrees. Step back to the starting position.

2. Lunge out at a 45-degree angle with your right leg, then return.

3. Lunge sideways with your right leg, then return.

4. Lunge backward at a 45-degree angle with your right leg, then return.

5. Lunge straight back with your right leg, then return. Step straight back with your left leg, then return. Lunge back at a 45-degree angle with your left leg, then return. Lunge sideways with your left leg, then return. Lunge forward at a 45-degree angle with your left leg, then return. Lunge forward with your left leg, then return. That's one complete set.

Dumbbell power clean and press

works back, shoulders, and arms

1. Grab a pair of dumbbells and squat with your feet shoulder-width apart. Hold the dumbbells straight down at arm's length, palms facing your feet.

2. In one motion, pull the dumbbells up to your shoulders as you rise from the squat and then dip your body down to "catch" the weights.

3. Push up to a standing position, then press the weights overhead. Pause, then lower the weights to shoulder level and return to the starting position.

Bench press

works chest, triceps, and front shoulders

1. Lie on your back on a flat bench and grab the bar with an overhand grip just beyond shoulder-width. Lift the bar so it's over your chin.

2. Lower the bar to your chest, pause, then push it back up over your chin.

Nonlockout squat works quadriceps and gluteals

1. Set a bar on a squat rack and step under it so the bar rests across your upper back. Pull your shoulders back as you grab the bar with an overhand grip. It should sit comfortably on your upper trapezius muscles. Lift the bar off the rack and step back. Set your feet shoulder-width apart, and keep your knees slightly bent, your back straight, and your eyes focused straight ahead.

2. Slowly lower your body as if you were sitting back into a chair, keeping your back in its natural alignment and your lower legs nearly perpendicular to the floor. When your thighs are parallel to the floor, pause. Return to the starting position without completely straightening your legs. Repeat the exercise without pausing at the top of the movement.

Bent-over row works upper back and arms

1. Grab a barbell with an overhand grip that's just beyond shoulder-width, and hold it down at arm's length. Stand with your feet shoulder-width apart and your knees slightly bent. Bend at the hips, lowering your torso about 45 degrees, and let the bar hang straight down from your shoulders.

2. Pull the bar up to your torso, pause, then slowly lower it.

PHASE 6: Workout-A-and-B Training Log

		Repetitions		Week 1		Week 2		Week 3	
	WORKOUT A	BEGINNER	ADVANCED	WEIGHT	REPS	WEIGHT	REPS	WEIGHT	REPS
AB ROUTINE: CONTROL	**Reverse crunch**	10–15	10–15						
	Situp	10–15	10–15						
	Cycling twist or Russian twist	10–15	10–15						
	Toe touch	10–15	10–15						
	Modified V-sit	10–15	10–15						
	Aerobic station	—	—						
	Jump squat	10–15	8–12						
	Aerobic station	—	—						
	Pullup or overhand lat pulldown	10–15	8–12						
	Aerobic station	—	—						
	Shoulder press	10–15	8–12						
	Aerobic station	—	—						
	WORKOUT B	BEGINNER	ADVANCED	WEIGHT	REPS	WEIGHT	REPS	WEIGHT	REPS
AB ROUTINE: POWER	**Reverse crunch**	10–15	10–15						
	Situp	10–15	10–15						
	Anchored Russian twist	10–15	10–15						
	Toe touch	10–15	10–15						
	Modified V-sit	10–15	10–15						
	Aerobic station	—	—						
	Walking lunge	10–15	8–12						
	Aerobic station	—	—						
	Dip or bench dip	10–15	8–12						
	Aerobic station	—	—						
	Windmill lunge	1*	1*						
	Aerobic station	—	—						
	Underhand lat pulldown	10–15	8–12						
	Aerobic station	—	—						

* Each repetition includes five lunges with each leg, which constitutes a complete set. If you do more than one set in a workout, alternate the leg you start off with (if you start with your left leg on the first set, start with your right on the second set).

PHASE 6: Workout-C Training Log

		REPETITIONS		WEEK 1		WEEK 2		WEEK 3	
		BEGINNER	ADVANCED	WEIGHT	REPS	WEIGHT	REPS	WEIGHT	REPS
AB ROUTINE: ENDURANCE	Reverse crunch	15–20	15–20						
	Situp	15–20	15–20						
	Cycling twist or Russian twist	15–20	15–20						
	Toe touch	15–20	15–20						
	Modified V-sit	15–20	15–20						
	Aerobic station	—	—						
	Dumbbell power clean and press	10–15	8–12						
	Aerobic station	—	—						
	Bench press	10–15	8–12						
	Aerobic station	—	—						
	Nonlockout squat	10–15	10–15						
	Aerobic station	—	—						
	Bent-over row	10–15	8–12						
	Aerobic station	—	—						

FEED THE

PART FOUR

When you build your dream house, you don't use cheap material just because it's easier to deal with. Same with building your leaner, meaner body. Eating any old thing will get you nowhere, no matter how much you exercise. Instead, you need to eat plenty of high-grade concrete, reinforced steel, and redwood four-by-fours.

Okay, not really—though we've often suspected that some NFL linebackers do their grocery shopping at Home Depot.

The real raw materials for your dream body are the right amounts of the right foods to fuel your workouts, build your muscles, and minimize body fat.

Mom had the right idea when she insisted that you eat right. But exercise nutrition probably wasn't her specialty. Lucky for you, it's ours. Keep reading and it'll be yours, too.

BEAST

MH•QUIZ

Do You Eat Right?

What are the best foods to fuel fitness and weight loss? For starters, if you want to lose your gut, you need plenty of fiber from fruits, vegetables, and whole grains. Fiber fills you up, so you eat less. You also need complex carbohydrates and protein for energy and muscle-building power, plus nutrients like riboflavin and magnesium to ensure optimum muscle function.

To see whether you're eating the right foods for getting fit, check off the items filling your fridge and then read how they rate.

1 In the door . . .

- [ ] Dozen eggs
- [ ] Tomato sauce
- [ ] Mayo
- [ ] Low-fat yogurt
- [ ] Butter

2 On the shelves . . .

- [ ] 2% milk
- [ ] Six-pack of Bud
- [ ] Fruit juice
- [ ] White bread
- [ ] Shredded cheese

3 In the meat bin . . .

- [ ] Chicken breasts
- [ ] Pastrami
- [ ] Ground beef
- [ ] Fish filets

4 In the fruit-and-vegetable bin . . .

- [ ] Iceberg lettuce
- [ ] Pears
- [ ] Potatoes
- [ ] Red peppers
- [ ] Broccoli

HOW YOUR FOOD CHOICES RATE

1. If you checked . . .

Dozen eggs: Eggs are an excellent source of the protein that's essential for building muscle. But they're also high in fat, some of it saturated. A couple a day is okay, but probably not three or four folded over a pile of Cheddar cheese.

Tomato sauce: Add lean ground beef and pair it with whole grain pasta for a post-workout meal that's high in carbs and protein.

Mayo: One tablespoon contains 100 calories and 11 grams of fat. Switch to light mayo and cut those numbers in half.

Low-fat yogurt: Loaded with protein and calcium for muscle contraction, low-fat yogurt is a great choice for the active guy. The fruit-on-the bottom yogurts are loaded with calories—about 240 per serving. Toss fresh berries or banana into plain yogurt and save 70 calories.

Butter: Both butter and margarine contain heart-clogging fats, but butter is your better choice, says Sue Saunders, R.D., director of nutrition at dietsmart.com. Buy "lite" whipped butter, which is lower in saturated fat. If you're a hard-nosed margarine man, use soft tub margarine, which has fewer trans fats than the stick kind.

2. If you checked . . .

2% milk: Milk is a great source of riboflavin (a B vitamin necessary for energy), plus calcium and protein. Remember to wipe off the white mustache before heading for the gym.

Six-pack of Bud: Trade it for a six-pack of abs. Beer contains empty calories that go right to your gut.

Fruit juice: Juices are high in calories and often contain added sugar. That means you get a quick sugar spike into your bloodstream, which in turn signals the release of insulin. The insulin causes a dip in blood sugar, which tells your body that it's low on fuel, making you crave even more. It's better to eat whole fruit; you'll get fewer calories, plus fiber to help you feel full.

White bread: Whole grain breads and cereals are lower in calories and provide more fiber. They're also good sources of thiamin, a B vitamin essential for utilizing energy. Plus, unlike processed breads, whole grains help keep your insulin at an even keel. That prevents dips in mood and energy as well as spikes in appetite.

Shredded cheese: A great source of calcium and protein . . . that's loaded with fat. Switch to extra-sharp Cheddar. It's more flavorful, so you'll use less. Or try the reduced-fat variety.

3. If you checked . . .

Chicken breasts: A good source of protein, they're a staple for any muscle-building man. Serve hot and whole, or cook ahead of time and slice cold over salad.

Pastrami: As lunchmeats go, pastrami is off the charts in fat and sodium. Instead, try lean-cut roast beef, which has less than a third of the fat and less than half of the sodium, plus more than 6 grams of protein per slice.

Ground beef: You already know beef is a great source of protein. It also has zinc and iron—two minerals you lose in sweat and urine when you exercise. Eating beef helps replenish your supply. Look for lean meat that's 7 to 10 percent fat.

Fish filets: Fish like tuna and salmon are rich in protein, plus they provide heart-healthy omega-3 fatty acids. Freeze the fish if you don't plan to eat it the same day, or it'll become raunchier than a Martin Lawrence monologue.

4. If you checked . . .

Iceberg lettuce: Regardless of whether you're as big as the Titanic, steer clear of the iceberg. It's pretty much void of nutrition, not to mention taste. Instead, eat spinach. It has magnesium, which is vital for muscle contraction, and the B vitamins riboflavin and B_6, which are necessary for using energy efficiently. Incorporate spinach into as many meals as possible—omelets, sandwiches, salad, tacos, pizza.

Pears: Now we know why partridges hang out in pear trees—they've heard that the fruit contains a type of fiber called lignans. Lignans not only help you eat less (because they fill you up) but also help lower cholesterol. And a pear's portability makes it a great snack when you're on the go, especially before a workout.

Potatoes: We love potatoes, and we hear they go great with meat. They also cause quite an insulin spike, so save them for post-workout meals.

Red peppers: The red bell pepper not only is sweeter-tasting than its green cousin but also packs more than three times the vitamin C. Some research has suggested that extra vitamin C may boost endurance and increase work capacity.

Broccoli: When food gurus talk about dark green vegetables, think broccoli. It has endurance-boosting vitamin C as well as calcium and magnesium for your muscles.

—DEANNA PORTZ

BY THOMAS INCLEDON, R.D., C.S.C.S.,
AND RICHARD LALIBERTE

Laws of LEANNESS

Eat your way to bigger muscles and a smaller waist

Think of getting into shape as a major renovation/remodeling project: You're constructing new muscle to both improve structural integrity and make things look better while simultaneously dumping fat like plaster debris. Projects like this require—in addition to time—abundant supplies of two essential commodities: raw material and energy. To get both, you need good nutrition.

"The nutrition component of any training program is just as important as the physical component," says Becky Schneider, R.D., a nutrition educator and personal chef in Indianapolis. "But athletes at all levels of training often fail to follow through with it."

When you eat the right balance of nutrients, your body fuels muscles more efficiently, builds bulk faster, and repairs injuries more easily. The bottom line is that you'll be stronger, faster, and longer-lasting if you eat right. Doing so isn't difficult, but it does call for a bit of know-how. What's important? "There are two basic things to look at: composition and timing," says nutritionist Ellen Coleman, R.D., of Riverside Cardiac Fitness Center in California.

The best muscle-building diet includes beef, pork, poultry, and fish, according to a study published in the *American Journal of Clinical Nutrition*. The reason is simple: Animal protein builds muscle better than soy or vegetable protein does, and buying it satisfies your primal urge to boss around big guys in bloody aprons.

The amount of protein you need is always debated, but the most reliable research shows that to build muscle during a strength-training program, you need 0.60 to 0.82 gram of protein per pound of body weight daily. If you weigh 200 pounds, that means taking in 120 to 164 grams of protein each day.

Say you choose 150 grams as your daily goal. Split it up so you eat 25 grams in each of six small meals. Breakfast might be two eggs, milk, and oatmeal. Lunch could be tuna on whole wheat. Grilled-chicken salad would be a good dinner.

Eat This

Composition is the cornerstone of any eating plan. There are six basic classes of nutrients, each of which matter for different reasons.

Carbohydrates. You need them. But not the fun kind. Consumption of high-fructose corn syrup and other sugary sweeteners, which went up more than 21 percent between 1970 and 1997, has possibly done more to expand America's waistlines than anything else. And it's fueled an anticarbohydrate mania that has sucked in everyone from Oprah to Al Gore.

That's too bad. The carbohydrates in fruits, vegetables, and whole grains are crucial to your health, give you energy, and help you build and repair muscle after workouts.

How much is enough? If your main goal is to be lean, try for 30 to 50 percent carbohydrate in your diet.

Protein. Remember: Meat equals muscle.

Fat. Fat still occupies that tiny prison cell at the tip of the Food Guide Pyramid, but its health benefits are hugely underrated.

A diet with 21 percent of its calories from monounsaturated fat reduces your risk of cardiovascular disease by 25 percent, according to a Pennsylvania State University study. And research has shown that men eating a diet with 40 percent fat have higher testosterone than those eating 20 percent. So chomp on those macadamia nuts and drench your salad with olive oil. You'll not only enjoy your food more but also live longer and have more sex.

Water. Even though it has no calories, it's the most critical of nutrients. Water carries all-important oxygen and nutritional fuel to working muscles, clears out waste, and dissipates body heat, to name just a few of its vital functions. It's also lost at a rapid rate when you exercise.

There's nothing complicated about drinking water, so long as you get enough. That means drinking not only while you're working out but all day long. A typical guy should drink six to eight 8-ounce glasses of water a day. If you're bigger or more active than the common Joe, drink more. And don't wait for thirst to hit before imbibing. By the time you're thirsty, you're already slightly dehydrated.

Vitamins. The word is derived from *vitality*, but vitamins have no usable energy of their own. Rather, they make possible a wide array of complicated processes involving energy creation from other nutrients, along with cell function, muscle and bone growth,

Three Laws to Break

You diet. You exercise. So why is your gut still hanging over your belt? Because of these common pitfalls.

❶ You Inhale Food

If you were a rat, you'd chow down for about 15 minutes, feel full, and stop eating. But you aren't. You probably eat so fast that your stomach hardly has time to alert your brain to tell your mouth to quit chewing before your stomach explodes.

▶**Solution:** Try this drill during your next meal. On every bite, chew, swallow, put down your fork, and take a sip of water. See how long it takes you to eat. During subsequent meals, take just as long to eat, only without the drill.

❷ You Think Fitness Trumps Fatness

Exercise alone won't make you thin. A recent study of military personnel who increased their exercise during a 3-year period found that they gained weight despite their extra efforts. Why? Food, most likely. They simply ate more than they burned off.

▶**Solution:** Controlling portion size is absolutely essential to weight loss. And the best way to control portion size is to limit how often you eat out.

According to the *Tufts University Health and Nutrition Letter*, a single restaurant meal often could feed an entire family. A pasta dish at an Italian restaurant may include eight 1-cup servings. A rib dish may consist of a pound of meat—more than five servings. A side of fries may have 70 of the little devils, which is seven servings.

Eat at home whenever possible, and when you do eat out, don't try to clean your plate. Why do you think doggie bags were invented?

❸ You're Cocky

It happens all the time: Guy drops 10 or 20 pounds and starts thinking he's Joe Weight Loss. Next thing you know, he's back to beer and pizza—and his original weight.

▶**Solution:** Remember that scene in *Patton* when George C. Scott refuses to pull his troops back, saying he doesn't like to pay twice for the same real estate? Okay, you're Patton, and every 10 pounds of fat you shed is real estate you own outright. Don't give it back.

With each 10 pounds you drop, sit down and reassess your diet and exercise program. If you calculated your food intake and exercise volume when you started, run a new set of numbers, based on your new weight and activity level.

blood formation, brain/muscle interaction—the kind of stuff your biology teachers used to fill entire blackboards with. We've known that vitamins are important ever since our moms fed us chewables. But what do we need now?

Research suggests that an exercising body uses certain vitamins differently than a sedentary one does, but it isn't clear whether this translates to an increased need, or whether taking extra doses of vitamins will improve physical performance. A number of studies over the years, for example, have suggested that taking vitamin C in amounts ranging from 50 to 200 milligrams a day boosts endurance and increases work capacity. But, as one research review points out, most studies involving vitamins and performance have not been designed or controlled well, making any conclusions . . . well, inconclusive.

One thing researchers agree on, however, is that it's important to get vitamins in food, not pills, because food contains other substances that either make vitamins work better or provide beneficial effects all their own. "Variety is very important," says Roseann Lyle, Ph.D., associate professor of health and food science at Purdue University in West Lafayette, Indiana. "You'll get everything you need if you eat a lot of fruits and vegetables and foods that are high in starch." The U.S. Department of Agriculture's ubiquitous food pyramid recommends three to five servings of vegetables and two to four servings of fruit every day.

Minerals. Last and least are minerals. We say least not because minerals aren't important—they're crucial for providing structure for bones, for maintaining vital functions like heartbeat and muscle contraction, and for regulating things like cell activity. But the body needs minerals only in tiny amounts. In fact, in excess, many minerals—including sodium, magnesium, and iron—can have harmful effects.

PEAK performance

Food Labels 101

Here's a quick primer on the language of labels.

Free. **As in *fat-free* or *sugar-free*. This means one serving has so little of the stuff in question that it won't make a blip on your dietary screen.**

Low-. **As in *low-calorie* or *low-fat*. This means the product doesn't have a lot of a particular substance, but it still has enough that it could make a difference in your diet. Specifically, low-calorie means 40 calories or less per serving; low-fat means 3 grams or less of total fat; low saturated fat means 1 gram or less; and low-cholesterol means less than 20 milligrams.**

Lean or extra-lean. **These terms refer to meat. Lean means one serving has less than 10 grams of total fat, less than 4 grams of saturated fat, and less than 95 milligrams of cholesterol. Extra-lean means one serving has less than 5 grams of total fat, less than 2 grams of saturated fat, and less than 95 milligrams of cholesterol.**

Reduced- or less. **This means there's 25 percent less of a certain ingredient or nutrient as compared with a similar product. *Reduced-* means the product was nutritionally altered to meet the claim. The term *less*, by contrast, is often used for comparisons, as in: "Our pretzels have 25 percent *less* sodium than potato chips."**

The most important thing to know about minerals is that a good diet, balanced as we've outlined here, will give you all you need. There is one mineral, however, that is of special concern for active men, and that's zinc. This single mineral is important for an astonishing number of different metabolic functions, including digestion, wound healing, and taste. Exercise makes the body lose zinc in sweat and also boosts the amount excreted in urine. One of several studies on zinc loss in athletes and military trainees found that 23 percent of male runners had below-normal concentrations of zinc in their blood. So try to eat foods high in zinc, such as moderate amounts of lean beef and pork, skinless poultry, and seafood such as oysters, crabmeat, and tuna, recommends Schneider. Whole grains, beans, and legumes are also good sources. Avoid supplements: Too much zinc can hinder the body's absorption of copper and can lower levels of "good" HDL cholesterol. If you do take supplements, don't take more than the Daily Value of 15 milligrams a day.

TOUGH TALK

"Don't tell people you're trying to lose weight. Too often, instead of getting support, you'll wind up getting misinformation and bad advice."

—MARK C. DAVIS, *MEN'S HEALTH* BELLY-OFF CLUB MEMBER, ON LOSING 168 POUNDS

When to Eat

If you get the basics of composition down, timing is a secondary concern, but a real one if you're interested in being in great shape. There are several basic principles.

Eat before you exercise. You increase muscle mass in two ways: by building up muscles and by preventing them from breaking down. If you eat some protein an hour or two before your workout, you'll have more amino acids available to your muscles during exercise. This prevents the muscle tissue from breaking down as much as it otherwise would.

You also need pre-exercise carbohydrates to ensure you'll have enough energy during your workout. Without this type of fuel, your muscles could break down the amino acids in your muscles for energy.

The perfect pre-workout meal is a small shake with juice or fruit, milk, and yogurt and/or a scoop of protein power. Fat and fiber slow digestion, so limit them before a workout.

And eat afterward. After a workout, you want to wolf down some muscle chow containing both carbohydrates and protein. This is the one time of day when you benefit from eating fast-acting, easily digestible carbohydrates such as white bread, instant rice, and baked potatoes.

Here's why: After exercise, your muscles are more sensitive to insulin, the rapid-transit system for the protein and carbohydrates your muscles need for growth, repair, and fuel. And the faster you digest the carbohydrates you eat, the faster your body can put them to use.

The best post-exercise meal is a shake made with a meal-replacement powder that contains protein and a fast-moving carbohydrate like maltodextrin. Don't want to go the supplement route? Try the shake described above; it works after exercise, too.

Drink fluids constantly. If you're hungry right before a workout, have a small snack such as fruit or juice instead of eating a meal. Immediately before exercising, drink at least one cup of water, then keep sipping one-half to one-quarter cup every 15 to 20 minutes during exercise. Top off your workout with another full cup. Remember, throughout the day you should get a total of at least six 8-ounce glasses.

Eat breakfast. It's vital for replenishing blood glucose and glycogen stores depleted while you sleep. Men should eat 300 to 400 calories at breakfast—an amount easily covered by toast and jam, cereal with milk, and fruit.

Be a nutritional Boy Scout. You're going to get hungry every 2 to 3 hours, guaranteed. So be prepared. If you know you're going to be away from decent food, take some healthy snacks with you. Nuts and dried fruit are clean and compact, and require no special preparation or refrigeration. If you need to pack something more meal-like, try a peanut-butter-and-jelly sandwich on whole grain bread. Keep apples in hand's reach everywhere you go; if you make it through one a day, the pectin will keep you too full to crave anything really awful.

Eat before bed. If you're trying to build muscle while losing weight, you may need some food right before sleep to keep your body from breaking down muscle tissue as you snooze. Planning this snack will help you resist the temptation to inhale an entire chocolate fudge cake at midnight.

If you're trying to gain weight, your bedtime snack will help you maximize muscle growth. In either case, limit this snack to about 500 calories. Don't make it too high in protein, though; that can kick your brain into overdrive, creating intense dreams and waking you up. A half-cup of ice cream with some nuts and fruit is a nice way to end the day.

Lean Measures for a Hard Body

Here are three strategies to tip the scales in your favor.

1 Pretend You're a Tailor

Measure everything—your neck, chest, waist, arms, thighs, calves. (Skip your inseam, unless you can talk an aerobics instructor into measuring it for you.) Write it all down and put it someplace where you'll have to look at it every day. Record your weight, too, although that's less important.

▶**Your goal:** Maintain or reduce the size of your waist while increasing the size of everything else. Repeat your measurements every 4 weeks (every 2 weeks, if the aerobics instructor is a really good sport).

2 To Change Your Weight, Follow the 15/500 Rule

Changing your diet radically—starving yourself to lose weight or stuffing yourself to gain—is futile. If you're trying to lose weight, you'll slow your metabolism to a crawl. If you're trying to gain, the excess calories will produce a lot of fat.

Here's a more sensible strategy.

▶**To lose weight:** Cut your daily food intake by a maximum of 15 percent or 500 calories, whichever is less.

▶**To gain weight:** Increase your daily intake by 15 percent or 500 calories, whichever is less. And daily means every day. Increasing your intake only 1 or 2 days a week won't work.

3 Take Notes

We've been hitting you with a lot of math here—500 calories of this, 0.82 gram of that. All of this is meaningless unless you know how much you actually consume.

For one day, try this: Measure everything you eat. That's right, pull out a measuring cup and see how much cereal you actually eat, count the slices or weigh the turkey breast you put on your sandwich, add up the bananas and dried apricots and Kit-Kat bars.

Then write it all down and calculate the total. We all know what we eat, but most of us have no idea how much. And it's the "how much" part that tells you whether you're heading toward a 32-inch waist or a volume discount at Big and Tall.

And learn to plan ahead: Calculate how much protein, fat, and carbohydrate you need. Write these numbers down, too, then figure out what foods you need to add or subtract.

Time-consuming? Sure. Boring? A bit. Instructive? Absolutely. Your body, your choice.

BY KELLY GARRETT

Get into the Drink

Bored by water? Never tasted a sports drink? Pal, you've got a drinking problem. Here's a 12-step program to turn it around

Step 1: Admit That You're Powerless

. . . until you start drinking a lot more fluid.

If you're like most guys, you don't even think about water unless you're parched. And during a workout, you figure unrelenting thirst just proves you're working hard.

Big mistake. The human body demands water to lubricate joints, digest food, transport nutrients, and flush wastes. The *exercising* human body needs it even more, because water helps carry oxygen and fuel to working muscles. And in the form of sweat, water keeps your body temperature from soaring when you push that last mile or bust that last set.

An underwatered workout is inefficient. You don't last as long, you achieve less, and you recover more slowly. You also run the risk of heat exhaustion, hallucinations, even heat stroke—especially in hot weather.

The physiology is simple. "When you lose fluid through sweat, you decrease your blood volume and therefore your oxygen availability," says Dale Huff, R.D., co-owner of Nutriformance, a sports-nutrition and personal-training company in St. Louis. "If you don't replace it, your body has to work harder to create the same amount of energy."

So go ahead, stand up and announce to the world: "My name is _____, and I need a drink."

Step 2: Accept a Higher Power

. . . by moving up to a sports drink.

There's a good reason why the jacked-up thirst quenchers once found only on football sidelines now take up half a supermarket aisle. They're more than a fitness fad or a prop for dousing head coaches. Sports drinks are important for the results-producing workouts you want.

They beat out water when it comes to helping you exercise longer, harder, and safer. Water's bloating effect actually makes it hard to drink enough. And, as you've surely noticed, plain water stimulates urination, so it's hard to retain enough. In contrast, sports drinks are less filling and less diuretic.

Trainers have even started to reconsider the standard recommendation that water is the best choice before and during exercise that lasts less than an hour. "Sports drinks help with moderate or strenuous exercise of any duration," says Huff. "Any guy who's fairly regular with his exercise needs a sports drink, not just plain water, for his workouts. It lets you keep improving instead of just hitting a wall and staying there."

Of course, water is preferable when you're trying to lose weight. While H_2O is calorie-free, sports drinks typically contain 50 to 80 calories per 8-ounce serving. Guzzling those extra calories will only defeat your purpose.

Step 3: Make a Decision

. . . about which sports drinks to slurp.

There are eight million sports drinks in the naked city. Which to choose? It comes down to carbs and taste.

Of Weights and Water

You don't see many weight lifters lugging oversized bottles from station to station. And in the weight room, you'll never see a table stocked with Gatorade paper cups.

There's a simple explanation for that: Weight lifters lose far less fluid than endurance athletes do—as much as four times less. Aerobic exercise requires more metabolic activity than anaerobic weight training does. That means more heat, which means more sweat, which means more fluid loss.

So when you train with weights, you don't need to drink as much as the aerobically inclined. But you still need to rehydrate, which is why even musclehead gyms have water coolers.

The next time you hit the one at your gym, enlighten that cute number in the spandex sports bra with this trivia tidbit: Depending on the type of exercise you do, your body will let you replace no more than a liter of fluid per hour. That leaves endurance athletes high and dry since they can lose up to 2 liters of fluid an hour. Weight lifters, on the other hand, are likely to lose only a half-liter in an hour, perhaps less. So even if you're pumping iron at a very high intensity, hitting the water cooler every 15 minutes for a mere half-cup (4 ounces) of water will keep you fully hydrated.

Gulping a sports drink during your workout may be an even better choice (though you'll miss your chance to chat with water cooler Wendi). Unlike water, sports drinks help you replenish the carbohydrates you burn while lifting weights. That's even more important after your workout, when your body is uniquely primed to replace the spent carbs.

In addition to providing fluid, sports drinks also contain fuel in the form of carbohydrates. Since sustained exercise depletes the fuel your muscles use for energy, you'll boost your workout if you replenish with a sports drink. And you won't have to waste time and energy on eating and digesting solid food.

Studies show that the most effective sports drinks are 5 to 8 percent carbohydrate, or 13 to 19 grams of carbs per 8-ounce serving. Any less won't be enough to top off your fuel stores. Any more will force your body to divert fluid to digest the carbs.

Okay, now you've got the choices down to four million. What do you do next? The same thing you do with beer and girlfriends: Keep trying new ones until you find a keeper. "If you like the taste, you're going to drink more," says Huff. "Find three or four that you like, so you don't get tired of drinking the same one."

PEAK performance

Mineral Matters

Exercising for an hour several times a week can cause mineral deficiencies severe enough to impair the immune system, according to a Danish study. The finding comes from analysis of a group of top-level athletes who had the mineral content of their blood tested three times during a year. "Deficiencies were most significant in athletes who spent the most time training but were also common enough to affect all men who regularly visit the gym," says Knut Flytlie, M.D., who conducted the research. Taking a multivitamin can help prevent the deficiencies.

Step 4: Make a Searching Inventory

. . . of the kind of sugar in your sports drink.

Check the ingredients list for fructose, one of the sugars that might make up the carbohydrate content of your sports drink. You don't want it, because it slows the release of fluid from the stomach, hampering hydration and defeating the main purpose of a sports drink. If fructose is listed in the midst of other sugars (such as sucrose, glucose, and maltodextrin), you're fine. If it's the first one listed (meaning it's the main sugar) or the only one listed, buy a different brand.

Step 5: Admit to Yourself and Others

. . . that you don't know what electrolytes are.

They're substances your body uses for acid-base balance and cell functioning. All you really need to know is that when you exercise you lose some key electrolytes—particularly sodium and potassium—through sweat.

The sodium and potassium in sports drinks not only replace these lost electrolytes but also help you absorb the sugars for energy and the water for hydration. Plus, they slow your urge to urinate. And the sodium, of course, promotes thirst, making it easy for you to drink more. You want to do that.

Simply check the label to make sure your sports drink provides 100 to 110 milligrams of sodium and 30 milligrams of potassium per 8-ounce serving. Most do.

Step 6: Be Ready to Remove the Defects

. . . by turning to drink.

Actually, there's just one defect to overcome: performance-sapping dehydration. The solution? DWE, or drinking while exercising. Hit your sports-drink bottle every 15 minutes throughout your workout. Each time, drink a bare minimum of 4 ounces (about half of a typical glass), up to a maximum of 12 ounces (a glass and a half). That's what you need to stay hydrated and get the 30 to 60 grams of carbs per hour that you need during exercise.

If you're not accustomed to taking in that much liquid, your stomach may not like it at first. Start off easy, says Huff, drinking the minimum at longer intervals—say, every half-hour. "Eventually it won't bother you," he says. As they say, one day at a time.

TOUGH TALK

"Look at my Corvette, a '98—one of the finest sports cars I've ever had. Would I put water in the gas tank?"

—FITNESS GURU JACK LA LANNE, ON THE JUNK PEOPLE PUT INTO THEIR BODIES

Step 7: Humbly Remove Your Shortcomings

. . . with a pre-workout double shot.

To make sure you're not short on fluids or carbs, drink 2 cups (16 ounces) of your sports drink before you start exercising. "It's not uncommon for someone to have last eaten as much as 5 hours prior to exercise," says Huff. "But you need to be adequately hydrated and nourished going in."

Remember, if weight loss is your goal, you can substitute calorie-less water—but you won't get the energizing carbs, not to mention the electrolytes and the good taste. Compromise with "fitness water" such as Gatorade's Propel. "Not a lot of calories (about 10), but you still get some glucose release into your blood, and some electrolytes," says Huff. "It's Gatorade lite."

Step 8: Make Amends

. . . by replacing lost nutrients with a postexercise drink.

Don't make the end of your workout an excuse to quit drinking. Rehydration matters at least as much after a workout as during it. Down 16 ounces of a sports drink when you're finished. And do it within 15 to 30 minutes. "That's the ideal time to replenish your system after exercise," says Huff.

Again, water is good, but a sports drink is better—for lots of reasons. Gulping that much water that fast can be inefficient without the retention-encouraging electrolytes you get in a sports drink. And you need to replace lost electrolytes anyway.

Also, after a workout you need the fast-acting carbs from a sports drink to replenish your fuel stores and avoid hypoglycemia (low blood sugar). You may need as much as a half-gram of carbohydrate per pound of body weight to do that, says Huff. Sixteen ounces of your usual sports drink won't give you that much, so if you exercise long and hard, you might consider a carb-rich blend for exclusive postworkout use.

Postexercise replenishment also calls for a sports drink with one part protein for every four parts carbohydrate. The only brand that provides this ratio is called Accelerate; it's available at GNC. Or you can enjoy a high-protein sports bar with your after-workout beverage. "At the very least, have your usual sports drink but make sure you eat a meal within an hour," says Huff.

Step 9: Make Direct Amends Wherever Possible

. . . by drinking plenty of liquids all day long.

Don't fall off the water wagon when you're not working out. Everything that's bad about dehydration when you're exercising is just as bad when you're not. In addition to his workout-related beverages, a fit and healthy guy needs at least six 8-ounce glasses of fluid daily. Eight 8-ounce glasses are even better; and if he's very big or very busy, he may need 10 to 12.

Don't worry, you're not locked in to 4 quarts of plain ol' agua. Juice, milk, and herbal tea also hydrate since they're mostly water. Huff usually recommends drinking four glasses of water daily, because other beverages will make up the difference (though they'll also tack on additional calories). To figure out exactly how much plain water you need to reach your liquid quota, keep track of the other fluids you slurp on a typical day. And when your renter's lease on the liquids is up, check out your pee. "If it's the color of apple juice, you're dehydrated," says Huff. You need to imbibe enough that you release a clear stream.

Step 10: Admit When You're Wrong

. . . about what counts as hydration.

Beer, wine, hard liquor, and coffee and other caffeinated beverages (including black or green tea and colas) giveth fluid but also taketh away due to their diuretic properties. Don't count them.

Speaking of caffeine, don't confuse "energy drinks" with sports drinks. Their energy boost usually relies on caffeine, which doesn't help your hydration effort.

Step 11: Improve Your Conscious Contact

. . . with potables.

So how do you remember to suck it up during the day, thirsty or not? Hey, nobody said beating your drinking problem would be easy.

You can do it (and like it) by making water part of your daily routine. Keep a 32-ounce bottle of water with you and sip it till it's empty. Or get in the habit of quaffing a glass of water before each meal. Especially in summer, fill a pitcher with ice water flavored with a little lemon, lime, or other fruit. Keep it at eye-level in the fridge.

Step 12: Carry the Message

. . . to your dry brethren.

Now that you're lubricating your way to better fitness, are you going to keep the secret to yourself? Have an intervention in which you get some of the guys together to talk about their drinking problems. Call it Dehydrators Anonymous.

BY THOMAS INCLEDON, R.D., C.S.C.S.

The Hard-Muscle Diet

Pack on some grade-A beef with this all-day meal plan

One good meal a day is easy. Most of us do that by accident. Throw some raisins on your cereal with low-fat milk and, as Emeril would say, "Bam!" Two good meals a day is trickier. And how often do you get three perfect meals in one day? Or four? Probably about as often as you share a mud bath with Jessica Alba.

Here's why you should: Muscle happens all day, every day. After one good workout, your body will spend the next 48 to 72 hours building and repairing your muscle cells. Work out three or four times a week and your little cellular-repair teams are going at it three shifts a day, Monday through Sunday.

If they're going to put in all that OT, the least you can do is give them the best materials to work with: high-quality protein to build and repair muscles, the most nutrient-dense carbohydrates to provide energy, and heart-healthy, testosterone-friendly unsaturated fats to help you feel full longer.

And instead of giving your body the three big meals a day you grew up with, you should eat six smaller meals. Frequent meals prevent you from storing food as love handles and keep your body from tapping into your muscle protein for energy during workouts or between meals.

Hate to plan? Don't worry. Putting together frequent, healthful meals doesn't take as much preparation as you think. To show you how simple and easy it is, we created a plan with 3,080 calories for a thin guy who wants to add a few gigabytes to his mainframe. (If you weigh more than 200 pounds and want to lose weight, see "Lean Day" on page 166 for a version of this diet that will help you lose the gut and keep the biceps.)

Try eating right for 24 hours (and check out the substitutions that stretch this plan beyond a day). We think you'll like the changes. We know your muscles will.

8:00 A.M.: Meal #1

Cook (or order) . . .

Three eggs

½ cup of oatmeal with 1 cup of blueberries

1 cup of fat-free milk

Add a multivitamin/mineral supplement such as Centrum Performance or any other brand that supplies 100 percent of the Daily Values for the majority of its included vitamins and minerals.

Why this meal: The eggs and milk supply some of the highest-quality protein available. Oatmeal is a slow-burning carbohydrate, providing long-lasting energy and heart-protective soluble fiber. Berries contain some of the most potent antioxidants we know of, helping your body's cells recover from the damage caused by stress, pollution, and other unavoidable indignities.

What you can eat instead: Swap the oatmeal and berries for a high-fiber cereal with raisins and an orange. Cottage cheese or three low-fat turkey-sausage links can fill in for the eggs.

9:30 A.M.: Drink an 8-Ounce Glass of Water

Why water: Your muscles are about 60 percent water, so even slight dehydration impairs your physical performance. In addition, dehydration can cloud your thinking (if you don't notice, you can bet your boss will) and make you more vulnerable to colds and flu.

What you can drink instead: Your body can get the water it needs from anything wet, whether it's Mountain Dew or iceberg lettuce. But water, with no calories to account for, is the easiest on the waistline.

11:00 A.M.: Meal #2

Make a tuna-salad sandwich with . . .

½ can of tuna (use white or light water-packed tuna; drain the water), mixed with 1 teaspoon of mayo

Two slices of whole grain bread

2 cups of salad (you can mix your own or buy some premixed; dark green lettuce, carrots, chopped bell peppers, tomatoes, and onions are all good ingredients to throw in)

1 tablespoon of olive oil in whatever dressing you choose (a tablespoon of olive oil contains 14 grams of fat, so if you're using a bottled dressing containing olive oil, use whatever serving size gets you to 14 grams)

One large orange (eaten separately or as part of the salad)

Drink a glass of water.

Why this meal: Tuna is a terrific source of protein. Dark green vegetables are stocked with magnesium, a mineral crucial to muscle function and testosterone production. The other vegetables provide a mix of fiber (great for appetite control) and antioxidants. Olive oil is mostly a monounsaturated fat, known to preserve HDL cholesterol (the "good" one) and to lower triglycerides (blood fats linked to heart disease). The orange gives you a nice splash of vitamin C, which can help lower your body's production of cortisol, a stress hormone that breaks down muscle.

What you can eat instead: Swap the tuna for lean roast beef with grainy mustard (keep the whole grain bread, of course). If you get sick of the greens, quarter two tomatoes and mix them with a handful of chickpeas, some chopped fresh basil, and a teaspoon of olive oil. Half a cantaloupe stands in pretty nicely for the orange.

12:45 P.M.: Drink a Glass of Water

2:00 P.M.: Meal #3

Make a chicken sandwich with . . .

3 ounces of sliced chicken breast

Two slices of whole grain bread

1 tablespoon of mayonnaise

Add some lettuce, and sliced green bell pepper, onion, or tomato

Drink a glass of water.

Why this meal: Chicken and turkey are both great protein sources. Whole grains provide slow-burning carbohydrates, and they'll help you feel full longer. There's nothing good to say about mayonnaise except that it adds some rich flavor.

What you can eat instead: Any kind of lean deli meat will be fine in a sandwich. If you don't want to eat a sandwich, try a big (16-ounce) can of soup—minestrone, for example—and add 3 ounces of turkey or chicken.

3:15 P.M.: Drink Another Glass of Water

4:30 P.M.: Meal #4 (Pre-Workout)

Make a shake or smoothie with . . .

One scoop of whey protein powder (that's about 20 grams)

1 cup of fat-free milk

1 cup of fresh or frozen berries

1 cup of orange juice

1 teaspoon of flaxseed oil (keep refrigerated)

1 teaspoon of olive oil

Why this meal: Whey protein (derived from milk products) is considered the gold-standard muscle-building supplement. It ranks very high in "bioavailability," a measure of how easily your body can use it. (If a protein isn't bioavailable,

your body sends it into the municipal sewer system.) Just about any whey protein powder will do. The two oils give you a combination of the polyunsaturated and monounsaturated fats that your body uses easily for energy and that also help your brain think clearly.

What you can eat instead: If you don't have access to a blender and a refrigerator at 4:30, substitute a cup of fat-free milk, an apple, and either an ounce of nuts or 2 tablespoons of peanut butter. You'll be light on protein, so you'll need to add an ounce of chicken or turkey breast to the previous meal and an ounce of salmon to the next one.

A second option is to mix a packet of a meal-replacement powder (such as Met-Rx or Myoplex) with water and olive oil. All you need for that is a shaker cup; you can get one wherever you buy the protein powder. This shake will give you a little more protein than you need, so you can

Lean Day

If you're a 200-pound guy working out hard three or four times a week, here's a 2,300-calorie, 1-day plan for losing about a pound a week. (A 180-pounder would lose about a pound a month; a 220-pounder would drop about 5 a month.) Of course, that's just the numbers on the scale. Anyone on this plan will lose fat and gain muscle, meaning he'll like what he sees in the mirror whether he drops pounds, maintains his current weight, or beefs up.

8:00 A.M.: Meal #1

Cook (or order) . . .

Two eggs

½ cup of oatmeal with ½ cup of berries (fresh or frozen)

1 cup of fat-free milk

Add a multivitamin/mineral supplement such as Centrum Performance or any other brand that supplies 100 percent of the Daily Values for the majority of its included vitamins and minerals.

9:30 A.M.: Drink a Glass of Water

11:00 A.M.: Meal #2

Make a salad with . . .

1 of can tuna (use white or light water-packed tuna and drain the water)

2 cups of salad (you can mix your own or buy some premixed greens; dark green lettuce, carrots, chopped bell peppers, tomatoes, and onions are all good ingredients to throw in)

1 tablespoon of olive oil in whatever dressing you choose (a tablespoon of olive oil contains 14 grams of fat, so if you're using a bottled dressing containing olive oil, use whatever serving size gets you to 14 grams)

One medium orange (eaten separately or as part of the salad)

Drink a glass of water.

What you can eat instead: You can substitute any type of meat—lean sirloin steak, for excut the whey in your post-workout shake to one scoop.

5:30 P.M.

Hit the gym. For serious muscle-building workouts, check out The King of All Workouts on page 84, or order our "Total-Body Workbook" series at www.menshealth.com (click on "Marketplace").

6:45 P.M.: Meal #5

Make a shake or smoothie with . . .

1½ scoops of whey protein powder (about 30 grams)

2 cups of fruit juice

Why this meal: After a hard workout, your body is in a catabolic state, meaning that it's breaking down muscle tissue. But with an immediate infusion of carbohydrates and protein, you can stop catabolism and start the reverse process, anabolism, better known as muscle building. The fruit juice supplies the carbohydrates, while the whey protein takes care of the rest.

ample—for the tuna on the salad. Or, if you get sick of the greens, try sliced tomatoes with mozzarella cheese. Sprinkle basil on top, and top it with a tablespoon of olive oil. Instead of an orange, you can have some cantaloupe, although it has just half the vitamin C. Some of the best vegetable sources of C are red bell pepper, broccoli, and spinach.

12:45 P.M.: Drink a Glass of Water

2:00 P.M.: Meal #3

Make a chicken sandwich with . . .

3 ounces of sliced chicken

Two slices of whole grain bread

1 tablespoon of mayonnaise

3:15 P.M.: Drink a Glass of Water

4:30 P.M.: Meal #4

Make a shake or smoothie with . . .

One scoop of whey protein powder (that's about 20 grams)

1 cup of fat-free milk

1 cup of fresh or frozen berries

1 teaspoon of flaxseed oil (keep refrigerated)

1 teaspoon of olive oil

5:30 P.M.

Hit the gym. Drink water throughout.

6:45 P.M.: Meal #5

Make a shake or smoothie with . . .

1½ scoops of whey protein powder (about 30 grams)

1 cup of fruit juice

8:30 P.M.: Meal #6

Cook or order . . .

3 ounces of salmon, grilled or poached

One small baked sweet potato

2 cups of salad (with the same ingredients you used before)

1 tablespoon of olive oil in dressing of your choice

Drink a glass of water.

11:00 P.M.

Hit the sack. You'll sleep like a rock and wake up a leaner man.

What you can eat instead: Try 2 cups of plain nonfat yogurt blended with a cup of strawberries. There are endless combinations of ingredients you can use to concoct liquid meals based on alternative protein sources—yogurt (as mentioned), tofu, powdered milk, and egg substitutes are just a few. But most men quickly discover that the best, most convenient substitute for a protein shake is . . . a protein shake.

8:30 P.M.: Meal #6

Cook or order . . .

6 ounces of salmon, grilled or poached

One medium baked sweet potato

1 cup of whole grain rice

2 cups of salad (with the same ingredients you used before)

1 tablespoon of olive oil in dressing of your choice

Drink a glass of water.

Why this meal: Salmon gives you two great nutrients: protein and polyunsaturated fat. Since it's not a predator fish, it's also relatively safe from mercury. The baked sweet potato is rich in potassium to help your body use protein for muscle.

What you can eat instead: Any type of lean meat will work here—steak, pork loin, chicken breast. If sweet potatoes give you too many baby-food flashbacks, try a banana, dried apricots, or dried figs.

11:00 P.M.

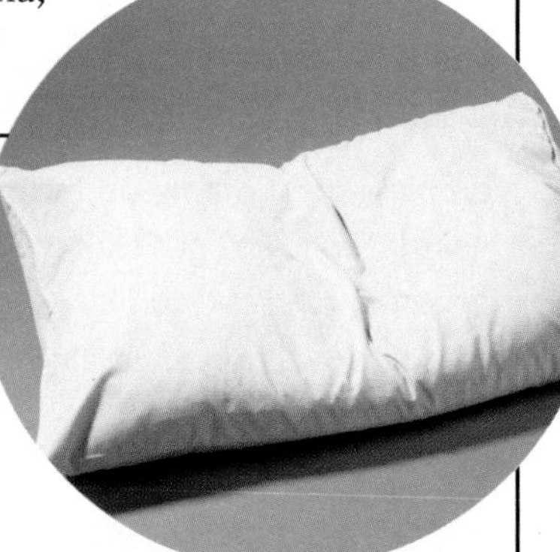

Lights out. You'll wake up with some muscle that wasn't there the day before.

Customizing the Diet

We realize that different guys have different goals. Say you weigh more than 160 and want to put on a pound a week. Simply add about 200 calories to your meal plan for every 10 pounds you weigh over 160. So if you weigh 170, add a cup of milk, a slice of whole grain bread, and a medium orange.

We also understand that only a small percentage of guys can actually time every meal around a 5:30 workout. Use the timing as a model. For example:

- If you work out in the morning, have the pre-workout shake as soon as you wake up, exercise an hour after you get up, and then have the post-workout shake immediately after. What we call Meal #1 would follow 2 hours after the post-workout shake.
- If you work out at noon, have Meal #1 as described, then the pre-workout shake at 11:00, followed by the other shake after the workout, followed by Meal #2, 2 hours later.

BY HOWARD M. SHAPIRO, D.O.

Eat More, Weigh Less

Here's how to make more food equal fewer pounds

We men eat when our stomachs say it's time to. Then we keep eating until there's nothing left. This is why, after dinner, we often can't find our dates.

The problem with this approach? It can make you fat. Really fat—unless you know how it can make you skinny.

And that's what we're about to tell you. We have visual proof that cutting calories from your diet—the key to losing weight—doesn't have to mean limiting your intake to delightfully marinated chunks of balsa wood. On the contrary, when you pick the right foods, eating fewer calories can mean feasting on a whole lot more. We're talking portions the size of your date's head—and then some.

So start loading up your plate—with the foods on the right, not the left. Remember: If you make more substitutions, you'll fill up with fewer calories and weigh less. It's better to fill your plate than to fill your pants.

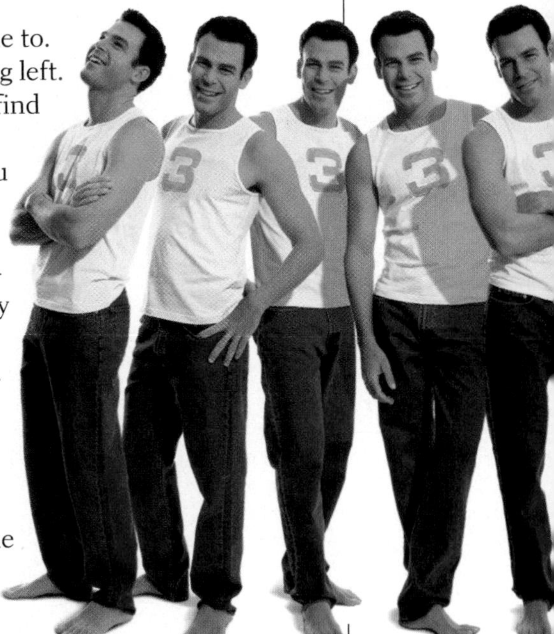

FOR BREAKFAST

YOU CAN EAT THIS . . .		OR THIS . . .	
½ dry bagel	= 200 calories	2 light waffles, 2 Tbsp of light syrup, and berries	= 200 calories
9-ounce fat-free, sugar-free muffin	= 720 calories	1 pineapple, ½ cantaloupe, ½ kiwifruit, ½ papaya, grapes, 2 pears, and 2 whole wheat rolls	= 720 calories
6-oz corn muffin	= 530 calories	4 English muffins	= 530 calories
1 large fat-free café latte (no sugar)	= 180 calories	6 large hazelnut coffees, each with low-calorie sweetener and 2 Tbsp milk	= 180 calories

FOR LUNCH

YOU CAN EAT THIS . . .		OR THIS . . .	
1 chicken nugget	= 80 calories	1¼ cups of vegetable-lentil soup	= 80 calories
1 turkey sandwich (8 oz of turkey) with 2 Tbsp mayo on rye	= 740 calories	2 turkey sandwiches (3 oz of turkey each) with lettuce, tomato, and mustard on rye	= 620 calories

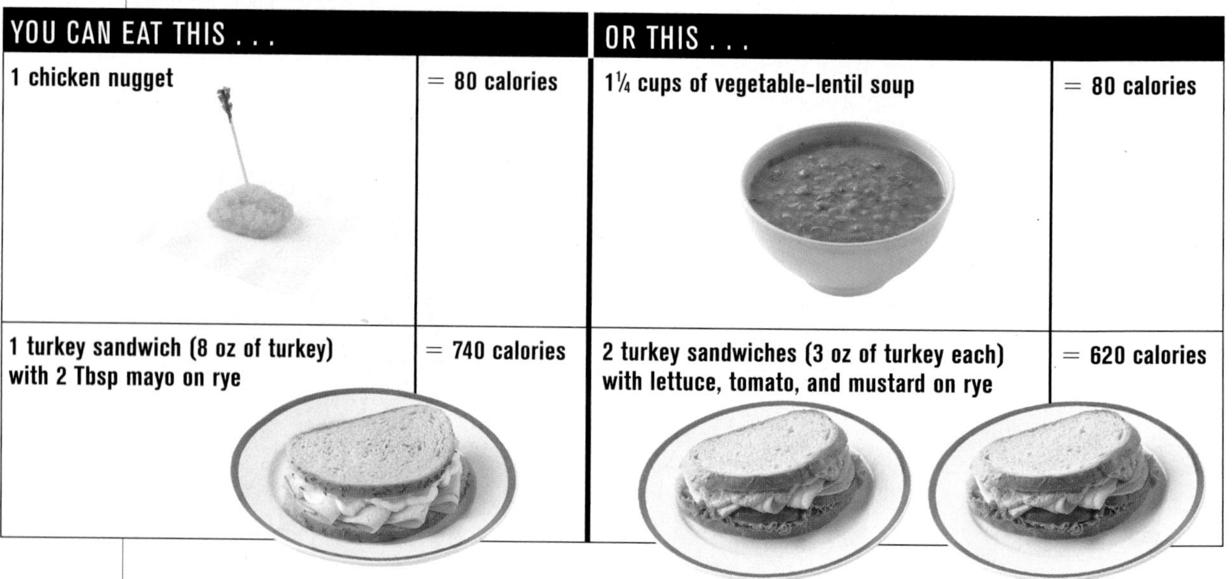

FOR LUNCH

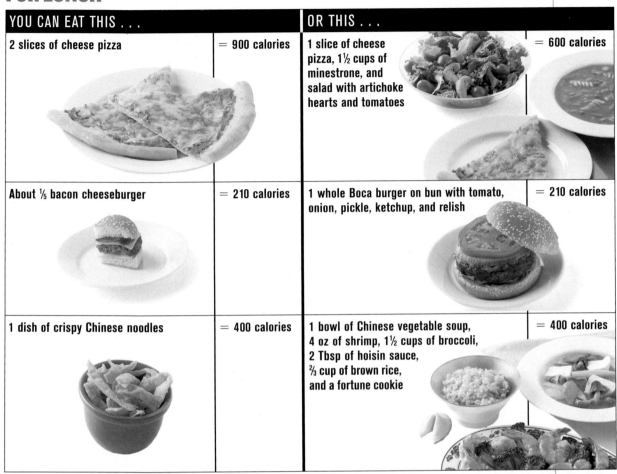

YOU CAN EAT THIS . . .		OR THIS . . .	
2 slices of cheese pizza	= 900 calories	1 slice of cheese pizza, 1½ cups of minestrone, and salad with artichoke hearts and tomatoes	= 600 calories
About ⅕ bacon cheeseburger	= 210 calories	1 whole Boca burger on bun with tomato, onion, pickle, ketchup, and relish	= 210 calories
1 dish of crispy Chinese noodles	= 400 calories	1 bowl of Chinese vegetable soup, 4 oz of shrimp, 1½ cups of broccoli, 2 Tbsp of hoisin sauce, ⅔ cup of brown rice, and a fortune cookie	= 400 calories

FOR A SNACK

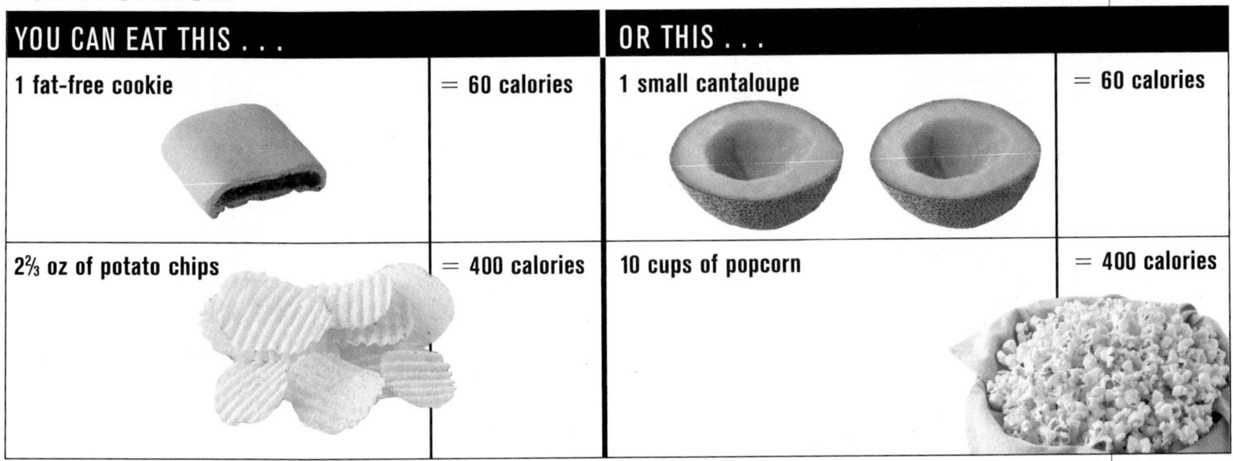

YOU CAN EAT THIS . . .		OR THIS . . .	
1 fat-free cookie	= 60 calories	1 small cantaloupe	= 60 calories
2⅔ oz of potato chips	= 400 calories	10 cups of popcorn	= 400 calories

FOR DINNER

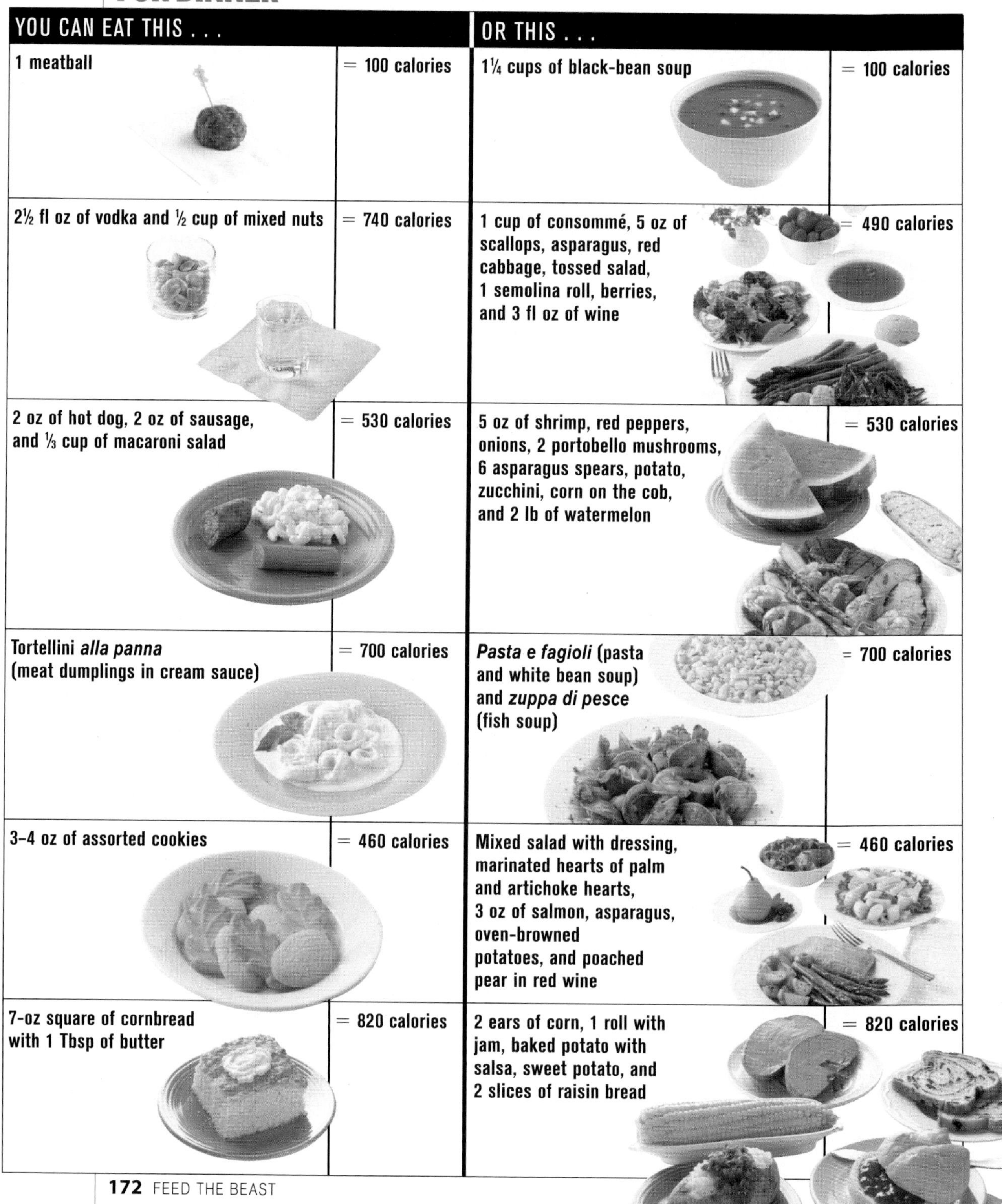

YOU CAN EAT THIS . . .		OR THIS . . .	
1 meatball	= 100 calories	1¼ cups of black-bean soup	= 100 calories
2½ fl oz of vodka and ½ cup of mixed nuts	= 740 calories	1 cup of consommé, 5 oz of scallops, asparagus, red cabbage, tossed salad, 1 semolina roll, berries, and 3 fl oz of wine	= 490 calories
2 oz of hot dog, 2 oz of sausage, and ⅓ cup of macaroni salad	= 530 calories	5 oz of shrimp, red peppers, onions, 2 portobello mushrooms, 6 asparagus spears, potato, zucchini, corn on the cob, and 2 lb of watermelon	= 530 calories
Tortellini *alla panna* (meat dumplings in cream sauce)	= 700 calories	*Pasta e fagioli* (pasta and white bean soup) and *zuppa di pesce* (fish soup)	= 700 calories
3–4 oz of assorted cookies	= 460 calories	Mixed salad with dressing, marinated hearts of palm and artichoke hearts, 3 oz of salmon, asparagus, oven-browned potatoes, and poached pear in red wine	= 460 calories
7-oz square of cornbread with 1 Tbsp of butter	= 820 calories	2 ears of corn, 1 roll with jam, baked potato with salsa, sweet potato, and 2 slices of raisin bread	= 820 calories

FOR DESSERT

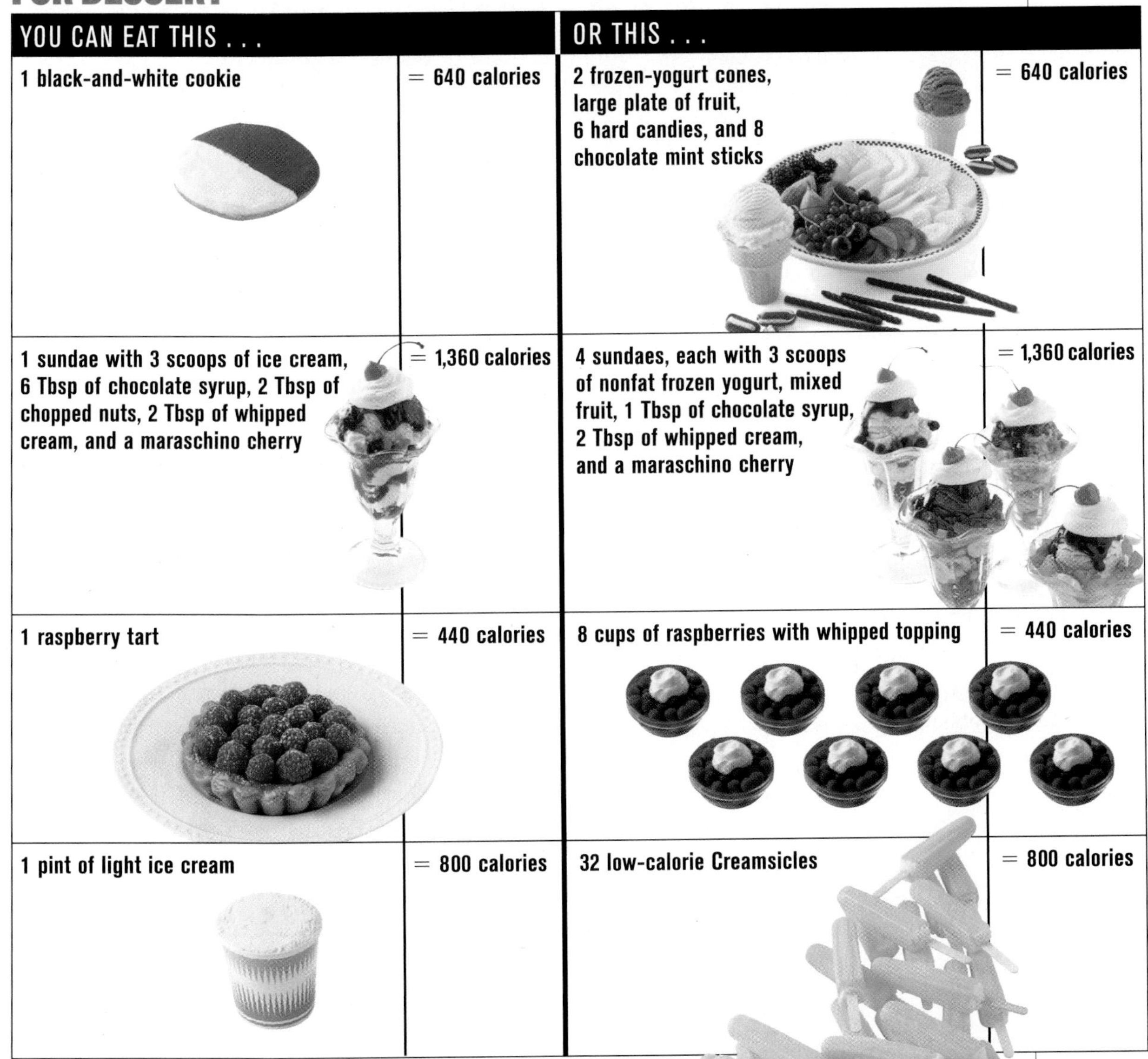

YOU CAN EAT THIS . . .		OR THIS . . .	
1 black-and-white cookie	= 640 calories	2 frozen-yogurt cones, large plate of fruit, 6 hard candies, and 8 chocolate mint sticks	= 640 calories
1 sundae with 3 scoops of ice cream, 6 Tbsp of chocolate syrup, 2 Tbsp of chopped nuts, 2 Tbsp of whipped cream, and a maraschino cherry	= 1,360 calories	4 sundaes, each with 3 scoops of nonfat frozen yogurt, mixed fruit, 1 Tbsp of chocolate syrup, 2 Tbsp of whipped cream, and a maraschino cherry	= 1,360 calories
1 raspberry tart	= 440 calories	8 cups of raspberries with whipped topping	= 440 calories
1 pint of light ice cream	= 800 calories	32 low-calorie Creamsicles	= 800 calories

Trainer's Forum

with MICHAEL MEJIA

CHOW TIMES

Q Does *when* I eat matter for losing weight? What about for gaining muscle?

J. P., ALPINE, TENNESSEE

A Although the most important factor for weight loss is total caloric balance (calories in versus calories out), meal timing can also impact your results. For instance, if fat loss is your primary goal, your best bet is to eat the bulk of your calories earlier in the day, when you're more active. Start with a good breakfast, then gradually taper the size of each meal as the day wears on. Aim to eat every 3 hours, for a total of at least four meals a day. It's a much better alternative to starving yourself until you get home and then eating everything in sight.

Besides helping to regulate blood-sugar levels, eating this way also lets you burn off more calories with minimal effort. By contrast, eating large meals late in the day or evening, when many of us tend to just sit around, increases the chance of those calories being stored as fat.

To build muscle, eat several smaller meals throughout the day to provide your muscles with a continuous supply of protein. How you eat after your workout is also important. Right after your workout is the best—and perhaps only—time to purposely increase your consumption of fast-acting carbohydrates such as fruits and fruit juices. When these carbs are mixed with a high-quality protein like whey, the resulting insulin surge helps deliver key nutrients your muscles need to replenish and grow. This is why many nutritionists recommend at least a 2:1 ratio of carbs to protein in any post-workout drink.

OUR KIND OF GUY

Extreme Eating

Joe Decker says it's okay to enjoy junk food one day a week. If you're working out regularly, satisfying a craving can help keep you honest for the rest of the week.

In one 24-hour period last December, the 5-foot-9, 195-pound Decker ate potato chips, candy bars, hamburgers, doughnuts, muffins, and peanut-butter cups. Lots of peanut-butter cups.

Between meals, he earned the title of World's Fittest Man, according to Guinness (the book, not the beer). He did it by cycling, running, hiking, swimming, kayaking, walking, and rowing, for a total of 153 miles (that's not even mentioning the 278,540 pounds of weights he lifted or the thousands of jumping jacks he did).

His lesson is a good one: During a normal week, he eats lots of fruits, vegetables, chicken, and fish, and drinks gallons of water. On the weekend, he welcomes the pizza and beer.

"What are you guys having?"

WE ATE IT, WE RATE IT

Bar Fight

Frankly, we prefer our muscle-building protein in the form of a 16-ounce rib eye. But that's not always possible (or advised), which is why low-fat protein bars have become post-workout substitutes. Our favorites:

►Balance chocolate (200 calories, 14 grams (g) protein, 6 g fat). The first bite tastes like raspberry-chocolate cake, and the coating is the most candylike of all the bars we tried. Downside: It's a little dry and grainy.

►Source-One by MET-Rx chocolate roasted peanut (170 calories, 15 g protein, 5 g fat). It has a peanut-butter-cup taste, and it's soft and chewy. Eat it quickly and you won't notice that it's slightly bitter.

►Zone Perfect almond crunch (190 calories, 14 g protein, 6 g fat). It starts out tasting like a Bit-O-Honey bar. But after a few chews, it reminds us of seven-grain bread sprinkled with honey. Real almonds—nice touch.

►Premier Eight cookies and cream (270 calories, 31 g protein, 6 g fat). Smells like a tree-bark scratch-and-sniff sticker, but the sweet icing masks the bar's otherwise bland flavor. Thirty-one grams of protein makes it one of the best in its class.

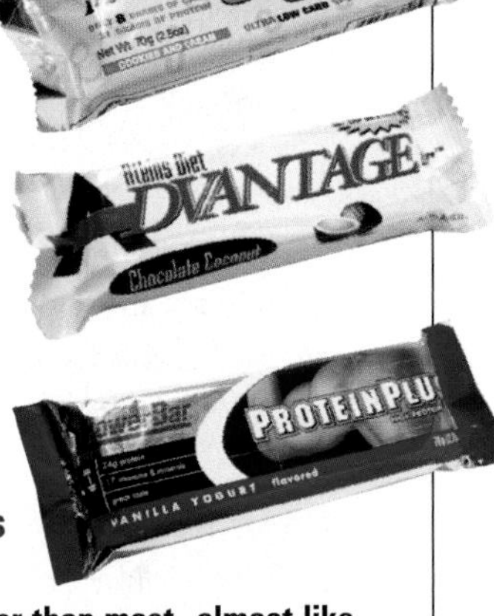

►Advantage chocolate coconut (250 calories, 18 g protein, 13 g fat). A bit slimy, but the coconut flavor masks the aftertaste that's pretty typical in most bars. Think of it as a Mounds bar you left in a hot car too long.

►PowerBar Protein Plus vanilla yogurt (290 calories, 24 g protein, 5 g fat). It's sweeter than most—almost like cookie batter and icing. The vanilla is a nice change from the more traditional chocolate.

TREAT YOURSELF

Q I don't want to completely give up foods like beer, potato chips, and ice cream. How much of these can I have each week without hurting my progress?

W. J., RUTLAND VERMONT

A It's difficult to quantify how much of a certain food a person can eat before it impacts results. Everyone's metabolism is different: What's too much for one guy may be just right for another. Therefore, I can't really recommend a specific amount with any degree of confidence.

What I can tell you is that it's important to eat favorite foods every now and then so you don't feel deprived in the long run. Usually, when people make up their minds to lose weight, they do so out of utter disgust. Hell-bent on making radical changes, they swear off the foods they believe contributed to their problem in the first place. Then, after weeks of feeling deprived, they binge. Afterward, thinking this one setback has somehow sabotaged their results, they allow it to snowball and end up right back where they started—if not heavier. So you're right to be wary of giving up your treats.

CONTINUED

MEATLESS MIGHT

Q I'm a vegetarian who wants to build muscle. What kinds of foods should I eat to bulk up? Will I be able to get big as fast as a meat eater?

T. S., MISSOULA, MONTANA

A To be perfectly honest, it's pretty tough to bulk up on a vegetarian diet—not impossible, but tough. The first thing you're going to need is plenty of high-quality protein. And unlike some of your carnivorous friends, you may have trouble getting all the protein you need. Some of the best vegetarian protein sources include tofu, beans and legumes, whey, soy milk, and eggs. These are known as complete proteins because each of them contains all nine of the essential amino acids that are vital to your quest for muscle. You can also combine several "incomplete" proteins such as rice and beans, or peanut butter and whole wheat bread, to form complete proteins.

You won't have trouble getting enough carbohydrates and fats. Good carbohydrate sources such as pasta, rice, potatoes, and vitamin-rich fruits and vegetables will go a long way toward helping you get big. Combine those with quality fats like olive, canola, flaxseed, and peanut oils, along with avocados and nuts, and you'll have virtually everything you need to muscle up. One caveat: Even consuming these foods, you probably won't be able to keep up with us meat eaters when it comes to building muscle.

TOUGH TALK

"Stop before you're stuffed. I stop eating while I'm still a little hungry, but the hunger goes away within 20 minutes, when your brain registers that you have food in your stomach."

—MARTY EDWARDS, *MEN'S HEALTH* BELLY-OFF CLUB MEMBER, ON LOSING NEARLY 200 POUNDS

HARD TRUTH

Monounsaturated fats. **Found mainly in vegetable and nut oils, such as olive and canola, these are often referred to as good fats because they help reduce blood-cholesterol levels and protect against heart disease.**

Polyunsaturated fats. **These contain the essential nutrient linoleic acid and are found in the fat from plants, such as safflower and corn oils. Like monounsaturated fats, these also tend to reduce blood-cholesterol levels.**

Saturated fats. **These are found in all foods that come from animal sources, including meats and dairy products. They are also in oils such as coconut and palm-kernel oils. Saturated fats pose a higher risk for heart disease and some types of cancer.**

Hydrogenated fats. **These are lipid oils that have been chemically altered to a semisolid state. Margarine and vegetable shortening are prime examples. Hydrogenated fats are thought to clog coronary arteries, which places them in the "bad" category.**

Feast Lean on World Cuisine

7 Ways to Find Healthy Ethnic Eats

These days, bistros, trattorias, and sushi shacks pop up as quickly as reality TV shows. Here are seven ways to eat smart à la carte—helpful for, say, the next time your out-of-town clients choose lunch at the new dim-sum palace near your office.

CUISINE	FAT-BELLY CHOICES	FLAT-BELLY OPTIONS
1. Chinese	Deep-fried egg rolls, barbecued pork ribs, and fried rice	Wonton soup, steamed vegetables or rice, and fish
2. French	Croissants and any creamy sauce	Consommé, vegetable salads, crusty bread (easy on the butter), and anything grilled, broiled, or roasted
3. Greek	Feta cheese, phyllo dough, and anchovies	Pita bread, rice, fish, chicken, nuts, olives, and *tzatziki* (yogurt and cucumbers)
4. Indian	*Poori* (fried bread) and *samosa* (fried pastries)	*Chapati* (baked bread)
5. Italian	Antipasto, parmigiana, and Alfredo or other creamy sauces	Pasta and tomato sauce with garlic
6. Japanese	Tempura, miso soup, and anything *agemono* (deep-fried)	Natto soup, chicken teriyaki, sushi, and anything *yakimono* (broiled) or *nabemono* (boiled)
7. Mexican	Crispy tacos, chorizo, refried beans, tortilla chips, and sour cream	Soft corn tortillas, grilled fish, chicken fajitas, guacamole, and salsa

—STEPHEN GEORGE

CONQUER THE

PART FIVE

Getting fit is its own reward. As is whipping the assorted butts of all who dare to challenge you athletically. So why not do both? Better yet, why not actually tailor a fitness program to get that competitive edge on your chosen field of glory?

Training for excellence in a particular sport takes a little know-how. If sport-specific training were simple and obvious, those other guys would be doing it and claiming their share of bragging rights. Get beyond some false preconceptions about the fitness demands of your sport and you'll stay well ahead of the pack.

We offer you some top-notch fitness programs that will pay dividends during competition. Keep reading—then reap the benefits. If you humiliate your opponents in the process, well, that's their problem.

COMPETITION

MH • QUIZ

Are You a Winner?

Question: What separates champs from chumps? ***Answer:*** The ability to perform under pressure. We talked to four guys who help athletes stay calm in the clutch. Take this quiz to find out whether you'll choke or meet the challenge.

1 When I cut the grass, I usually . . .
- ☐ Finish fast
- ☐ Try to make the yard look good
- ☐ Mow down any small animals that get in my way

2 The night before a big game, I . . .
- ☐ Hit the sack earlier than usual
- ☐ Check in at my usual time—after 11:30 P.M.
- ☐ Don't remember. I guess I drank a few more beers than I thought

3 When I'm in a big match-up, I feel . . .
- ☐ Pumped
- ☐ Nauseated
- ☐ Oh yeah, today's the big game—I knew that

4 When I'm on deck, I'm thinking . . .
- ☐ "I'm 0 for my last 15. If I don't whack this one, coach is gonna bench me."
- ☐ Thinking?

5 I play better when I'm . . .
- ☐ Mad
- ☐ Relaxed

6 After I make a mistake . . .
- ☐ My whole game goes downhill
- ☐ I keep playing without a hitch

7 Sometimes I lose track of time during a game.
- ☐ True
- ☐ False

WHAT YOUR ANSWERS SAY ABOUT YOU

1. Fast finishers stress out easily and have impatient type-A personalities. "They're the players who rush through the drills in practice and arch their backs when they bench press just so they can hurry up or put up more weight," says sports psychologist Robert Troutwine, Ph.D., who designed a personality test that assesses how you'll play under pressure. (You can pay to take it at www.tapsport.com.)

The guy with the pristine yard will outthink, not outpower, his opponent. Like Tiger Woods, he focuses on his A-game, staying calm and confident under pressure.

The guy who mows down anything in his way likely uses force over finesse to win. If he picks positions that suit his personality (such as football lineman or basketball center) he may do fine, as long as he doesn't draw too many penalties.

2. You have to be at the top of your game physically in order to have the mental edge. The two are so intertwined they simply cannot be separated, says sports psychologist Jim Loehr, Ed.D., who has worked with the likes of Eric Lindros, Grant Hill, and Ernie Els, to name just a few. "If you become fatigued, if you don't fuel with the right diet, or if your blood-sugar stores are low and glycogen in the muscles breaks down, I don't care how brilliant, talented, and skilled you are, it's not going to happen," he says.

That's because fatigue—not to mention a hangover—clouds your concentration. "You've got to be able to make quick decisions and respond fast to get that rebound or snag the line drive," Loehr says.

3. On the nervousness continuum, you'll find "freaked out" at one end and "laid back" at the other. "If you're too excited, too over-amped, you're going to choke," says sports psychologist Alan Goldberg, Ed.D., of the athletic department at the University of Connecticut in Farmington. "On the other hand, if you're too relaxed because you're overconfident, your performance will be flat." You want to be right in the middle—pumped to the point that you'll perform at your best.

For most guys, the challenge is staying calm. Focus on what you can do in the moment to defeat the jitters. Stretch, joke around with teammates, tie the batboy's shoelaces together.

4. Yogi Berra once said, "You can't think and hit at the same time."

Whether swinging a bat, shooting a free throw, or catching a pass, you need to focus, not muddy your mind with self-talk. You can bet Mark McGwire never said, "I gotta break Roger Maris's record," every time he slugged the ball over the fence. If he had, he never would have come close.

"When you do what I call time-traveling, which is when you think about your past mistakes and the future outcome, you're going to try too hard and do worse," says Goldberg. "Instead, keep your head in the moment." If you can't completely clear your head of thoughts, tell yourself things like "Stay loose. Breathe."

5. Anger translates into tighter muscles—an athlete's kiss of death. You want to stay loose, relaxed, and focused on your game, not get steamed about your opponent's uncalled foul. "If you're mad, you're focusing on the wrong thing. You need to focus on your performance, whether that's proper technique on a tennis serve or shaving minutes off your race time," says Troutwine.

In contrast, staying relaxed and in control of your emotions allows you to play at your peak in every match.

6. The funny thing about a mistake is that if you dwell on it, you're bound to make another one. You dig your own grave when you force yourself to play preoccupied.

To avoid making a string of mistakes, you first need to realize you've lost your focus, says Goldberg. Then you can take steps to regain it quickly, whether you're distracted by an error, an official's bad call, or a teammate's injury. Some pro athletes use this centering exercise from martial arts: Focus on your center of gravity, located an inch or two below your belly button. Relax, inhale through your nose, and exhale through your mouth, concentrating on breathing from that center spot. Repeat for several minutes three or four times a day. "You need to practice it for it to be an effective tool come game time," says Goldberg.

7. If you answered "True," either you need to get yourself a watch or you've made it to the zone, pal. "When athletes are in the zone, they actually go into a hypnotic kind of a trance where they lose sense of time and their perceptions change," says Goldberg. "Football players talk about seeing the opposing linemen come at them in slow motion."

When you're in the zone, you stop thinking and let your body take over. In fact, research shows that when you perform at your peak, your brain activity actually *slows*, says sports psychologist Joel Kirsch, Ph.D., director of the American Sports Institute. "In a sense, you get the hell out of your own way," he says, "and that allows great things to happen."

—DEANNA PORTZ

ESSENTIAL READING 16

BY RICHARD LALIBERTE
AND KENNETH WINSTON CAINE

Shoot and SCORE

Make your basketball game a slam dunk

You want to shoot farther, quicker, and with pro precision.

You want to sprint faster.

You want to heighten your jump.

You want to grab the rebound, pivot, and pass in a split second.

You want deadly accuracy and speed when you dribble and pass.

You want to increase your endurance and stamina so you can keep up with—and even outperform—your basketball buddies and, especially, the competition, as the clock ticks past 30, 40 minutes. This is a game where you move, move, move. You sprint, you block, you chase, you grab, you run, you jump, you shoot, you score. Basketball is not for the meek. You know that.

If you regularly play full-court ball, you're probably in pretty good aerobic condition. But if you're not strength training, you're only playing at a portion of your potential.

Why Strength Train

You'll never know what kind of basketball you can really play until you've done a strength program.

Why? Listen to *Sports Strength* author Ken Sprague, who is also a coach and strength trainer, the former owner and operator of the original Gold's Gym, and a physical monster of a man who trained alongside Kareem Abdul-Jabbar when Jabbar was playing pro.

"The stronger someone becomes, the more power he produces at a given moment," says Sprague. "Basketball is a real contact sport, so the stronger the player—especially inside players, forwards, and centers—the better. Strength becomes integral to your game.

"Reaching for a ball on a rebound is a good example," he continues. "The stronger fellow is going to pull that rebound away from a weaker fellow. Also, strength extends the effective range of your shot. If you can make the shot with only 50 percent of your strength instead of, say, 100 percent, then you have a lot of strength left that you can apply to controlling the ball."

The General Program

Underlying most of the program, says Sprague, is increased power for jumping. Leg, thigh, and calf work obviously adds power to your jump. To develop the power to snap your back straight and thrust your hips forward explosively during the jump, add some deadlifts and box jumps. The latter exercise refers simply to jumping on and off a short box, such as a milk carton, to get used to takeoff and impact.

Nobody minds the ripples achieved from abdominal work. Crunches give you clean-cut, muscular abdominals that stabilize your torso upon landing. So there's your free bonus: abs of steel.

This is a program you stick with year-round, in-season and out, though you vary its intensity. You quickly lose the edge and strength gains if you lay off the program when you're not playing, says Sprague.

Sprague advises using a periodization program for maximum benefits during the off-

Mix It Up

You've probably noticed that if you stick with the same workout intensity for any length of time, your muscles catch on and quit adapting as efficiently. Essentially, you hit a plateau. To ensure maximum progress, some trainers recommend a *periodization* schedule. This kind of program mixes up the intensity of your workout, keeping your muscles constantly on edge, always adapting.

Schedules vary. Some trainers recommend three cycles; some recommend more. All periodization programs feature an active-rest phase, a period in which you do little or no weight training at all. Instead you use the bulk of your training time for other fitness activities, such as sports or aerobics. The active-rest period should be the same length as the other cycles.

To show you how periodization can shake up a workout, here's a five-cycle periodization program developed by *Sports Strength* author Ken Sprague. Each cycle could be as short as a week or as long as a month. The length is up to you. Complete all five phases then start again.

Muscular-endurance phase	**2 or 3 sets**	**12–20 reps (light weights)**
Muscle-building phase	**3–5 sets**	**8–12 reps (moderate weights)**
Strength phase	**3–5 sets**	**3–8 reps (moderate to heavy weights)**

Then, to step beyond the basic principles, Sprague recommends the following:

"Peak" phase	**1–3 sets**	**1–3 reps (heavy weights)**
Active-rest phase	**(cross-training, racquet sports, basketball, etc.)**	

season. That's a program of altering your weights and repetition count constantly. (See "Mix It Up" on page 183.) In season, balance court time with gym time, but be sure to get in two weight-lifting sessions per week, doing two sets of 10 reps with a weight that challenges you to finish the reps while maintaining good form. And be sure to schedule at least 2 days' rest time before a game, he says. Otherwise, you'll overtrain and actually lose ground.

The Exercises

These are the specific strength-training exercises that Sprague recommends for basketball players. (See The Strongest Man Wins on page 207 for photos and descriptions.) Pencil out these 11 exercises into a periodization program, and you'll have your exact off-season ongoing workout routine.

- Squats for leg and hip thrust
- Dumbbell lunges for leg and hip thrust
- Box jumps for leg and hip thrust
- Leg curls to strengthen hamstrings and protect from injury
- Bench presses (narrow grip) for upper-body thrust
- Pullups for upper-body pull
- Deadlifts for back extension
- Straight-leg raises for knee lift and torso stabilization
- Grip strengtheners for ball control
- Toe raises for ankle extension
- Crunches, for ab strength and torso stabilization

Carioca drill

This foot drill develops side-to-side agility and strength. Cross one foot over the other, again and again and again, moving quickly from side to side on the court.

Box hop

To build your jump, stand on a box or bench with your knees bent and your feet about a foot apart. Jump forward to the floor

Beyond Strength Training

Obviously, all that strength won't do you much good if you don't have the heart-and-lung conditioning to apply it over and over and over, for hour after hour of Saturday pickup ball. It's often the best-conditioned player who wins the game with the last-second breakaway layup. So to have the stamina you need to be a true basketball master, you need to be in top aerobic shape, says *Sports Injury Handbook* coauthor Allan M. Levy, M.D., who is also an orthopedic surgeon in Woodcliff Lake, New Jersey. That means an ongoing program of running, bicycling, or whatever your aerobic pleasure, preferably with three vigorous sessions per week. Dr. Levy recommends running. Once you can comfortably run 3 to 5 miles several times a week, you should add in sprints or interval training. Wind sprints develop the endurance and explosive bursts of speed that come in so handy in basketball.

Also, the amount of twisting, turning, pushing, and shoving that occurs in a basketball game means flexibility is crucial to avoid injury, says Dr. Levy. Before any workout and before and after every game, go through a basic stretching routine that covers all parts of the body. Do some warmup work first, though, before doing your pre-workout or pre-game stretching.

Get Your Skills on the Ball

All that strength and stamina will be wasted if you don't develop good ball-handling skills. "At its best, basketball is a game where five players move the ball as a team," says *Basketball: Steps to Success* author Hal Wissel, who is also an advance scout for the Dallas Mavericks and the founder of basketballworld.com. That means great passing, smart dribbling, good peripheral vision, and much more.

or ground, bending your knees when you land. Spin to face the box and jump back onto it, deeply bending your knees again. Repeat to exhaustion.

Moon walking

Leap your way up and down the court several times in smooth, giant, bounding steps, as though playing on the moon, free of the Earth's gravity.

Ball handling

This warmup consists of passing and catching the ball, going from one hand to the other. There are five basic moves here.

1. Over your head
2. Around your head
3. Around your waist
4. Around one leg, then the other
5. Figure eight through your legs

Begin with your body in a balanced stance. Forcefully pass the ball from one hand to the other by flexing your fingers and wrists. Do a complete follow-through on each pass, pointing your passing fingers at your catching hand.

Practice each move 10 times in one direction, then reverse direction and do 10 more. Your goal is to get through all five parts, both directions, in 3 minutes with a maximum of three errors.

This five-part warmup develops dribbling ability and strengthens your fingers and forearms.

1. Crossover. In a balanced stance, change the ball from one hand to the other, dribbling it lower and not wider than your knees. Keep your nondribbling hand up as a guard, and change the position of your feet and body to protect the ball. Alternating from left to right and right to left, complete 20 repetitions.

2. Figure eight. Dribble the ball in a figure eight from back to front through the middle of your legs. Change from one hand to the other after the ball goes through your legs. After 10 repetitions, change direction and do 10 more.

3. One knee. Continue to dribble the ball as you kneel down on one knee. Starting in front of your knee, dribble around to one side and under your raised knee. Change hands and dribble behind your back leg. Again change from one hand to the other and continue to the starting point in front of your knee. Dribble in a figure eight for 10 repetitions in one direction; change directions and do 10 more.

4. Sitting. Continue to dribble as you sit down. Dribble for 10 repetitions on one side. Raise your legs, dribble the ball under them to your other side, and dribble on that side for 10 repetitions.

5. Lying down. Continue dribbling as you lie down on your back. While lying down, dribble for 10 reps on one side. Sit up, raise your legs, dribble the ball under your legs to the other side, lie down, and dribble for 10 more reps.

How Shaq Does It

Basketball superstar Shaquille O'Neal swears by strength training. For 20 minutes 3 or 4 days a week, he does crunches followed by weighted situps, seated leg tucks, and lumbar extensions. Before he incorporated the ab routine into his workout, he sometimes had back problems. But he adds, "Not anymore."

O'Neal's legwork involves time on a leg-press machine and 5 to 10 minutes of strides across the court; he also does sprints throughout practice to develop and maintain speed.

And stretching gets top priority. "I stretch at least 20 minutes every day, no exceptions," he says. He focuses on stretching his legs, back, and shoulders, improving range of motion and, thus, revving up more power.

Dribbling two balls at once is tough but fun. There are six parts to this approach.

1. Together. Simultaneously dribble two basketballs below knee level.

2. Alternate one up and one down. Simultaneously dribble two basketballs below knee level, so that one is up when the other is down.

3. Crossover. While dribbling two balls low and close to your body, cross them back and forth, changing them from one hand to the other. Alternate which hand reaches in front.

4. Inside-out. An inside-out dribble is a fake change of direction. Dribble the two balls to the sides of your body. With one, start a dribble toward the front of your body, but then rotate your hand over the ball to dribble it back to your side. Do it with one ball at a time, and then with both.

5. Through your legs. Dribble first one ball, then the other, and then both balls through your legs.

6. Side-pull forward and back. Dribble a ball at each side of your body. Then dribble them backward and forward, using your fingers and wrists as though pulling them back and forth.

Shoot and Dunk like a Pro

The swish of a ball sailing through the net is much more satisfying than the boing of a ball hitting the rim or backboard. Here are former streetball world champ David Jensen's secrets for perpetual swishhood.

▶**Face the basket.** "Get your chest and feet square with the basket," he says. It may not look fancy, but it works.

▶**Favor one hand.** Both hands bring the ball up, but get your weak hand off the ball before you release. That's the southpaw hand if you're a right-hander. You have better control and speed when you use your dominant hand.

▶**Let the wrist do the precision work.** Release from the wrist. Let the ball roll from your fingertips, slipping off the index and middle fingers last. If you're shoving the ball with your arms, you don't have much precision. Think wrists, fingers.

Then there's the matter of the dunk.

Here we defer to Chip Sigmon, strength-and-conditioning coach for the Charlotte Hornets and the WNBA's Charlotte Sting. His advice? Well, it's what a big part of this chapter is all about: strength training and jumping work.

▶**Powerful legs.** Obviously, you need great leg muscles for jumping. You get that from squats, lunges, and leg presses.

▶**Powerful shoulders.** Upper-body work, especially shoulder-strengthening routines, add a lot of zip to your jump, says Sigmon. They help pull your arms and the rest of your body upward.

▶**Jumping drills.** Sigmon recommends the rim jump: Pick a spot on a wall or tree limb, about 6 inches higher than you can reach. Jump up and try to touch it with your dominant hand. When you land, immediately spring back up with another jump and try to slap the spot with your other hand. Keep alternating hands, and do two sets of 10 jumps each. As you improve your ability, raise the target spot and keep at it, he says.

▶**Practice, practice.** First from underneath the rim, later with a running start. Use both feet to push off, and extend your legs, back, and arms fully through the jump, he says.

BY STEPHEN GEORGE

Be a Two-Wheel Wonder

Get the cycling skills you need to be king of the road . . . or mountain

Anyone who has bought a bicycle within the past decade knows that the market has split into two camps: road cycling and mountain biking. Different mentalities, different bike styles, different pleasures, different goals. The road cyclist covers the miles, gets into a rhythm, and stays locked in, often for hours. The mountain biker is into the thrill, the flight, the risk, the bursts of power.

You can love one or the other or both. We take no stand on which is more fun. What's certain is that the fitness needs of the two differ. If you want to ride a bicycle to your peak level, you first must determine how exactly you want to ride.

"Figuring out the right program for you depends first on the type of cycling you like to do. If you're strictly a road cyclist, you have issues of endurance and form to contend with," says Bill Strickland, executive editor at *Bicycling* magazine and coauthor of several of the magazine's books of cycling hints and tips. You need a training program that emphasizes proper form while also building cardiovascular and lower-body power.

These are also important issues for mountain bikers. And because of the rough-and-tumble nature of off-road cycling, you need to work extra-hard to develop the skills and reflexes necessary to surmount countless obstacles and trail hazards. You also need to use equipment and conditioning techniques that will help minimize the pounding your body is bound to take on a mountain-bike trail.

Take It on the Road

Road cyclists find the most pleasure in the exhilaration of getting into a good pedaling rhythm and just cranking down the road. That said, it's always wise to pay attention to form. Improper body alignment—and improper bike settings, for that matter—hurt performance and can cause injury. If you have any doubts about your form, get expert advice from a local cycling club or professional bike shop.

Whether you're joyriding or competing, the only way to find that rhythm, maintain a good speed, and keep your body in cycling trim is to get out there at least twice a week. The more you bike, the more natural you feel doing it. Here are some tips for peak road-cycling performance.

Find your cadence. Pedaling fast and well is the basis of powerful cycling. The trick is maintaining a consistent, even, speedy cadence—or leg speed—throughout a ride. Elite cyclists try to maintain a cadence where they are "spinning"—that is, a cadence that falls between 80 and 100 revolutions per minute (rpm). If you're training to be a fast road cyclist, you should work to get your cadence up to those levels, too.

Casual riders only need to keep their cadence to around 50 rpm; keep that number firmly in mind as your training minimum. To determine your cadence, you can either hop on a stationary cycle with an rpm register or simply count the number of times your right foot comes to the top of your pedal stroke. Do this for 30 seconds, then multiply the number you get by two. That's your cadence.

Each week, work to increase your cadence by at least 10 rpm, until you find a rhythm than works for you.

Stay narrow. The more your elbows and knees wing out away from your body, the more drag you create, and the slower you go. Instead, make a point of keeping your elbows tucked in as you ride, says Strickland. And if your knees bow out every time you pedal, take a look at your seat height—chances are it's too low for you.

Get flat. Even amateur cyclists know they should try to ride as low in the saddle as possible. Even though you feel like you're riding low, chances are you have an arch in your back, and that hump makes you less aerodynamic.

Practice flattening out your back and making adjustments in your form to make you even flatter, says Strickland. For example, rotating your hips forward in the saddle can help you straighten out and fly right. If you have an indoor wind-trainer or stationary cycle, set it up in front of a mirror. Or get someone to watch you on your bike.

Don't stand for it. When you come upon a steep hill, the natural temptation is to immediately stand up in the saddle and crank furi-

Proper Road-Cycling Form

ously until you're over the top. The problem is that this position causes your heart rate to go way up, and you end up burning energy you may need later in the ride.

Instead, stay seated as long as possible. Switch to a lower gear if you have to, but keep your butt planted. The longer you wait before standing, the more power you conserve. Practice this often enough and you may find you won't need to stand up at all.

Use the big gears. One tip cycling coaches recommend is deliberately cycling in the lower, or bigger, gears. This increases the resistance when you pedal and gives your legs a great workout. If you're going down a hill, don't shift to a higher gear. Stay in the big gear and pedal as fast as possible—it's a good speed-training technique, says Strickland.

Success on the Mountain

You don't need to be very streamlined on a mountain bike, but you sure need good form. "In mountain biking, good form means getting to the bottom of the hill in one piece," says Don Cuerdon, former writer at *Mountain Bike* magazine.

That means building sharp reflexes and plenty of upper-body strength to help you steer the bike over outrageous obstacles. Good lower-body and cardiovascular power, meanwhile, will enable you to enjoy many hours of churning up and down hills and up and over logs, stumps, and rocks. Here are a few wise words to help you accomplish all these goals.

Be a part-time roadie. Although some diehard mountain bikers look down their noses at road cycling, doing so robs them of a great cardiovascular workout. "Road cycling helps train your heart and lungs better. Believe me, that will come in handy when you're out in the woods trying to make it up a good, steep, crumbling hill," says Cuerdon.

Develop foresight. A mountain-bike trail is absolutely studded with obstacles. "It wouldn't be a mountain-bike trail—and it wouldn't be fun—if it wasn't," says Cuerdon. What's not fun is hitting a rock or root and doing an endo (short for *end over end*) because you weren't prepared for it.

This most often happens because you overfocus on one object—the one right in front of you—and not enough on the rest of the trail. Train yourself to see all the potential pitfalls on the next several feet of the trail, not just what's about to go under your wheel. "The trick is to see the log just ahead as well as the rocks 2 feet beyond that and the roots 5 feet beyond that," says Cuerdon.

Use the granny gear. When you're trying to crank up a hill, don't be afraid to shift up to the smallest front gear, also known as the granny.

"I think the name makes guys shy away from it. But it's there for a reason: to make your life easier. Go ahead and use it," says Cuerdon. To make your climb easier, lean forward, almost putting your chest to the handlebars.

Stay padded. In mountain biking, you might take harder knocks than you did in high school football—and you wore a lot more padding in football. To protect against some of the most common mountain-bike traumas, wear padded gloves and some sort of padding for your nether regions. "You don't have to be one of the shiny blue people, wearing those skin-tight, padded cycling shorts," says Cuerdon. If you want to be more discrete, you can buy padded underwear-like liners for your usual shorts. Your butt will thank you.

Descend smartly. You're going down a steep hill, your speed's picking up, the bike's bounding on rocks and sticks. Unless you learn how to control your descent, you may end up paying a steep price. Here's what to do, according to our experts.

▶Make sure your bike is in a high gear and pointed in the general direction of where you want to go. As you start downhill, don't let your weight slide forward—if you hit a big rut, you'll go flying. Instead, extend your arms and slide your butt back off the back end of the saddle. Keep your pedals parallel to the ground to avoid catching them on low obstacles.

▶For better control, squeeze the saddle with your thighs and pump the brakes, relying mostly on your front brake. Don't jam on them. When you get to the bottom of the hill, resume your normal position and start cranking.

PEAK performance

Cycle through the Great Indoors

Performance Technique Rollers ($119) work like a treadmill for your bike. Ride on top of them and you'll feel as if you're riding outside, because you have to stay balanced. Use them to train indoors during bad weather. Because they offer little resistance and you have to keep pedaling to keep yourself upright, they help improve your speed, says Gil Hatton, who trained world-champion cyclist Marty Nothstein. First-time users should place the rollers next to a wall or a sturdy chair to help themselves balance.

Inexperienced cyclists can try the Performance Technique Rollers Front Stabilizer ($39.99). It essentially converts the rollers into a stationary trainer by increasing resistance and stabilizing the bike.

Order either of these products at www.performancebike.com.

Strength Training for Cyclists

"Cyclists used to think all they had to do for training was just ride their bicycle—a lot. But nowadays, no matter what type of bicycling they do, cyclists are seeing the value of strength training and conditioning off the bike. That's what will help them ride better and avoid injury when they're on the bike," says John Graham, C.S.C.S., one of the directors of the Allentown Sports Medicine and Human Performance Center in Pennsylvania and the strength trainer of world-champion cyclist Marty Nothstein.

Whether you're a road cyclist or a mountain biker, your workout is going to be pretty much the same.

"Cycling is universally hard on the legs and lower back. But because you're using your upper body to steer and help control the bike, you'll also want to pay attention to the muscles there—that's something a lot of cyclists forget," says Cuerdon.

Include the following exercises in your workout, says Graham. (See The Strongest Man Wins on page 207 for photos and descriptions.) Do one to three sets of 12 to 20 reps. Select a weight that challenges you to finish 12 to 20 reps while maintaining good form.

- One-arm dumbbell rows for upper back
- Bent-over rows for upper back
- Bench presses for upper body
- Alternating presses with dumbbells for chest
- Biceps curls
- Concentration curls for biceps
- Lying triceps extensions
- Wrist curls
- Reverse wrist curls
- Leg presses for quads and hamstrings
- Squats for quads and hamstrings
- Leg curls for hamstrings

▶Abductor/adductor moves for inner and outer thighs

▶Crunches for abs

When to Exercise

If you're the least bit competitive in your cycling—or you want to be—you need to partition your workouts according to the cycling season, off-season, and pre-season.

Traditionally, the off-season, which runs from October to January, is your time to focus on weight training. Do it 3 or 4 days a week. Keep your cycling muscles limber on a stationary bike or wind-trainer—use that as a warmup or aerobic workout.

In February, you'll start to move into the pre-season phase. Here, Graham suggests riding more and cutting back weight training to two or three times a week. "Don't go easy on those days. Keep up the intensity of your weight training," he admonishes.

By April, you'll be getting into prime cycling season, and most of your exercise time will probably be devoted to riding. Don't abandon weight training, though. Graham recommends continuing to lift 2 days a week throughout the season. That should be enough to maintain your muscle until you get back into the off-season. Again.

Cycling Essentials

Don't pedal another inch without these velo vitals, says Don Cuerdon, former writer at *Mountain Bike* magazine.

▶**Helmet.** Most fatal or crippling cycling injuries are the result of not wearing a bicycle helmet. 'Nuf said. For around $25, you can buy a basic helmet and look smart. For around $100, you can buy the latest, aerodynamic, shock-resistant helmet and look smart *and* cool.

▶**First-aid kit.** Skid on pavement or down a rocky slope even one time, and thereafter you'll be convinced of the need for a few medical necessities. Carry a few large adhesive strips, or a small roll of gauze and some waterproof adhesive tape. Also carry some antiseptic wipes for cleaning out dirt and crud in cases of "road rash," if you're luckless enough to take a spill.

▶**Patch kit.** Put enough miles on your bike and you're bound to suffer a flat. "Murphy's Law of Cycling absolutely dictates that it will happen at the moment you are absolutely the farthest away from civilization," says Cuerdon. A patch kit will at least help you cope with the most obvious punctures. If you mountain bike with any regularity, consider carrying a spare tube—insurance against the kind of off-road rips no patch kit can cure.

▶**Bicycle pump.** The patch kit is useless without it.

▶**Water bottle.** Feeling the coolness of the breeze against your skin may make you forget that you're sweating up a storm with all that pedaling. Be sure to carry at least one filled water bottle with you. Drink from it often—at least every 10 minutes.

▶**Snack.** When you're cycling, you are your own engine. Don't be caught in the middle of nowhere when you run out of fuel. Instead, take your own, in the form of a sports bar, fig bars, or even fruit.

▶**Cash.** In case you forgot to pack a snack, a few bills tucked into a sock or sleeve could come in handy. At the very least, carry a couple of quarters so if you or your bike gets hurt, you can call for a ride home. That's assuming you can find a pay phone 5 miles from the trailhead.

BY KENNETH WINSTON CAINE

GOLF like a PRO

Keep your game out of the rough

For too long, golfers got no respect. If you mentioned to a nonplayer that you golfed, you'd inevitably get teased about the ugly plaid pants that had to be hanging in your closet.

Thanks to Tiger, things have changed. Golf is getting more and more popular. Nearly everybody who tries it likes it. Golf, people are realizing, is a fun, challenging game of skill, played in a truly beautiful setting. Respect has arrived.

Or so you'd think. Don't try selling golf as great exercise. Carrying a full golf bag for 18 holes . . . well, yes, that's very good for you. The actual game, taking up to 6 hours to hit the ball fewer than 150 times (let us hope), with at least half of those hits being putts or chips, is not exactly a day at the gym.

A golf swing puts extraordinary torsion (twisting or wrenching force) on your back and spine—up to eight times your body weight during a swing, says *Golf Injury Handbook* coauthor Allan M. Levy, M.D., who is also an orthopedic surgeon in Woodcliff Lake, New Jersey. If you aren't warmed up and flexible, the sudden, swift torsion is jarring. It's likely to tax and strain muscles, leaving you uncomfortable the next day, says Dr. Levy.

Also, every golf swing is in the same direction, so what muscle building it does is lopsided. And players often suffer lower-back pain from the constant one-direction torsion, adds New York City chiropractor Joseph Askinasi.

Working Out for Golf

Practice improves your skills, but a powerful swing and a pain-resistant body require workout time away from the course. To be your best at golf, be like the pros: Do general conditioning and golf-specific strength building.

"Muscles from the head to the toe are involved in a golf swing, and a long drive requires strength," says *Sports Strength* author Ken Sprague, who is also a coach and strength trainer, and the former owner and operator of the original Gold's Gym. "The strength with which you hit the ball contributes to its speed, which in turn determines how far the ball travels down the fairway."

Just as important, trainers put a tremendous emphasis on flexibility, flexibility, flexibility, notes Dr. Levy. Pro players, he says, spend 45 minutes warming up and stretching before they tee off. Flexibility is your best defense against back injury.

And provided you forgo the golf cart, you'll need some endurance training so you won't be huffing and puffing by the 18th hole. Walking 18 holes on a golf course is well over 4 miles.

If your partners will chug along with you, turn the distance to your advantage and transform golf into a minor workout. "Carry your own clubs and move as rapidly as possible from tee to the ball to the next tee. That's a practical way of working on developing the stamina specific to the game," says Sprague.

What to Do

Start with a core routine for general strength. It should include the following: squats, bench presses, one-arm dumbbell rows, alternating presses with dumbbells, concentration curls, and lying triceps extensions. (See The Strongest Man Wins on page 207 for photos and descriptions of these exercises as well as the ones mentioned below.)

The only area you really don't want to build excessively is the chest, says Sprague. Too much bulk there will interfere with your swing.

Here is what golfers need to pay particular attention to and why, according to Dr. Levy.

- Toe raises for legs
- Leg extensions
- Leg curls
- Oblique crunches for torso and back
- Oblique twists for torso and back
- Crunches for abs
- Side lateral raises for shoulders
- Shoulder extensions
- Forearm curls
- Reverse forearm curls
- Wrist rolls
- Grip strengtheners

Also, palm-up and palm-down elbow stretches lengthen the extensor and flexor muscles of the wrist so you can avoid a form of tennis elbow to which golfers are prone.

A Pro Trainer's Top Tips

Randy Myers, head trainer at the PGA National Resort and Spa in Palm Beach Gardens, Florida, works with more than 40 touring professionals. What they do, you should do, he says. And the biggest thing they do that he doesn't see recreational golfers doing?

"Stretching," he says. Stretch before and after a round. And "instead of sitting around drinking beer on the 19th hole, find a place where you can at least get crossover stretching—trunk rotation—for the lower back," he says.

"What's amazing about golf," says Myers, "is that if you're a golfer, you'll spare no expense to buy the clubs that Greg Norman uses or the wedge that Fred Couples uses." But, he says, there's more to Norman's and Couples's games than good equipment. "These people are also doing conditioning activities—stretching and different things. And if Greg Norman is doing stretching, you should be, too."

For his players, Myers also develops strength-training programs similar to the one we recommend. And he offers an insider's tip: "You heard it here first: The best upper-body conditioning exercise for golf, bar none, is an inclined pushup. I'll tell you why: It strengthens the upper chest and mid-back, keeps you in a good postural position, and also gets extension for the biceps and forearms."

What equipment do you need? A desk, a sturdy table, or a bathtub. An inclined pushup is simply a pushup done on an incline. You plant your hands on the edge of the furniture instead of on the floor.

The Pre-Game Routine

You arrive at the course at 7:40 A.M. and have 20 minutes to tee time. You (a) get a small bucket of balls and start whacking; (b) get some scrambled eggs and coffee; or (c) do a thorough warmup and stretching routine to get your body ready.

You know the right answer.

Here's how to proceed.

First, you warm up with jumping jacks, running in place, or walking vigorously. The object, says Dr. Levy, is not necessarily to get your heart pumping hard but to get blood flowing in your muscles before you subject them to stretching and tension. Just 2 to 3 minutes of warmup is all you need. It's an important step, says Dr. Levy. Don't skip it.

Next, you stretch. See page 200 for an on-the-course stretching routine adapted from the recommendations of DeDe Owens and Linda K. Bunker in their book *Golf: Steps to Success*. You'll need your driver for some of them.

For the Hard Core

Want to talk really serious golf muscles—the kind you get only in a gym? Talk to Sprague. "Specific strength training can really help your game," he says.

Here's his specialized full-body training program for golfers.

Off-season, Sprague wants to see you in the gym 2 or 3 days a week, doing the exercises below. (Again, see The Strongest Man Wins on page 207 for photos and descriptions.) In season, stick to 2 days each week and do two sets of each exercise, eight reps per set. Select a weight that challenges you to finish eight reps while maintaining good form.

- Dumbbell lunges for hip and leg thrust
- Dumbbell stepups for hip and leg thrust

- ▶Oblique twists for strong torso rotation
- ▶Upright rows for shoulder development
- ▶Deadlifts for back extension
- ▶Forearm curls
- ▶Grip strengtheners
- ▶Pullups for upper-body pull
- ▶Crunches for a stronger abdomen

TOUGH TALK

"If you play well and lose, then I think sometimes you learn less. But if you . . . really throw up all over yourself and lose that way, then obviously you're gonna learn an awful lot about yourself."

—TIGER WOODS

Watch It

Want to play better golf? Watch TV. That is, watch *yourself* on TV.

This is the advice of former bank chief executive Dick Noel, who shaved his handicap in half in two seasons with this and a few other tricks we'll let you in on.

Before turning on the tube, Noel says, buy a rubber golf mat and set it up in your backyard. Then unwind each evening by hitting plastic golf balls—the kind that won't take out your neighbors' windows. So what if they're toys? The swing is the same. So is the slice and the hook. Fifteen minutes a night, each work night. That's Noel's prescription.

Now, time for the TV. Almost. First, set up a video camera next to the practice mat to record your swings. Tape yourself once every couple of weeks. Indicate to the camera when you hit a good shot.

Now watch TV. You'll probably see some things you don't like. And you'll fix them. Because a picture is worth a thousand words.

Noel also recommends comparing your best swings to that of a great pro teacher on a video. He likes *Golf with Al Geiberger* from SyberVision.

Other tips?

- ▶Play with people who are just a bit better than you, advises Noel. This keeps you on your toes.
- ▶Hit the links by 6:45 A.M. a couple of days a week. Play five or six holes, and play two or three balls each hole. Drop some balls in the traps and the deep rough. Playing the extra shots does wonders for your short game, Noel says. You're at work by 8:30, he adds.
- ▶Do a full-body weight-lifting routine and a stretching routine. (We already told you this.) Noel lifts on Mondays, Wednesdays, and Fridays for 45 minutes. He does 15 minutes of stretching on Tuesdays and Thursdays. Within 3 weeks, he saw the payoff. He was hitting balls farther and was more chipper after 18 holes.

Stretch and Deliver

Neck stretch

Stand straight and relaxed. Rest one hand on a golf club whose head (or handle) is resting in front of one foot. Turn your head and neck to the golf-club side of your body. With your other hand, gently push against your jaw so you chin touches your shoulder. Hold for 15 seconds. Relax, and switch sides. Do this a total of six times in each direction.

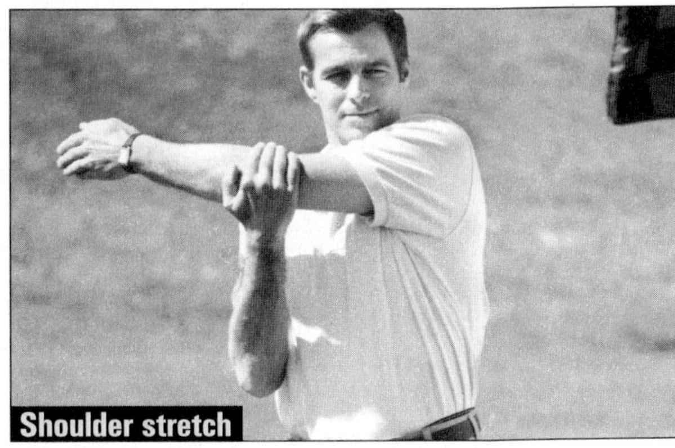

Shoulder stretch

Stand with your heels close, toes pointed out at a 45-degree angle. Draw your left arm across your chest at shoulder height and, with your right hand on your left elbow, gently pull your arm closer to your chest. Hold the stretch for 10 seconds, then reverse arms. Do a total of six for each arm.

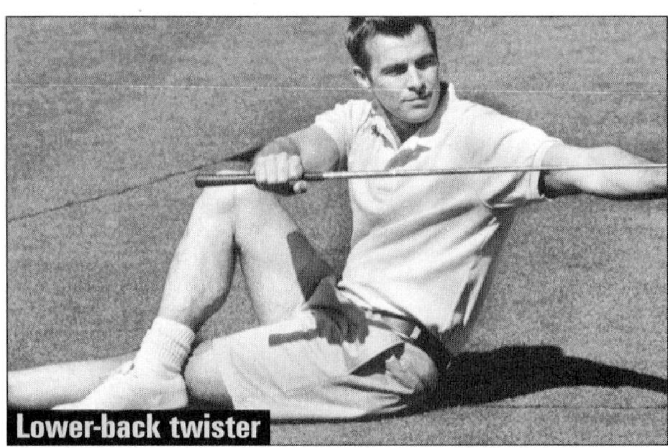

Lower-back twister

Sit on the ground with your legs stretched in front of you. Bend your right knee and put your right foot on the ground outside your left knee. Grasp a golf club, hands on each end, hold it at shoulder height, and turn to the left as far as is comfortable. Hold for a count of 10. Do this six times. Repeat on the other side.

Couple this stretch with the back primer or side twister.

Back primer

Place the club behind your neck, across your shoulders. Hold it at each end. Keeping your hips facing forward, twist your torso in one direction as far as is comfortable and hold for 15 seconds. Then twist in the other direction and hold. Do six on each side. Don't just rock back and forth. That actually tightens your muscles. Twist, hold, and stretch.

Side twister

Stand with your feet slightly apart. Grasp the golf club midway up the shaft with both hands, and lift your arms straight up in the air. Bend your upper body to your right as far as is comfortable for a count of 10, then to the left for the same time. Do six reps on each side.

Hand-and-arm builder

Stand with your legs shoulder-width apart, arms close to your body. Grip the club in the center of the shaft with your right hand and bend your elbow so your forearm and palm are parallel to the ground. Rotate your wrist a half-circle to the right, then back to center. Do 10, then switch hands and repeat, rotating your arm to the left. Do six sets of 10 repetitions for each arm.

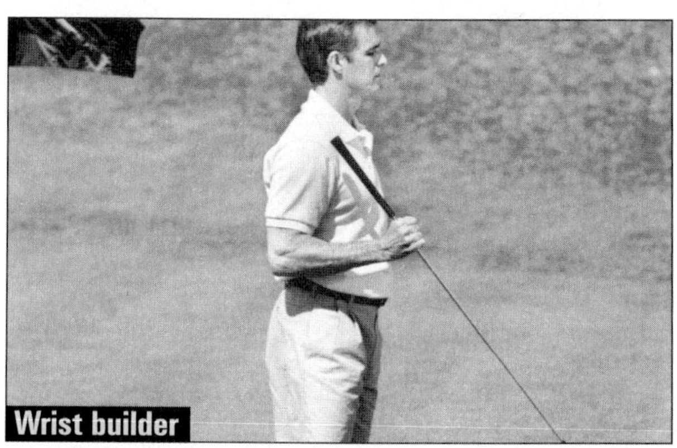
Wrist builder

Stand with your legs shoulder-width apart, arms close to your body, one arm bent at the elbow so your forearm is parallel to the ground but your palm faces inward. Grip a club so its ends point up and down. Gently rock it forward and back a few times, then switch arms and repeat.

Leg stretcher

Stand with your right foot crossed over your left. Holding a golf club at the ends, gently bend forward, relaxing your upper body and letting the club reach as close to the ground as is comfortable. Hold for 10 seconds. Repeat six times. Then reverse the foot position and repeat six times.

BY KENNETH WINSTON CAINE

Better RUN

Prep your body to run better, faster, longer

There's a simplicity, an almost Zen purity to the sport of running. You, your shoes, the open road. Nothing more, nothing less. Doing what man and animal have done for thousands of years. The most natural exercise of all.

There's more to this passion than meets the eye. There's a science to it all: how to train, how to prevent injury, how to breathe, how to condition your body for maximum results. Sure, you can go outside and just run. Children do it every day. But if you want to run well, you must do more.

Developing the skill, strength, and endurance of a good runner—and keeping your knees, ankles, hips, and hamstrings as injury-free as possible—requires a well-conceived training program, says Budd Coates, marathon runner, trainer, exercise physiologist, and special consultant to *Runner's World* magazine.

The precise nature of the program depends upon what level of runner you are, of course. In general, "what you need to do over a 7-day period is introduce the body to endurance training, quality training, and rest," says Coates. When you do this in the right manner, at the right level of stress, you'll improve.

How Much Should You Run?

Coates notes that the majority of runners average 16 to 20 miles per week. If you're among them, Coates recommends the following runs each week.

- One long run of about 8 miles.
- One medium run of 5 to 6 miles that includes what Coates calls quality. "Quality is basically a run that involves more effort than the others," he says. "You could include cruise intervals, tempo runs, track intervals, some hill work."
- Two or three shorter runs of 2 to 4 miles, done at a comfortable pace.
- Two or 3 days of rest alternated into the schedule.

In all, it should add up to about 20 miles, says Coates.

Coates notes that all runners need to adapt the basic 7-day-per-week running program to their own levels of strength and endurance. "The fact is, everybody needs to do endurance work; everybody needs to rest; and everybody needs to do quality work," he says. "The exact ratio or recipe is really dependent upon where you're at and what you've done before."

The recommended program "could bury someone who has just started running and could be totally tedious for an experienced runner," he says.

For the more advanced runner, Coates says he "wouldn't make many changes—just

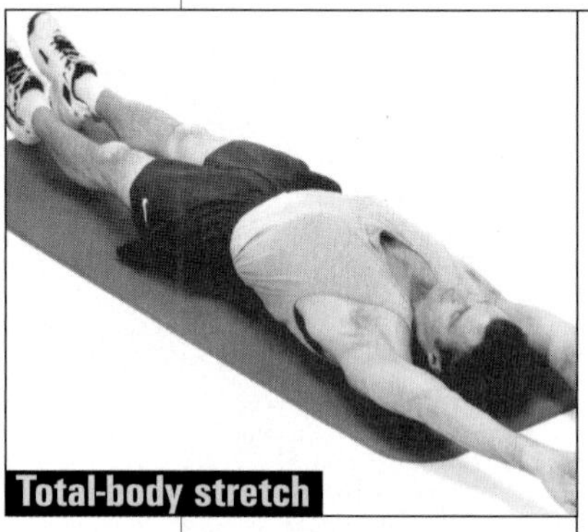

Total-body stretch

Lie on your back. Fully extend your arms and legs. Tense and stretch as far as possible for 5 seconds, then relax. Repeat three to five times. Do this to begin and end your stretching routine.

Toe touches

Stand with your feet shoulder-width apart. Slowly bend at your hips until you feel a pull at the back of your legs. Make sure your knees are not locked. Hold the position for up to 20 seconds. If you can't actually touch your toes, that's okay. This stretch is good for the lower back, hips, groin, and hamstrings and guards against pulls and injuries in those areas.

Ankle pulls

You'll need a towel for this stretch. Lie on your stomach with one leg straight and the other bent at the knee, pointing toward the ceiling. Loop the towel or a strap around your bent leg and hold the ends with your hands, behind your back. Curl your neck and shoulders upward, and attempt to straighten your bent leg against the tension from the towel until the thigh is taut. Hold for 20 seconds, then relax. Repeat three times, then switch legs and repeat. This exercise is good for the thigh muscles.

the quantity. The long runs become longer. Rest days can be an hour easy run, and moderate days can be 12 to 15 miles. A hard day can be 15 to 20 miles with a variety of quality inside that mileage."

A beginning runner, on the other hand, should start off with walking and, after a couple of weeks, alternate between walking and jogging. After a couple more weeks, he should alternate between walking and running and, eventually, over a 2-month period, work up to a steady run, says Coates.

Stretching

As with any workout, it's important to get your blood flowing and your muscles primed with a short warmup before diving into the main event.

Coates suggests that you save stretches for the end of the workout, which is what he does. "The key," he explains, "is that if you stretch after you work out, you will be ready for the next day's run."

Occasionally, he says, you may need to stretch early in your run "if you feel a muscle that's being kind of a squeaky wheel.

"But if everything is fine, after 10 to 15 minutes of comfortable running, just progress into the hard run and then stretch everything in general after the workout," Coates says.

Above are six stretches that Coates recommends as a good routine.

Strength Training

Coates suggests you supplement your running workout with appropriate strength training. "Appropriate" means a good overall workout, he says. It also means experimenting a bit to find what works for you.

Straight-knee calf stretch

Stand about 2 to 3 feet from a wall and rest your palms on it. Bend one leg at the knee, lifting that heel off the ground. Keep the other foot flat on the ground and that knee and hip, as well as your back, straight. Bend at your ankles and elbows until you feel the extended calf tighten. Hold for up to 20 seconds, then relax. Alternate from leg to leg and repeat three times with each leg. This strengthens, stretches, and works out pain in the calves and Achilles tendons.

Groin stretch

Lie on your back with the soles of your feet touching firmly. Let your knees and hips relax and hold the position for 40 seconds. This relaxes the body and helps prevent groin pulls.

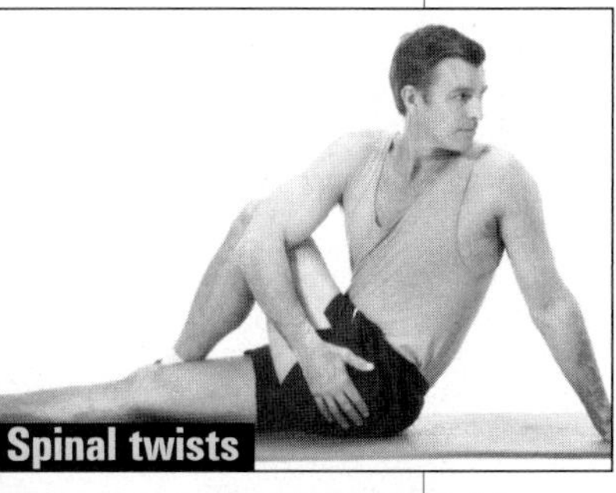

Spinal twists

Sit with your right leg straight. Cross your left leg over your right so your left foot rests on the outside of your right knee. Bend your right elbow, resting it on the outside of your left thigh. Rest your left hand on the ground behind you. Slowly turn your head to look over your left shoulder while rotating your upper body toward your left arm. Hold for up to 20 seconds, then stretch the other side. This is good for the hips, back, and rib cage and reduces or prevents back and hip pain.

"The biggest thing with strength training is that you need to listen to your body while you're running," says Coates. "You know when you're creating a muscle imbalance and trying to run with it. You don't feel biomechanically fluid anymore. Or if you feel you're carrying around extra baggage—your upper body is feeling bulky—you're probably overdoing it.

"Lift like you're a runner; don't lift like you're a lifter. You're always looking at lifting through a runner's eyes. You're not looking at lifting to get so many more pounds on the bench and so many more pounds on the arm curl and to flex in front of the mirror. The program that works is the one that makes you feel good when you're out running. You find it on your own. Pick a sound overall program, and with a little bit of trial and error, find what works for you."

A few specific strengthening exercises are recommended for runners by *Sports Strength* author Ken Sprague, who is also a coach and strength trainer, and the former owner and operator of the original Gold's Gym. "Some strength training can help runners avoid injury," Sprague says. Most runners, he says, experience at least one relatively serious injury a year.

The exercises he recommends can be done with free weights or with gym equipment. (See The Stongest Man Wins on page 207 for photos and descriptions.) For each exercise, do two sets of 10 reps, twice a week. Select a weight that challenges you to finish 10 reps while maintaining good form.

PEAK performance

Chafe Protection

Two new pals for your buds. During a marathon, the typical male nipple brushes against its shirt approximately 50,000 times, causing burning and embarrassing bleeding. The usual fixes don't work: Petroleum jelly rubs off, and Band-Aids adhere painfully to chest hair. That's why Bob Kocher, a long-distance runner in Arlington, Virginia, invented NipGuards. These quarter-size patches stick safely and securely to your nipples and shield them from chafing. A pack of 10 pairs costs about $9 at running stores or at www.nipguards.com. Tassels not included.

Sprague's program for runners includes:

▶Dumbbell lunges for hip and leg thrust

▶Dumbbell stepups for hip and leg thrust

▶Leg curls to prevent hamstring injuries

▶Deadlifts for torso stability

▶Bench presses with close grip to improve arm drive

▶Heel raises with seated-leg-press machine for ankle extension

▶Pullups for upper-body strength

▶Leg raises with ankle weights or dumbbells

Runner's Terminology

Do-it-yourselfers and those relatively new to running may be unfamiliar with the following training techniques. Give them a try, suggests Budd Coates, marathon runner, trainer, exercise physiologist, and special consultant to *Runner's World* magazine.

▶**Intervals.** These are periods of hard running alternated with easier "rest" periods of jogging. They're great for increasing speed, says Coates. Hard-running periods can last from 30 seconds to 5 minutes, and rest periods should be about the same length. Or you may be able to cut rest intervals down to half the time of the hard-run intervals.

▶**Cruise intervals.** You'll need to have a good grasp of your speed and endurance capacities for these. Run at a pace that is 15- to 20-seconds-per-mile slower than your 10-K race pace; then jog for 20 to 30 percent as long (for example, 10 minutes of running, 2 minutes of jogging). Repeat three or four times, consecutively. The purpose is to increase endurance by raising the point at which muscle-tiring lactic acid begins to build up in your blood. Increase distance, but not speed, as the training gets comfortable, advises Coates.

▶**Tempo runs.** After warming up, run for 15 to 30 minutes at a pace 20- to 30-seconds-per-mile slower than your 10-K pace. The object is the same as with cruise intervals, says Coates.

▶**Hill work.** Run up hills at 85 to 90 percent effort, then jog down as a rest; repeat several times. The uphill part should take from 30 seconds to 5 minutes, and the recovery (downhill) portion 1½ to 2 times longer. You may want to add a 30- to 60-second surge in the middle of the downhill portion. The object is to increase your efficiency at running hills.

The STRONGEST Man Wins

You'll kick some serious butt with these exercises

By now, you know why it's important to put muscle on your bones if you want to be the best in your game: to pummel the competition, of course.

We put all the sports-related exercises in one place. Your job? Do 'em. Then have the other team for lunch.

Note: All exercises are with free weights unless indicated.

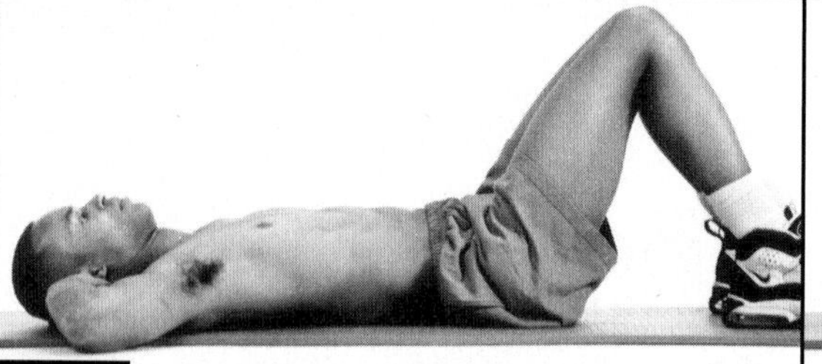

Crunch

Lie flat on your back with your hands cupped behind your ears or crossed over your chest—never pull on your neck during a crunch, because you could end up injuring your neck or upper back. Keep your feet together, flat on the floor and about 6 inches from your butt. Bend your knees at about a 45-degree angle, and keep your legs slightly apart.

Curl your upper torso toward your knees until your shoulder blades are as high off the ground as you can get them. Only your shoulders should lift—not your lower back. Feel your abs contract, and hold the raise for a second. Lower to the starting position, then continue with your next rep without relaxing in between. As your abs get stronger, you can hold a light weight plate across your chest for added resistance.

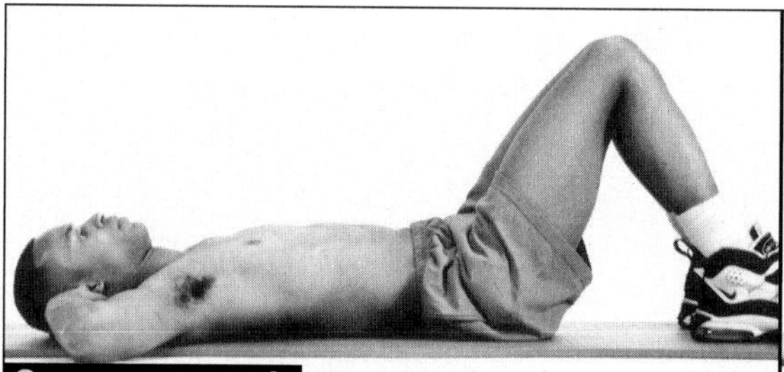

Crossover crunch

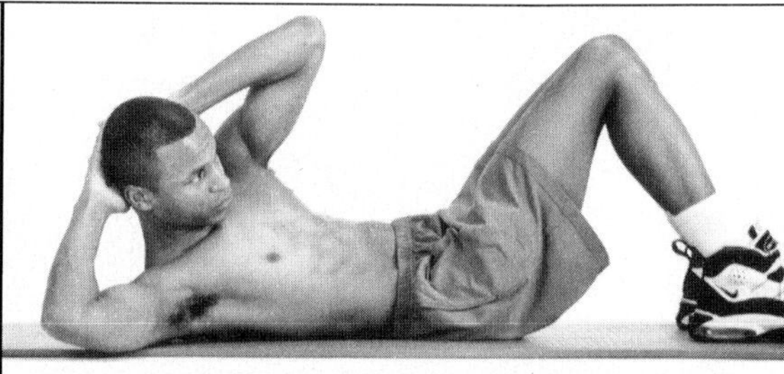

Lie on your back with your feet flat and your knees at about a 45-degree angle. Keep your feet about hip-width apart and cup your hands behind your ears.

Raise your torso up, lifting your shoulders and shoulder blades off the ground. Without pausing at the top, slightly twist to the left. Hold the contraction for a second, then lower to the starting position. Repeat, but this time twist to the right. Don't relax between reps.

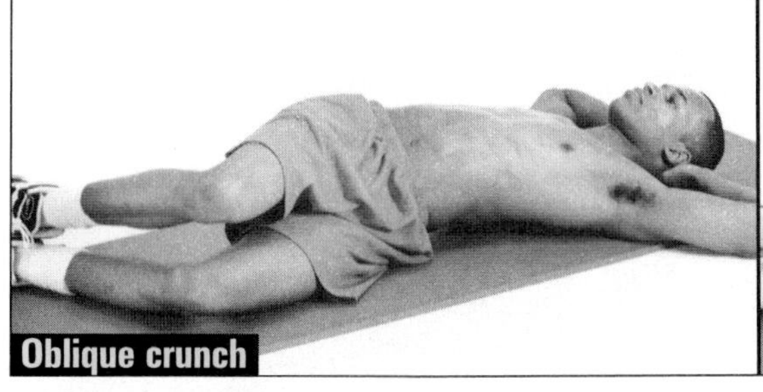

Oblique crunch

Lie flat on your back with your knees bent and your hands cupped behind your ears. Let your legs fall as far as they can to your left side so that your upper body is flat on the floor and your lower body is on its side.

Keeping your shoulders as parallel to the floor as possible, lift your upper torso until your shoulder blades clear the ground. Concentrate on the oblique contraction and hold for a second. Lower to the starting position and do your next rep. Don't rest between crunches—keep your abs tight. After one set on this side, switch to the other.

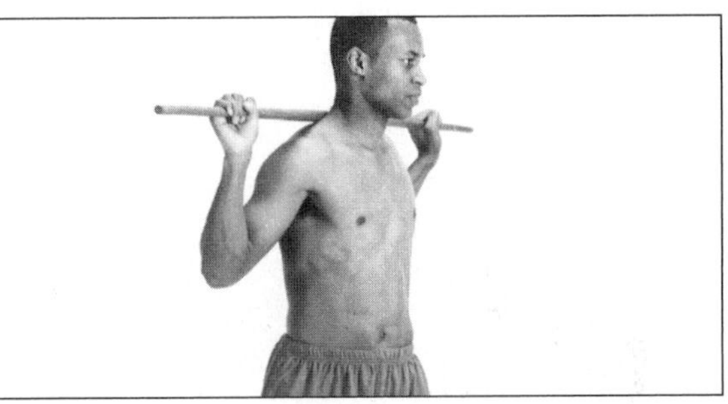

Oblique twist

Stand upright with your feet about shoulder-width apart, hips facing forward and knees unlocked. Hold a broomstick across your shoulders, behind your neck, so it's resting on your trapezius and upper deltoid muscles. Your hands should grasp the ends or outer portions of the broomstick.

Keeping your hips still and facing forward, twist to your left as far as you can go. Then, without pausing, twist in the opposite direction. As you get used to the exercise, do it faster, holding a medicine ball in front of your chest instead of using the broomstick.

Biceps curl

Stand holding an EZ-curl bar so your palms are facing up; your hands should be about shoulder-width apart. Extend your arms so the barbell is about thigh level.

With your back straight and your elbows close to your sides, lift the bar, curling it toward your collarbone. Lower it to the starting position. Keep your wrists straight and go slowly; if you move fast, your body will rock and momentum will do all the work.

Bench press

Lie on—what else?—a bench, with a barbell above your chest. Grasp the barbell with a medium or slightly wider grip, hands about shoulder-width apart. Your palms should face your legs and your feet should rest flat on the ground. Your back should be straight and against the bench.

Lower the barbell to your chest, at nipple level. Your elbows should point out while the rest of your body remains in position. Don't arch your back or bounce the bar off your chest. Raise to the starting position and repeat.

Concentration curl

Sit at the end of the bench with your feet shoulder-width apart. Holding a dumbbell with your palm facing up, lean forward and extend your right arm between your legs. Your elbow and upper arm should rest against your thigh. Keep your free hand on your other knee.

Slowly lift the dumbbell to your shoulder. Brace your elbow against your thigh and lean on your free hand if you need support.

Forearm curl

Sit at the end of the bench with your legs slightly wider than hip-width apart. Rest your right hand on your right knee, and grip a dumbbell palm-up with your left hand. Lay the top of your left forearm on your left thigh, the wrist slightly past your knee so you can bend it through its full range of motion. Keep your upper body upright (you may lean slightly into your left leg for comfort).

Curl the dumbbell up toward your body as far as you can. Don't let your arm rise off your thigh. At the top of the curl, hold for a second, then lower to the starting position. Finish your reps, then switch hands.

You can also do this with both hands and a barbell.

Reverse forearm curl

Sit at the end of the bench with your legs slightly wider than hip-width apart. Put your left hand on your left knee. Hold a dumbbell in your right hand, palm down. Rest the bottom of your forearm against your thigh, and hold your wrist slightly past your knee so you can bend it through its full range of motion. Hold your upper body fairly upright (you can lean slightly into your right leg for comfort).

Curl the dumbbell up toward your body as far as you can. Don't let your arm rise off your thigh. At the top of the curl, hold for a second, then lower to the starting position. Finish your reps, then switch hands.

Use a lighter weight for this lift than you would for a standard forearm curl. Also, you can modify this exercise using both hands and a barbell.

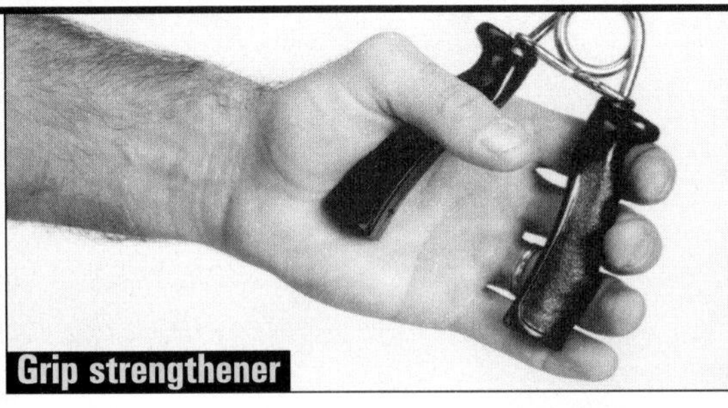
Grip strengthener

For a classic hand workout, get yourself a spring-loaded gripper device that offers moderate resistance. Squeeze it closed. Release and repeat. How's that for simple? Go for the most reps possible, then switch hands.

Lying triceps extension

Lie on the bench with your back in full contact with it. If your lower back arches when your feet are on the floor, pull your feet up to the end of the bench. Hold an EZ-curl bar above your chest, arms extended. Your hands should be only 4 to 6 inches apart, palms facing away from you.

Slowly lower the bar toward the top of your head, bending your arms at the elbows. Extend your arms back out to the starting position.

Pullup

Hang from a chinup bar with your palms facing forward, your hands 18 to 20 inches apart, and your arms extended. Your feet should be about 6 inches off the floor. It's okay to cross your feet or bend your knees; just don't kick your legs.

Pull yourself up until your chin clears the bar. Slowly return to the starting position so your arms are again fully extended.

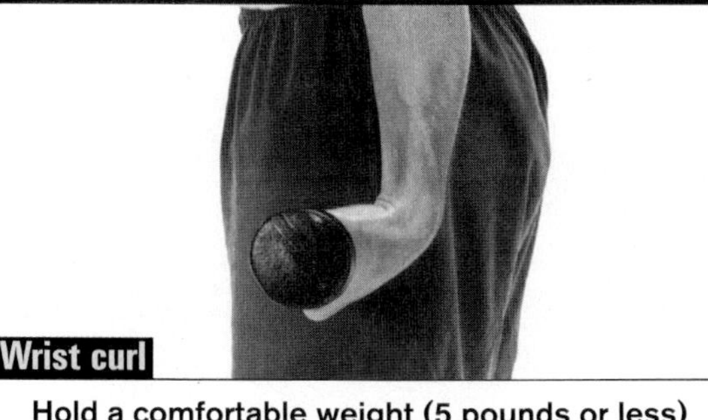
Wrist curl

Hold a comfortable weight (5 pounds or less) at your side. With your elbow locked and your palm facing forward, roll your wrist as far forward as it will go comfortably, then let it back down slowly. Repeat to muscle exhaustion.

Reverse wrist curl

Same as the wrist curl, except your palm faces backward. Flex your wrist forward as far as it will go comfortably, then let it down.

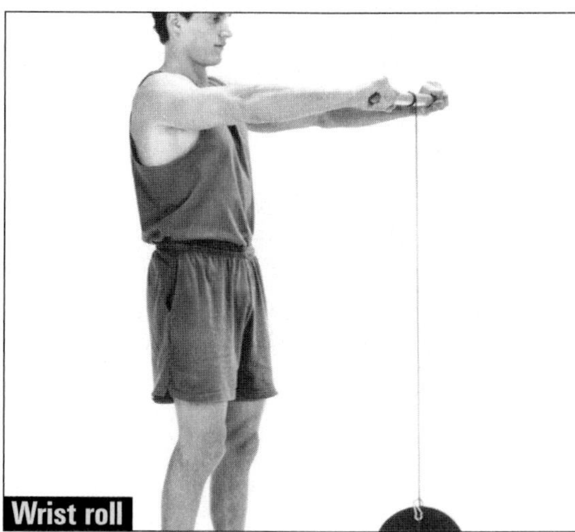
Wrist roll

Standing upright with your feet shoulder-width apart, hold a wrist roller in both hands, palms down, with your arms extended in front of you. The weight should dangle in front of you.

Slowly roll the weight up with your wrists. Use long, exaggerated up-and-down movements with your wrists to get their full range of motion. Keep the rest of your body stationary—don't sway your body or drop your arms. When the weight has reached the top, slowly lower it using the same motion.

Back extension

Position yourself in a back-extension machine with your ankles locked behind the padded bars and your groin area and upper thighs resting on the padded platform. Your hips should be over the edge of the platform, with your body held straight so it is at a roughly 20-degree angle to the floor. Fold your arms across your chest.

Bend at the hips, lowering your upper torso to a point a few inches above perpendicular to the floor. Your arms should still be crossed over your chest and the rest of your body should stay in the starting position. Raise to the starting position; repeat. If you need more of a challenge, do the back extension holding a weight in your arms.

Bent-over row

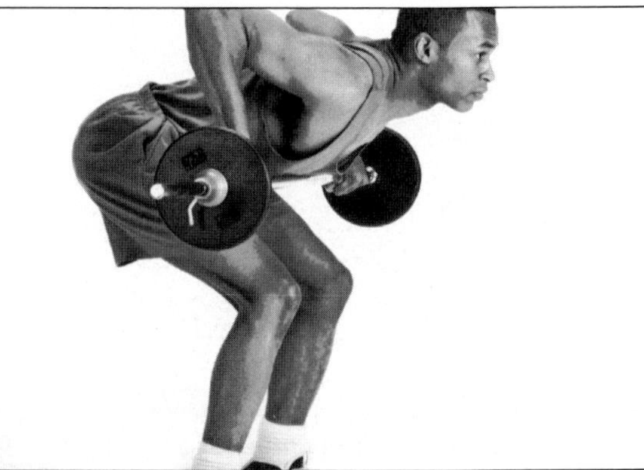

To work your upper back, stand bent over at your hips, back straight and hands gripping a barbell palms-down in a wide grip. Your feet should be shoulder-width apart.

Keeping your back straight, pull the barbell in toward your body so the bar touches your lower chest. Your elbows should point toward the ceiling.

One-arm dumbbell row

Stand partly over the bench with your body weight resting on your bent left leg and left hand, both of which should be on the center of the padded portion of the bench. With your right foot firmly on the floor, hold a dumbbell in your right hand. Keep your back straight and your eyes facing the ground. Extend your right arm toward the ground without locking your elbow.

Pull the weight toward your torso. Raise it as high as you can, bringing it in to your lower-chest muscles. Your right elbow should point toward the ceiling as you lift.

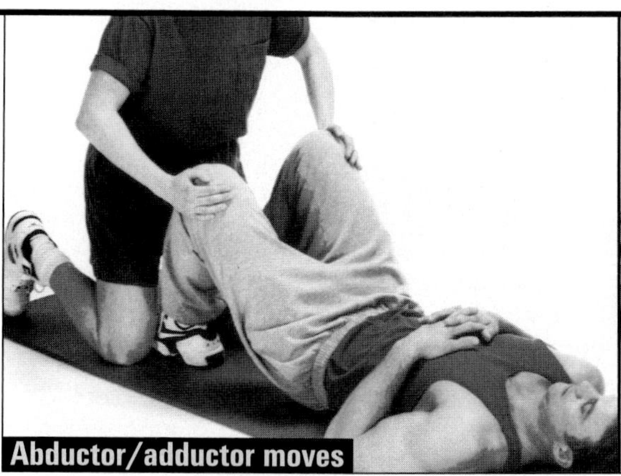

Abductor/adductor moves

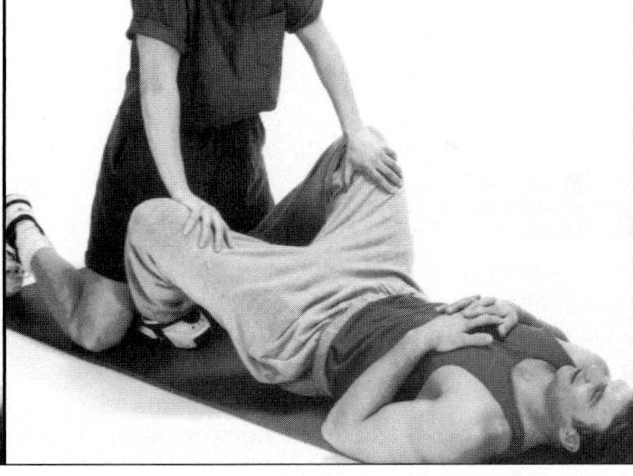

To work your outer-thigh muscles, lie on your back on the floor. Bend your legs and place your feet flat on the floor, knees together. Have a partner kneel opposite you with her hands on the outsides of your knees. Try to spread your legs, pushing your knees apart. While you do this, your partner should apply inward pressure.

For your inner-thigh muscles, assume the same position, only this time, put the soles of your feet together and point your knees outward. Your partner should apply pressure to the insides of your knees while you try to pull your legs together.

Do each exercise for a count of 12, then relax briefly and repeat.

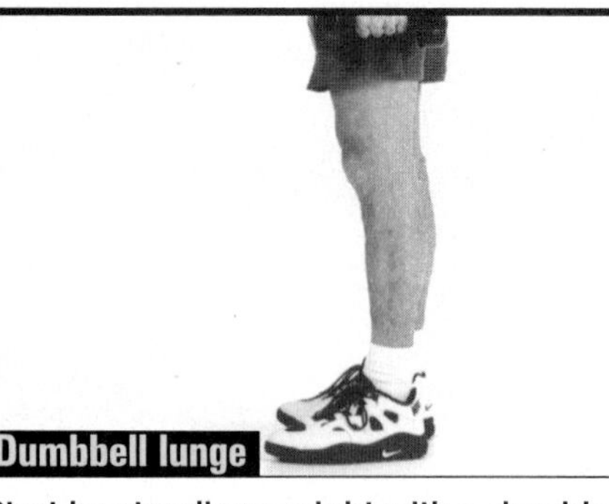

Dumbbell lunge

Start by standing upright with a dumbbell in each hand. Extend your arms down at your sides, palms facing in. Keep your feet about hip-width apart and your torso upright.

Step forward with your left leg, farther than you would in a normal step. Keep your torso upright and slightly forward. Bend your left leg 90 degrees; your knee shouldn't pass your toes. Your back knee should be bent. Keep your rear foot planted; it's okay if the heel is raised slightly.

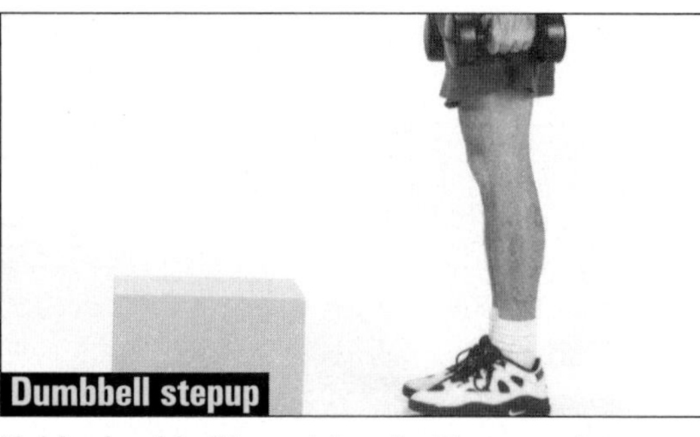

Dumbbell stepup

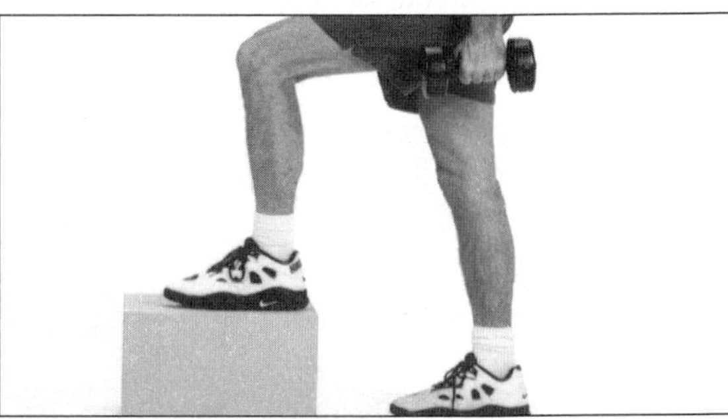

Hold a dumbbell in each hand with your palms facing your body and your arms extended down at your sides. Stand upright about one step away from a sturdy box that's 12 to 18 inches high. Keep your shoulders back and your chest out. It's best to do this on a nonslip floor so the box doesn't shift.

Step forward with your left foot, placing it in the center of the box as you step. Keep the dumbbells at your sides and your upper body straight and upright.

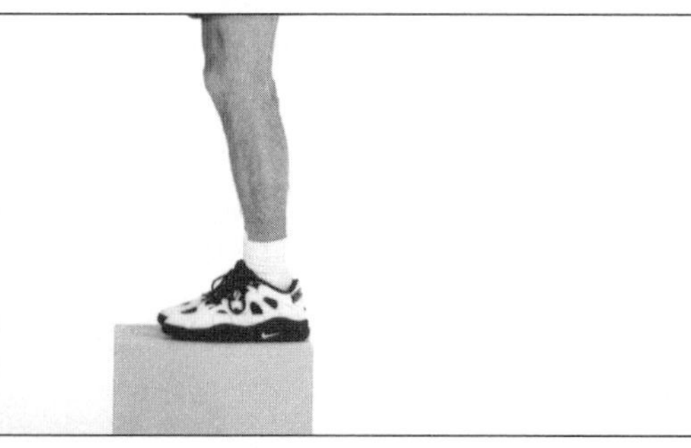

Push down with your left heel to complete the step so that you're standing on top of the box, feet together in the center. The dumbbells should hang at your sides; your body should be upright.

Step backward so your right foot is near the starting position. The step will be slightly longer than an average step. Then bring your left foot back to the starting position. Repeat, this time leading with your right leg.

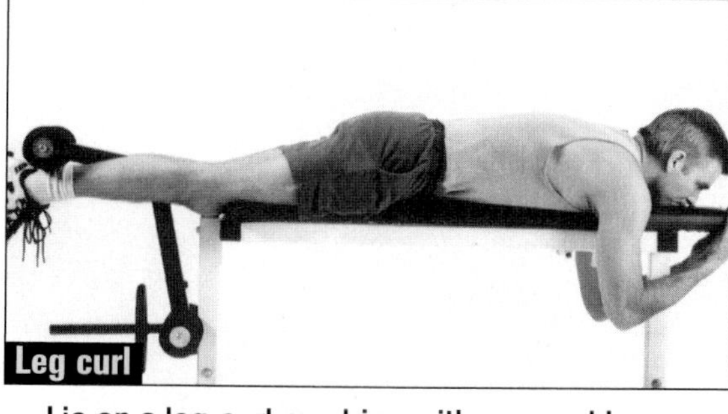
Leg curl

Lie on a leg-curl machine with your ankles hooked behind the lifting pads and your knees just past the bench's edge. Hold on to the bench or the machine's handlebars for support. Your legs should be fully extended, your toes pointing down.

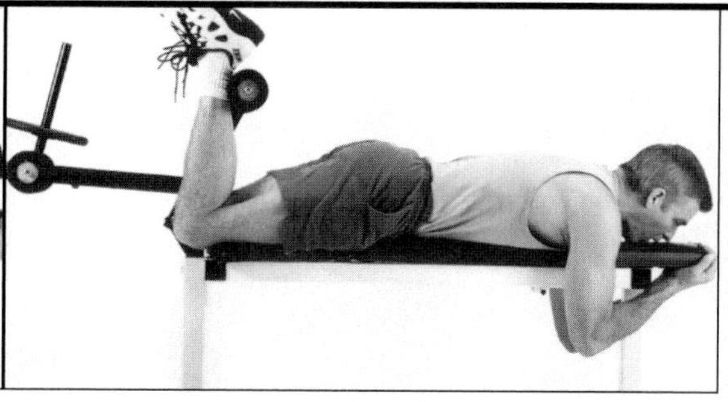

Keep your pelvis pressed against the bench and raise your heels up toward your butt so that your legs bend to about a 90-degree angle. Keep your feet pointing out away from your body.

Leg extension

Sit on an extension machine with your legs behind the lifting pads and your hands grasping the bench or the machine's handles. Bend your knees 90 degrees or slightly more, with your toes pointing in front of you.

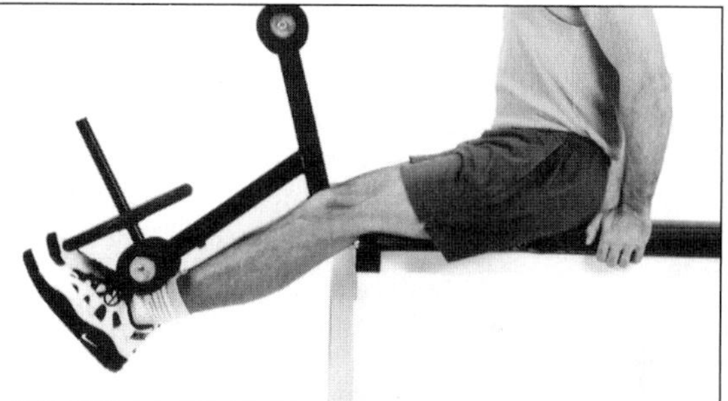

Straighten your legs by lifting with your ankles and contracting your quads. Don't lock your knees at full extension. Your toes should point up and slightly out. To work the muscles even more, do the lift using only one leg at a time.

Leg press

Sit with your back against the seat back. Place your feet flat on the plate with your legs bent 90 degrees or less and your arms holding the handrails.

Exhaling, push the plate until your legs are fully extended but your knees are not locked. Inhaling, slowly return your legs to a 90-degree angle.

Leg raise with ankle weights or dumbbells

Sit on the bench. Attach an ankle weight to each leg; or stand a low-weight dumbbell between your feet, holding your feet together so they can comfortably lift it. (You can increase the weight as strength develops.) Lie back, then extend your legs.

Raise both legs together, keeping them as straight as possible (it's okay to bend your knees at first until you attain the necessary flexibility to stretch them straight). Your feet should be directly above your hips, with your legs at a 90-degree angle to your torso. Slowly lower your legs to the starting position.

Narrow dumbbell squat

Hold a dumbbell in each hand with your arms at your sides, palms facing your body. Stand with your feet only a few inches apart.

Squat down, allowing your heels to come up off the floor, and feel the contraction in your quadriceps as you rise back up to the starting position. Stop if you feel any knee pain.

Squat

Hold a barbell with your palms facing forward and place it behind your neck—it should be even across your upper trapezius muscles. Stand straight, with your feet shoulder-width apart and your toes forward and slightly out.

Squat down as though you're about to sit in a chair. Your thighs should be parallel to the floor. Keep your feet flat. Rise to the starting position.

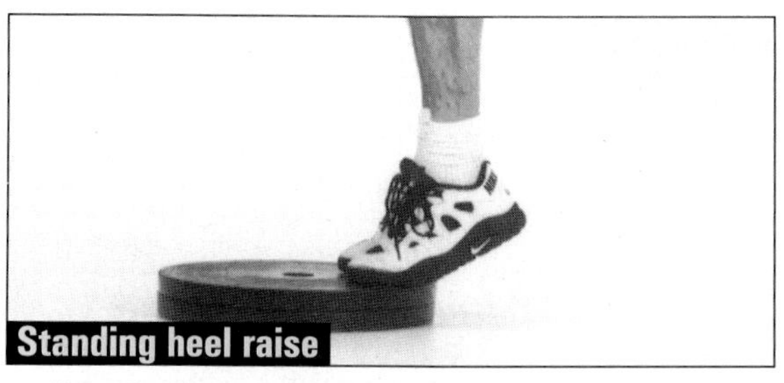

Standing heel raise

Stand with your toes on a 2- to 3-inch weight, platform, or block. Hold a dumbbell in each hand. Keep your feet hip-width apart, your heels on the floor, and your arms extended down at your sides. Put your weight on the balls of your feet so you lean forward slightly. Rise all the way up onto your toes. Feel the contraction in your calves and pause briefly at the top. Keep your arms extended; your body will probably be more upright. Lower.

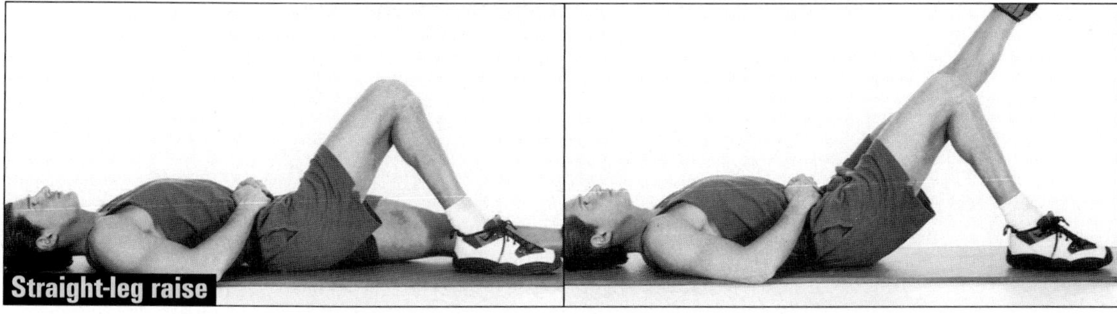

Straight-leg raise

Lie on your back with one leg extended. Bend the other leg so your foot is flat on the floor with the heel about 12 inches away from your butt.

Slowly raise your extended leg until it's as high as your bent knee. Then slowly lower it. Do two sets of 15 reps, resting 10 seconds in between, then repeat with the other leg. For more resistance, put an ankle weight on the extended leg, but don't make it any heavier than 15 percent of your body weight.

Toe raise

Stand upright with your heels on a 2- to 3-inch weight, platform, or block. Extend your toes as far out over the edge as you can, but maintain your posture and balance and keep your heels on the weight. If necessary, put one hand on a wall for balance.

Pull your toes in toward your shins as far as you can. Feel the contraction around your shins. Keep the rest of your body upright. Hold for a second, then lower and repeat.

Heel raise with seated-leg-press machine

Sit in a leg-press machine and push against the plate with your feet until your legs are fully extended.

Press forward with your toes and the balls of your feet, pushing the plate forward a few inches. Feel your calf muscles contract. Hold for a moment, then relax.

Alternating front lateral raise

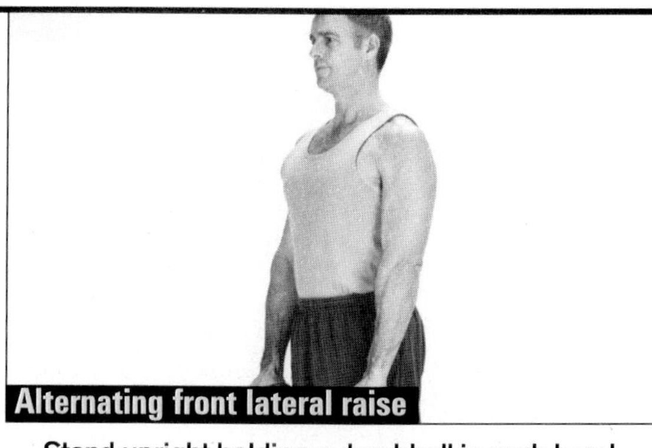

Stand upright holding a dumbbell in each hand, with your palms facing the fronts of your thighs and your elbows slightly bent. Keep your shoulders back, your chest out, and your lower back straight with a slight forward lean.

Raise one dumbbell toward the ceiling until it's shoulder level. Don't lock your elbow. Lower, then repeat with the other arm.

Alternating press with dumbbells

Grasping two dumbbells, sit at the end of the bench with your legs slightly apart. Your feet should be firmly on the floor, your arms raised. Hold the dumbbells in front of your shoulders, with your palms facing each other. Keep your shoulders back and your chest out.

Raise the left dumbbell up until your arm is straight, but don't lock your elbow. Lower, then repeat with your right arm.

Shoulder extension

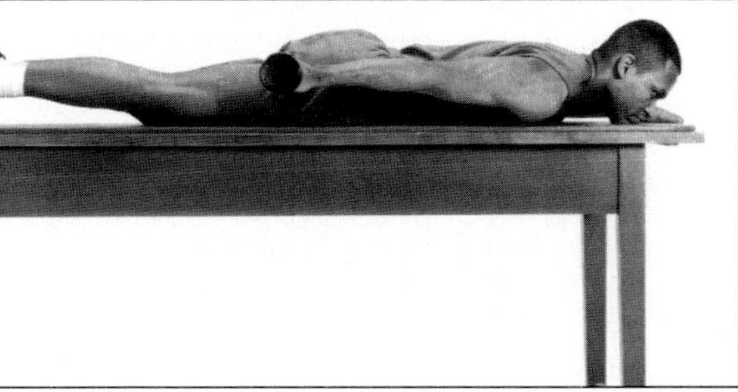

Lie facedown on a table, with one arm hanging straight to the floor. Hold a light dumbbell, or wear a hand- or wrist-weight, and point your thumb away from your body, with your palm facing forward.

Raise your arm straight back without bending your elbow. Stop at your hip—your arm should be fully extended. Lower and repeat.

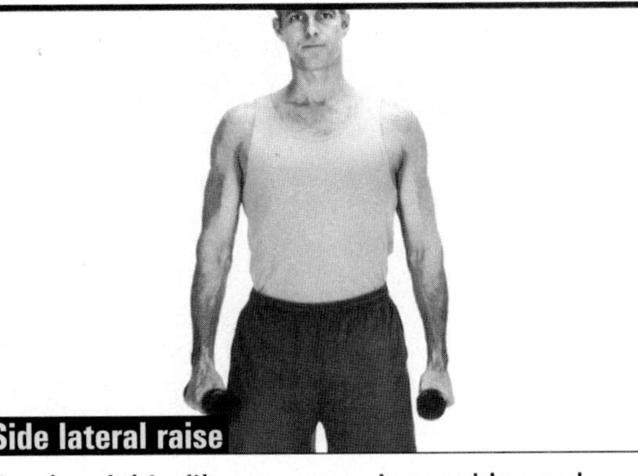

Side lateral raise

Stand upright with your arms at your sides and hold a dumbbell in each hand, palms facing your body and elbows slightly bent. Keep your shoulders back, your chest out, and your lower back straight with a slight forward lean. Your feet should be shoulder-width apart.

Raise both dumbbells straight out from your sides until they're shoulder level. Keep your elbows bent slightly. Pause, then lower.

Upright row

Stand upright and hold a barbell with your palms facing your body in a narrow grip. The barbell should be at upper-thigh level. Also try a shoulder-width grip, especially if the narrow one hurts your wrists.

Lift the bar up, pulling it toward your head until it's no higher than nipple level. Your elbows should point out. Don't sway or rock for momentum. Hold the lift for a count of three, then lower.

Deadlift

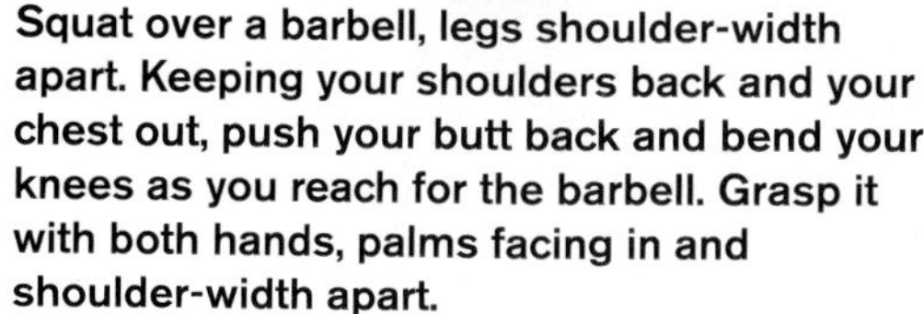

Squat over a barbell, legs shoulder-width apart. Keeping your shoulders back and your chest out, push your butt back and bend your knees as you reach for the barbell. Grasp it with both hands, palms facing in and shoulder-width apart.

Moving only from the hips and keeping your butt pushed back to maintain your balance, pull the bar up the fronts of your legs to your thighs. Slowly lower it along your thighs and shins.

Trainer's Forum

with MICHAEL MEJIA

LIFT FOR LONGEVITY

Q I've been lifting for years, but now that I'm over 50, I worry more about my health than my biceps. Should I switch to cardio exercise?

M. L., MARQUETTE, WISCONSIN

A Absolutely not! Even today, many people still think lifting weights is only for teenagers and muscleheads. Fact is, as you age, strength training becomes even more vital to your long-term health and well-being. As you get older, your metabolism slows and you lose muscle at an alarming rate—usually 5 to 10 pounds per decade after age 30. A slowed metabolic rate will likely increase your weight *and* your risk for cardiovascular disease and diabetes. Muscle loss decreases your strength and makes you more susceptible to injury.

Regular strength training not only helps offset this gradual loss of muscle but also improves your glucose metabolism, helping you control your weight. It also benefits your cardiovascular function and blood-lipid levels. Add to that the positive effect it has on your posture and overall appearance and it's easy to see why strength training should remain an important component of your fitness program. I'm not saying you should completely ignore cardiovascular exercise, just that it shouldn't be your focus.

TOUGH TALK

"No athlete is crowned but in the sweat of his brow."

—SAINT JEROME (A.D. 342–420)

HARD TRUTH

Save Your Head

Once you and your bike helmet have survived a crash together, the helmet's done, even if it looks fine. Give it your heartfelt thanks for protecting your noggin, then trash it and get yourself a new one.

PREVENTION

Kick Penalties

If your kid wants to play soccer with you, be sure to stretch your groin before heading onto the field. Groin strains and tears can happen easily because of the way players turn, run, and kick, says Peter Gerbino, M.D., a sports doctor at the Children's Hospital in Boston. Stand with your feet shoulder-width apart and lean back at about 45 degrees.

Shield yourself from injury.

STRATEGIES

Punch Up Your Spike

In beach volleyball, if you're going to spike effectively, the ball has to be in front of you. Many players move up on the ball too soon and end up trying to hit it when it's actually behind their head. "Wait for the ball to be set, and keep it in front of you," says Eric Fonoimoana, who won an Olympic gold medal in beach volleyball at the 2000 Olympics in Sydney.

QUICK FIX

Get 'Em In Line

If you've never done any maintenance to your inline skates apart from wiping off the blood, it's time for an inspection.

Rotate the wheels. **Move the two front ones to the rear, and vice versa. Flip all the wheels around—the inside edges wear faster than the outside. And replace any wheels that are chipped.**

Check your brakes. **There should be a clearly marked "wear" line on the each pad. If it's worn through (or close), with hard plastic coming through the rubber, give thanks that you made it through last summer alive—and then install a replacement brake.**

POOL POTENTIAL

Q I've heard that swimming is the best all-around exercise. If I swim three times a week, do I need to do anything else?

R. C., NORTH SMITHFIELD, RHODE ISLAND

A While swimming is definitely great exercise, it's not the be-all and end-all many tout it to be. For starters, it's not really the best way to build muscle. Not that swimming isn't rigorous exercise; it's just that water doesn't provide as much resistance as free weights or machines do.

Second, although swimming can provide an excellent cardiovascular workout, it's not necessarily a great way to burn body fat. While most swimmers tend to be thin, they're often not as lean as other athletes like sprinters and cyclists. That's because a swimmer's body becomes programmed to hold on to a certain amount of fat in order to regulate its temperature and stay afloat. Also, because swimming is such a mechanically inefficient activity, most beginners find it tough to exercise at an intensity or duration that burns enough fat. So while it's a worthwhile form of exercise, I wouldn't count on it as my sole means of keeping fit.

To integrate swimming into a more comprehensive fitness regimen, continue to swim three times a week, but spend half as much time in the pool. Devote the other half of your workout time to the weight room. If you do both workouts on the same day, don't swim immediately before lifting, because it will use up too much of the fuel you need for weight training.

MOTIVATION

Switch Sports

Winter is the most challenging time of year to maintain an exercise program. So don't try to. If you've been running or cycling all summer, switch to a different activity, like weight lifting, swimming, or even a martial art. The change of pace will renew your commitment and help make exercise fresh and fun again. Or buy a new piece of home fitness gear and let the MasterCard payments remind you to use it.

The Best Gear for Your Game

9 Pieces of Equipment Every Athlete Needs

If you're like us, you've probably kept the same baseball glove with which you caught that pop-up to win the final game of your varsity championship. Last fall, unbeknownst to you, your 2-year-old dropped it into the swimming pool. You found it Memorial Day weekend when you removed the tarp.

How do you even begin to replace it? Here's expert advice on getting the very best gear. If you never owned it . . . what are you waiting for?

1 *Softball glove.* Presoftened gloves allow you to buy a glove on your lunch hour and use it that evening. But beware: Some have leather that's very thin and so tenderized by chemicals that they can become rags after a season or two. Don't be cheap: If you spend less than $60 on a presoftened mitt, it won't last long.

2 *Softball bat.* Softball bats can cost from $50 to $250; hits go deepest at the high end.

The fit: Almost all bats are 34 inches long, but they can vary in weight from 26 ounces to 30 ounces. Lighter is better—you'll maintain more bat speed when you make contact.

3 *Football.* A good leather ball is tanned to feel a bit tacky but not quite as sticky as a Post-it note. It also has seams that are perfectly straight, a slightly squared-off nose, and two layers of woven leather (not vinyl) laces.

4 *Cleats.* Whether you're playing softball, rugby, or Ultimate Horseshoes, a good pair makes you a better player. Often you can use the same pair for every sport.

Heavier or less nimble players should look for higher-cut shoes that provide ankle stability. These also work best on wet fields. If you play mostly on dry turf, shorter cleats are better.

The fit: Get a half-inch of toe room and a snug heel.

5 *Tennis racket.* If you generate a lot of power, go with a smaller racket head, thinner beam (cross-section), and tighter stringing, says the International Tennis Federation's technical advisor, Howard Brody, Ph.D. Those factors will help you maintain ball control. If you have a slower, loopier stroke, you want a larger, thicker racket, along with softer stringing, to help provide power.

The fit: Don't buy a racket that feels too heavy in the shop. "You can always use lead ribbon later to add weight," Brody explains. On the grip, your fingers shouldn't touch the base of your thumb. A thicker handle makes for more palm contact, giving you more power and control during your swing.

6 *Basketball.* Three rules to remember: If you only play indoors, buy a leather ball. If you play outdoors on smooth asphalt, buy an indoor-outdoor ball made of synthetic material. If you only play outdoors on a rough surface, such as a concrete driveway, buy the best rubber ball you can find. A good rubber basketball feels very firm on the outside, meaning it has good windings inside.

Also, balls are shipped fully inflated, so it's a really bad sign if it's flat in the store.

The fit: Casual players tend to prefer deeper channels (the black rubber grooves) and pebbling (the nubby stuff), a softer cover, and a tackier surface, for basic ball control. "But competitive players like a pure release on the shot, so if there's too much tack or too deep a channel, they feel it's not releasing cleanly," says Dan Touhey, manager for basketball at Spalding Sports Worldwide.

7 *Flying disk.* Notice we didn't call it a Frisbee, which is Wham-O's trademarked version. And they get really fussy about that.

For casual throwing or to give your dog some exercise, go for a standard 110-gram disk. Ultimate Frisbee players want 175-gram disks for longer, straighter throws. Disk golfers use disks weighing around 170 grams but in varying sizes and thicknesses.

8 *Fishing rod.* Every type of fish and every type of water condition calls for a different combination of rod, reel, and line. "It's like potato chips—no one can have just one," says John Snow, former editor in chief of *Fishing and Hunting News*. That doesn't mean you need a dozen rods or reels if you fish a couple of times a year. A simple, medium-weight outfit will do just fine for most hook-related occasions. Besides a sturdy cooler, beer, and, well, more beer, here are three other things you want.

▶ A medium-weight, medium-action graphite spinning rod.

▶ A precision-machined reel with a ball-bearing mechanism. (Don't settle for metal construction.)

▶ Lifetime warranties on both of these items.

The fit: Here's something with sexual implications: A smaller rod is better. It has to be light enough to handle all afternoon.

9 *Bike.* The toughest decision is which type to buy: road or mountain. A hybrid bike is the typical compromise, but it generally will not be as well-built as a mountain bike, says Bill Strickland, executive editor at *Bicycling* magazine and coauthor of several of the magazine's books of cycling hints and tips. The best option for durability and comfort: Buy a mountain bike and swap the knobby tires for road tires (called slicks) when you take to asphalt. As for features, always buy the lightest frame you can afford. Consider lighter rims and Kevlar-beaded tires, too; you can upgrade other components later.

The fit: Make sure there's at least 4 inches of clearance when you straddle the top tube, and keep in mind that the length of the frame is as important as the height. Sit on the bike, put your hands on the grips, and look down. The handlebar should obscure the front hub.

—NOAH LIBERMAN

STAY IN THE

PART SIX

You can't get fit if you don't work out. And you can't work out if you're injured. The logical conclusion? Don't get hurt. And if you do, minimize damage and speed healing so you can get your butt out of a sling and back into the gym as soon as possible.

Pretty obvious, huh? So obvious, in fact, you'd think guys would do everything in their power to reduce risk and rev up recovery.

Think again. Every gym and playing field is littered with guys who never give a thought to training safely. And once these men take a hit, they shun treatment, try to come back prematurely, or otherwise engage in all manner of self-defeating behavior.

Do yourself a favor: Be smarter than that. Turn the page to learn how.

GAME

MH•QUIZ

Will You Get Hurt?

Every guy would like to believe he's like Cal Ripken Jr., major-league baseball's record holder for most consecutive games played. Here's how this fantasy typically plays out: Game after game, play after play, every minute, inning, or down, you're the go-to guy. The team knows they can count on you to be at every game, so you wind up schlepping the equipment. You complain, but it's a secret source of pride—you're the iron man with the mini-van.

As much as we'd all like to be as tough as Cal, the truth is, most of us are not. Sometimes a simple, boneheaded mistake—like forgetting to drink enough water—can bench you. Take this quiz to find out if you're bound for the sidelines—and pick up a few tips to help you stay on the field.

1 Do you mix it up with the guys only once or twice a month?

- ☐ Yes. That's all I have time for, but I make the most of it.
- ☐ No. I get out there as often as possible.

2 Do you go all-out every time you play?

- ☐ Naturally. Otherwise why bother?
- ☐ Nah. It's supposed to be fun.

3 Are you in a time-crunch that makes you avoid the gym?

- ☐ Yes. My weekend league gives me enough of a workout.
- ☐ No. I always make the time.

4 Do you play through pain?

- ☐ Of course. I'm tough.
- ☐ Nope. I'd rather sit out with a cold one.

5 Do you have any old high school/college/backseat/Sunday-afternoon-flag-football injuries?

- ☐ Wanna see the scar?
- ☐ So far, so good.

6 Do you frequently switch sports or vary the intensity and frequency of your workouts?

- ☐ Yes. I need to challenge myself in order to stay motivated.
- ☐ No. I keep myself on a pretty even keel.

7 Do you dive right in to play without warming up and stretching?

- ☐ Yes. With so little time, I want to give it all to the game.
- ☐ No. I warm up to get the blood pumping.

8 As soon as the pain is gone, do you go full-steam ahead?

- ☐ Why not? That means it's better, right?
- ☐ No. I take it easy.

9 Is your pee yellow?

- ☐ Um, yes. But that's a rather personal question.
- ☐ No.

10 Are you older than 35?

- ☐ Yes. Just don't tell that cute blonde sitting in the corner booth.
- ☐ No. But are some gray hairs showing, or what?

WHAT YOUR ANSWERS SAY ABOUT YOU

1. and 2. Gearing up for an all-out but occasional effort without adequate preparation is like gunning a car from zero to 60 after garaging it all winter. Sure, you can do it—but you'll pay with muscle strain and tears.

How to avoid a big bill? If it's a new routine or sport, or

if you've had a long layoff, start slow.

3. "You can't just grab your equipment, show up, and play," says Jon Schriner, D.O., an associate professor at Michigan State University College of Human Medicine in East Lansing. Make regular visits to the gym to strengthen all the major muscle groups. Many experts recommend three times a week with an off-day between sessions.

4. Tough guys play through pain, right? Wrong. *Dumb* guys play through pain. Pain is how your muscles talk. Your job is to listen. "If it's persistent, something's wrong and you need rest or treatment," says *Sports Injury Handbook* coauthor Allan M. Levy, M.D., who is also an orthopedic surgeon in Woodcliff Lake, New Jersey. "If you're running and you feel lousy for the first mile, you can stick it out if you feel better in the second mile," says Dr. Levy. "If you feel worse in the second mile, go home."

5. Some athletes have a weak link that makes them more prone to getting hurt. One of the most common weak links is an old injury. Sprain an ankle, for example, and you have a greater chance of twisting it again later. To prevent re-injury, see a sports-medicine specialist. He'll give you a personal exercise plan to strengthen your injury-prone areas. You also should use some sort of support device when you play.

6. Increasing the intensity, duration, or frequency of an activity too suddenly can cause overuse injuries. Prevent this by changing your workout gradually so that your body has time to adapt. A general rule of thumb: Never accelerate your workout program more than 10 percent a week.

7. "Without question, inadequate warmup is the major cause of injury," says Dr. Levy. You need to raise your body temperature about 2 degrees—enough to break into a light sweat—by doing 10 to 15 minutes of light calisthenics, jogging, walking briskly, or whatever it takes.

Once you warm your muscles, stretching them increases flexibility, further reducing injury risk. (For more on stretching, see page 50.)

8. Pain is good because it makes you stop playing. But just because the pain stops that doesn't mean you can start playing just yet. The good news: Muscles heal fairly quickly, depending on the extent of the injury, and usually rebound after no longer than a few weeks. Tendon or ligament injuries, on the other hand, take at least 6 weeks to heal. Worse, pain often subsides well before injured ligaments and tendons fully heal. Check with your doctor before resuming play.

9. Although you may prefer to keep this information between you and the porcelain, the color of your pee can help determine your susceptibility to injury. Yellow means you're not drinking enough water. Clear? You're properly hydrated. Drink 4 to 6 ounces of water every 15 to 20 minutes during physical activity, says Dr. Schriner. If you're not drinking enough water, you're more likely to get cramps and muscle tears.

10. According to the Consumer Products Safety Commission, guys between the ages of 35 and 54 are getting sports injuries at an unprecedented rate: 33 percent more in 1998 than in 1991. "A lot of guys out there have 16-year-old minds in 40-year-old bodies," says Dr. Schriner.

—DOUG DONALDSON

BY DOUG DONALDSON

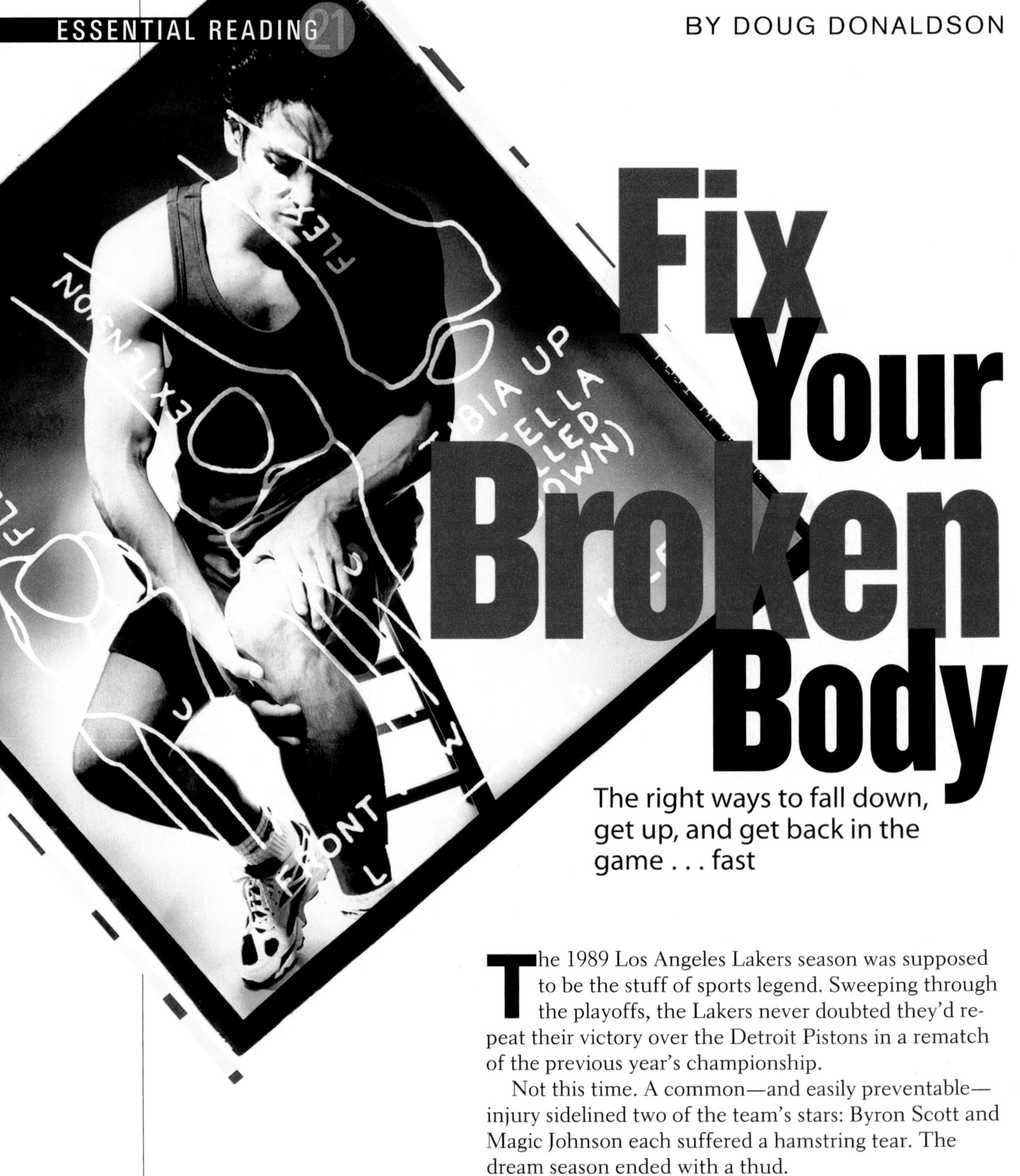

Fix Your Broken Body

The right ways to fall down, get up, and get back in the game . . . fast

The 1989 Los Angeles Lakers season was supposed to be the stuff of sports legend. Sweeping through the playoffs, the Lakers never doubted they'd repeat their victory over the Detroit Pistons in a rematch of the previous year's championship.

Not this time. A common—and easily preventable—injury sidelined two of the team's stars: Byron Scott and Magic Johnson each suffered a hamstring tear. The dream season ended with a thud.

The difference in this tough, physical series? Simple water.

The Lakers played their 5 stars almost exclusively for the whole series. They didn't have time to rest or rehydrate. The Pistons, on the other hand, rotated 10 players in and out. And on the Detroit bench, trainer Mike Abdenour made players drink bottle after bottle of the clear stuff. Smart man, that Abdenour: Dehydration contributes to muscle tears, says Dan Wathen, C.S.C.S., head athletic trainer at Youngstown University in Ohio and past president of the National Strength and Conditioning Association.

Learn how to treat and prevent the following common sports injuries, and you'll play healthier, longer, and stronger.

Torn Hamstring

The dead giveaway: First, your quads and other leg muscles cramp up. Next, you start feeling the effects of heat exhaustion, which means your muscles lack water, making them more likely to tear. (How to tell if you're suffering from heat exhaustion? You're panting even though Tyra Banks is nowhere in sight.) Finally, you feel sudden, stinging pain through your mid- and upper hamstring.

The quick fix: Take an anti-inflammatory such as ibuprofen, and apply ice for 20 minutes three or four times a day for 2 to 3 days. Avoid the temptation to treat with heat. Heat actually promotes inflammation.

Also, give yourself a rest. A muscle tear will get progressively worse if you try to play through it. "The first tear is a problem. The second tear is major. The third is a disaster," says Jon Schriner, D.O., an associate professor at Michigan State University College of Human Medicine in East Lansing.

When to see a doc: If your injury gets worse instead of healing in a matter of days, or if you're not sure what's wrong.

Don't let it happen again: Incorporate strength training and stretching into your workouts. Muscle weakness and inflexibility are major contributors to muscle tears, says Wathen. Torn muscles also result from dehydration. About 2 hours pre-exertion, guzzle 16 to 24 ounces of water. During exercise, drink 4 to 6 ounces of water every 15 to 20 minutes. Not sure if you're drinking enough? Take our favorite exam: the pee test. The clearer it is, the more hydrated you are. For an edge on your b-ball buddies, be the designated driver the night before the game. Those beers on Saturday night will rob your body of water on Sunday.

Tendinitis

The dead giveaway: A sudden spike of pain and tenderness near a joint.

The quick fix: Ice it immediately and then keep icing for 20 minutes at a time three or four times a day for 2 to 3 days. Take an anti-inflammatory such as ibuprofen. Once the pain subsides and you can do everyday lifting, work your way back up to your full-speed, full-strength game.

When to see a doc: When you have difficulty moving any joint.

Don't let it happen again: Two to 4 weeks

PEAK performance

Breathe Easy

If you have trouble breathing during cold-weather workouts, you could be suffering from a form of exercise-induced asthma. The condition is aggravated by frigid air constricting your bronchial tubes, resulting in tightness in the chest and that out-of-breath feeling. The solution is usually simple: Wrap a scarf or bandanna over your nose and mouth to warm the air as you inhale it. (Be sure to yell "Reach for the sky!" at any strangers you meet.) If you're wearing the scarf and still wheezing, see your doctor. There is specific medication for alleviating exercise-induced asthma—and, for that matter, antisocial thought patterns.

before you start playing, gradually strengthen the muscles surrounding your injured joint. Say you have tennis elbow: Hold a racket with your injured arm and go through all the normal stroke positions, but instead of swinging to hit a ball, push up against the racket with your other hand to create resistance. From here, you can progress to simulating your swing movement while holding light weights.

HARD TRUTH

No wonder so many of us have back problems

Number of bones that make up the spine:

33

Torn Rotator Cuff

The dead giveaway: Mild soreness in the shoulder area and a catching sensation when you rotate your arm.

The quick fix: Rest, and ice the shoulder three or four times a day for 20 minutes at a time. Use a sling to avoid discomfort. Three or four times a day, remove the sling and move your arm as much as possible to maintain range of motion. Build mobility by swinging your arm loosely in different directions.

When to see a doc: If you still feel pain after a day or two of reduced activity. Over 40? You're at greater risk for a complete rotator-cuff tear. A sure sign: The pain persists at night for several weeks. This needs attention from a pro.

Don't let it happen again: Once you have your doc's okay, you can do lateral and front raises with a 5-pound dumbbell to strengthen the smaller muscles in your shoulder. Also, stretch frequently by draping a towel over your shoulder, grasping it at each end, and pulling it up and down, as if you were drying your back. Do 10 reps on each shoulder.

Runner's Knee

The dead giveaway: Your knee aches, especially behind the kneecap.

The quick fix: Swallow an anti-inflammatory such as ibuprofen. Ice the knee three or four times a day for 2 to 3 days. Reduce your mileage and workout intensity until you're pain-free for 24 hours after light running. Focus on stretching your hamstrings and the muscles along the sides of your legs (the iliotibial bands). And strengthen your quad with straight-leg isometric exercises.

Refer to page 53 for a hamstring stretch.

To stretch your iliotibial bands, lie on your left side, bend your right knee, and grab the top of your right ankle with your right hand. Gently pull your right heel toward your buttocks as you move the inside of your knee down toward the floor. You should feel a stretch on the outside of your upper leg. Hold for 15 to 20 seconds. Repeat with your left leg.

To strengthen your quads, lie on your back with your left leg bent at the knee and your right leg out straight. Tighten the muscles in your right leg and lift it 5 to 7 inches off the ground, holding for 5 to 7 seconds. Do three sets of 12 on each side.

Gradually build back up to your normal running schedule.

Too Good to Be True

Remember hearing the story that a quick, karate-type shot to the nose could kill a man by pushing the bones into his brain? Sorry to break it to you, but that's a myth perpetuated by too many kung fu movies, says Sanford Archer, M.D., associate professor of otolaryngology at the University of Kentucky A. B. Chandler Medical Center in Lexington.

When to see a doc: If you still have swelling, a limp, or restricted movement after a few weeks of trying the above recommendations.

Don't let it happen again: Look at your running surface—concrete claims more knees than wood or turf.

And choose the right shoes. Pull out the insert and make sure it matches the curves of your foot. Once you get a shoe you like, don't let anyone—or any ad campaign—talk you out of it. Then, buy a duplicate pair.

TOUGH TALK

"Pain is temporary, pride is forever."

—ANONYMOUS

Ankle Sprain

The dead giveaway: Intense pain and weakness after you've twisted your ankle.

The quick fix: "If you have a minor sprain and try to walk it off, you can make it much worse," says orthopedic surgeon Nicholas A. DiNubile, M.D., who consults for the Philadelphia 76ers and the Pennsylvania Ballet. To prevent swelling, rest the ankle, elevate it above your heart, and ice it three or four times a day for at least 3 days. You can also take an anti-inflammatory such as ibuprofen.

When to see a doc: If you have significant swelling and your ankle won't support any weight.

Don't let it happen again: Once the swelling goes down and you have no ankle pain, build the ankle back up by stretching it and doing strength and balance exercises.

For starters, incorporate the ankle stretch on page 204 into your routine. Then, Dr. DiNubile recommends, use an elastic loop like a Thera-Band (which looks like a giant rubber band) to strengthen your ankle. Place one end around a chair or table leg and the other end around the ball of your foot. Move away from the chair or table just far enough to create some resistance. Flex your foot upward and hold for 10 to 15 seconds. Repeat, flexing downward, then inward, and finally outward. Do three sets of 10 repetitions.

For balance, stand on one foot with your arms straight out to the sides. Close your eyes and balance for 10 to 15 seconds. Rise to the ball of your foot and repeat. Switch to the other side.

When you're strong enough to return to the playing field, wear an ankle support and high-top sneakers.

Fractured Rib

The dead giveaway: You take a deep breath and feel stinging pain in your chest. It also hurts when you get up from bed or bend at the waist.

The not-so-quick fix: Don't wrap your ribs. Apply ice. And stay out of the game for at least 6 weeks for the injury to completely heal. The pain from a fractured rib may go away, but the rib will still be weak. Receive another shot to the ribs? You could wind up with a punctured lung.

When to see a doc: Always. Even if you think it's just a bruise, have it checked out. Tip: Fractured ribs often elude x-rays. If you've played a couple more games and still hurt, you probably have a fracture, even if your first x-ray was negative.

Don't let it happen again: Fractured ribs are common among weekend gridiron warriors. When you're on the field, pass on being quarterback. And when going long, don't run patterns over the middle of the field. That will leave you open to hits. Or wear a flak jacket. Try the Bike Rib-Lite Protector, available for $49.99 from www.sportsdepot.com.

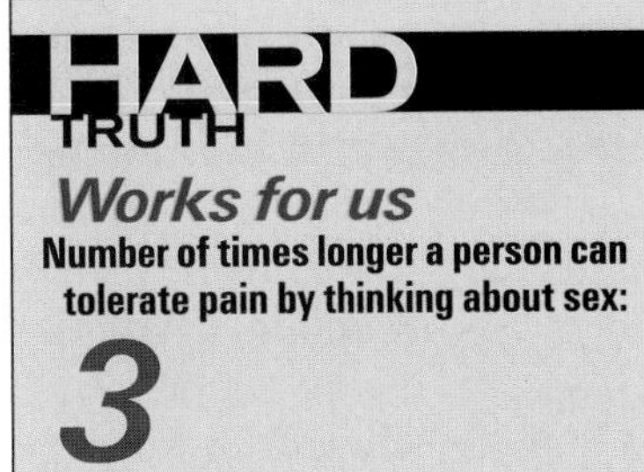

HARD
TRUTH
Works for us
Number of times longer a person can tolerate pain by thinking about sex:
3

Dumb Luck

In 1944, a desperate British pilot named Nicholas Alkemade jumped without a parachute from his flaming bomber 18,000 feet above Germany. He hit a fir tree, caromed into a snowbank, and walked away unscathed.

Don't try this at home.

Broken Nose

The dead giveaway: Pain, and your nose may bleed, swell, and bend at an odd angle.

The quick fix: Get off the field and stay there. Pinch your nose and lean your head back to stop bloodflow. Place a bag of ice on the bridge. Then, plug your nostril with cotton to absorb the blood.

When to see a doc: If your nose swells, bleeds, and is visibly displaced. If a hit was forceful enough to break your schnozz, you could have a more serious injury such as a concussion or neck fracture.

Don't let it happen again: Know your game. "The player who lacks knowledge about a game will get hurt more often," says Dr. Schriner. "He'll be less able to use his peripheral vision to get a sense of what's going on and brace for a hit."

One other word: *headgear.*

Stress Fracture

The dead giveaway: Very focused pain and tenderness directly over a bone. Stress fractures can affect any bone but most commonly afflict the lower part of the shinbone, above the ankle.

The not-so-quick fix: Most of the time, if you stop play for 4 to 8 weeks, the fracture will heal. If you keep playing on a stress fracture, it'll only get worse. Ice it intermittently and limit your activity. If the fracture is near your ankle, you can stay fit while it heals by doing upper-body strength training and bicycling. Check with your doctor to find out what's safe.

When to see a doc: If you're still sore after stopping all activity for a few days and then resuming at half your previous activity level. Or if you suspect a stress fracture at all. You may need crutches or a removable plastic shell to brace the fracture while it heals completely.

Don't let it happen again: Ask yourself, "Have I been pushing myself too hard?" Look carefully at your workout, and get a thorough evaluation by a exercise specialist who looks at not just the fracture but also your exercise program and body alignment.

Broken Collarbone

The dead giveaway: You scream and writhe in the dirt. And you realize you can't lift your hand over your head.

The quick fix: Apply ice intermittently for 20 to 30 minutes every hour. Relieve pain with ibuprofen.

When to see a doc: If your arm feels numb or your fingers feel cold or have turned an odd shade of blue, you've damaged the nerves and blood vessels bundled around the collarbone. Get to an emergency room within 4 hours. If you can't breathe without pain or are short of breath, you could have other injuries that need a doctor's attention. "If you see deformities around the shoulder, you shouldn't mess around," says David Johnson, M.D., president of the Wilderness Medical Associates in Bryant Pond, Maine.

Don't let it happen again: Wear body armor and learn how to tuck and roll. Here's how: If you've never tumbled, begin practicing from a kneeling position on a mat. Reach forward with your arms, then bend your wrists and elbows as you tuck your head and the shoulder closest to the mat. Roll across that shoulder and your back. The key is to let your arms collapse under the impact to dissipate the force. It should look like a lop-sided somersault. Once you get the hang of it, try it from different starting positions: First stand, then walk, and finally run and dive into it.

Bruise

The dead giveaway: Expletives burst from your mouth when you take an elbow in a little one-on-one with the neighbor. Look for a black-and-blue mark, pain, and swelling.

The quick fix: A bruise will continue to swell for 48 to 72 hours. Treat it with R.I.C.E.: rest, ice, compression, and elevation. The sooner you start, the less pain and discoloration you'll have, and the less range of motion you'll lose.

Rest, and apply ice for 15 minutes at a time once an hour for the first 4 hours, then as needed for the rest of the day. Along with ice, put pressure on the bruise to stop the internal bleeding, and elevate it above the level of your heart to help reduce "throbbing" pain. Don't take an anti-inflammatory immediately; stop the swelling first. "I would wait a full 24 hours or more from the time I began to treat the injury with R.I.C.E.," says Stephen Rice, M.D., director of the Jersey Shore Sports-Medicine Center in Neptune, New Jersey.

When to see a doc: If you develop massive swelling despite following these instructions or if you suddenly start to bruise easily and frequently. Both of these symptoms are possible signs of a blood disorder. Otherwise, don't bother.

Don't let it happen again: What, you think we're gonna tell you to play nice?

Dislocated Shoulder

The dead giveaway: Extreme pain, an inability to lift your shoulder, and possibly an indentation in the skin where your shoulder would normally fit into the joint. That, and your screams.

The quick fix: Ice it and beeline to the hospital. If you get there within 30 minutes, the doc can relocate your shoulder before too much swelling occurs. If it gets too swollen, you may need surgery.

When to see the doc: Don't try to coax it back on your own. Leave it to the pros.

Don't let it happen again: If you play a sport where you take a lot of spills, learn how to tuck your body and roll the way we described above.

Abrasions and Lacerations

The dead giveaway: Your road rage has turned into road rash.

The quick fix: Elevate the wound above your heart and apply firm pressure with a clean cloth to stop the bleeding. For a shallow cut, hold for about 5 minutes; for a deep wound, hold for 15 to 20 minutes. If the injury is minor and probably won't require stitches, remove any dirt and then cleanse the wound with plain soap and water. Rub on a thin layer of antibacterial ointment before applying a bandage.

When to see a doc: You may need stitches or a tetanus shot, so let a doc decide. He'll also treat any infection.

Don't let it happen again: Consider knitting?

He's a Real Band-Aid Man

When Simon and Schuster published *Doctor Dan the Bandage Man*, a children's Little Golden Book, publisher Richard Simon decided, at the last minute, to put a half-dozen adhesive bandages in each book as a gimmick. He wired a friend at Johnson & Johnson, saying, "Please ship two million Band-Aids immediately." The reply the next day said, "Band-Aids on their way. What the hell happened to you?"

Trainer's Forum

with MICHAEL MEJIA

REST UP

Q How can I tell for sure whether I'm overtraining?

W. S., AMARILLO, TEXAS

A Diminished performance is the best indication that you're overdoing it. Whether you're a runner, a weight lifter, or just a casual fitness enthusiast, your major training objective should be to improve from one workout to the next. If you add a few seconds to your usual time or fail to equal or better your number of repetitions with a given load, it usually means you're overtraining.

Also ask yourself these questions.

- "Am I irritable?"
- "Have I lost my appetite?"
- "Am I having trouble sleeping?"
- "Do I have aching muscles and joints?"

If you answered yes to any of these, consider a rest. Many top trainers and coaches recommend a week of total recovery at least once every 12 weeks. This not only gives your muscles and connective tissue a much-needed break but also gives your central nervous system a chance to recover. Whether you realize it or not, rigorous physical training imposes a tremendous demand on your nervous system. If you don't allow yourself to recover adequately, your coordination may suffer and you may lose strength and power.

TOUGH TALK

"I knew I wouldn't be totally healed until I got back in the water."

—47-YEAR-OLD SURFER AND AUTHOR KENNY DOUDT ON SURVIVING A SHARK ATTACK

QUICK FIX

Get Out of a Jam

Next time a flying ball goes head-to-head with an extended digit, grab the jammed finger with your thumb and index finger and pull for 5 seconds, rest for 5 seconds, then pull again, suggests orthopedic surgeon David H. Janda, M.D., who is director of the Institute for Preventive Sports Medicine in Ann Arbor, Michigan. That will stretch compressed tissue, align the joint better, and allow squished-out fluids to flow back in.

STRATEGIES

Joint Healing Effort

Don't return to the game with a sore knee—playing through a joint injury increases your chances of developing osteoarthritis later in life. In a study of former soccer players, researchers at England's Coventry University found that 49 percent of them had moderate or severe osteoarthritis in at least one joint, compared with just 10 percent of men in the general population. "Stretching ligaments in your knee when they're already injured creates scarring and tissue damage that your body can never repair," says Andy Turner, Ph.D., the study author.

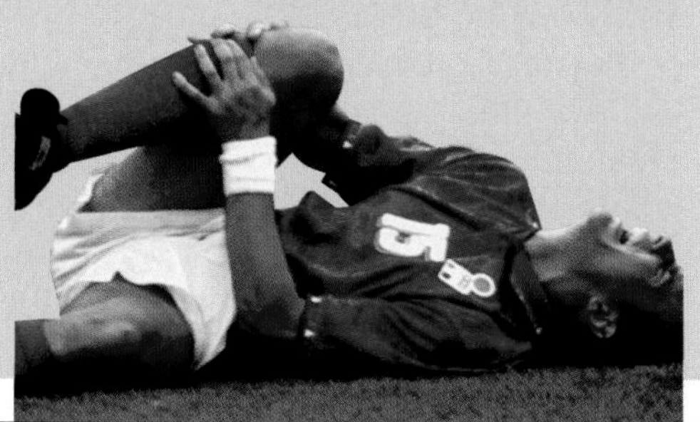

COOL STUFF

Illuminate Yourself

Exercising outdoors in the dark is dangerous, but it's often the only alternative for winter runners. You can look like a crossing guard in one of those dorky orange-and-yellow vests or stick reflective tape all over your body, or you can purchase some IllumiNITE reflective gear. IllumiNITE is a high-tech coating that embeds millions of microscopic, disklike particles into the weave of a fabric. These particles act as miniature mirrors to reflect car headlights up to 500 feet away. Look in sporting-goods stores for apparel that uses IllumiNITE.

HOME REMEDIES

Ace Pain

Don't use old tennis balls only to plug sinks and pelt rodents; use them for sore muscles. Here's how: Slice a 1-inch opening in a ball, fill it with water, and stick it in the freezer. When you have back pain, lie flat on your back, put the ice ball on the sore spot, and slowly roll your body over it. The ball will provide cold and pressure, both of which help heal sore muscles, says Arnie Scheller, M.D., team physician for the Boston Celtics and chief of sports medicine at New England Baptist Hospital. Ice the spot for 10 minutes every couple of hours.

BACK IN SHAPE

Q I've been lifting weights for only a few weeks. Lately, my lower back is tight or sore after I lift. I think I'm using good form, so what could be causing this and what should I do about it?

S. M., DESTIN, FLORIDA

A *Thinking* you use good form and actually doing so are often two entirely different things. I run into this problem quite often when I start working with a new client. As a test, I usually ask the client to show me his form on a few basic lifts (bench presses, lat pulldowns, lunges, etcetera). What I invariably find is that even if the person has been working out for several years, his form is usually not as polished as it should be. This holds true for even the most seasoned lifters—so expect it to be that much more so for someone like you who has recently embarked on a training program.

Despite the abundance of pithy catch phrases to the contrary, lifting weights is not supposed to be a painful experience. Lower-back pain is a definite sign that you're doing something wrong. My advice? Sign up for a few sessions with a knowledgeable trainer who can advise you on proper form. This way, you can ensure that the effort you're making in the gym isn't having a negative impact on your ability to function outside of it.

If the problem isn't in your form, you probably need to strengthen your abdominal and lower-back muscles—your core muscles. For starters, include back extensions (done off a hyperextension bench) and various crunches, keeping the reps within the 6-to-10 range to build strength. Holding weight plates across your chest to add extra resistance will help you power up.

Deadlifts and squats, which train the core muscles simultaneously rather than in an isolated manner, will also help.

HARD TRUTH

It must be the size of the ball

Number of eye injuries in 1999 from playing basketball:

8,383

From playing golf:

731

Be Prepared

15 First-Aid Fixes

In California, people drive around with cases of bottled water and canned chili in their trunks in case an earthquake suddenly hits.

Chances are you won't ever get caught in a quake while driving. Should you save your trunk for tailgating supplies? If you're an active guy, probably not. Instead, fill it with the tools you'll need to get yourself out of a more likely jam: a sports injury. Make a simple first-aid kit in a toolbox or tackle box, stash it in the trunk, and take it with you whenever you work out or hit the court. According to the American Red Cross, here's what you'll need.

1. ***Triangular bandage***
2. ***Adhesive bandages (assorted sizes)***
3. ***Gauze pads and roller gauze (assorted sizes)***
4. ***Adhesive tape***
5. ***Scissors***
6. ***Cold pack***
7. ***Plastic bags (handy for ice packs)***
8. ***Antiseptic ointment***
9. ***Hand cleaner***
10. ***Disposable gloves***
11. ***Tweezers***
12. ***Blanket***
13. ***Syrup of Ipecac (use only if instructed by Poison Control Center)***
14. ***Activated charcoal (use only if instructed by Poison Control Center)***
15. ***Flashlight and extra batteries***

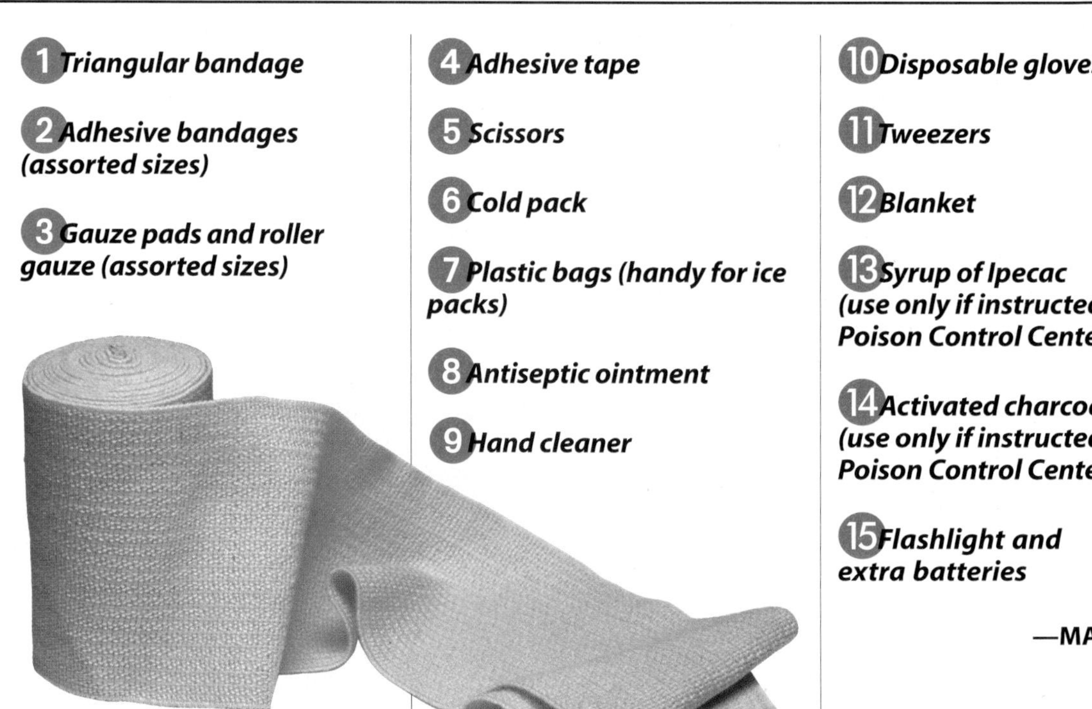

—MARC DAVIS

Credits

Cover Photograph

Alan Donatone; photographed by **Mitch Mandel/Rodale Images**

Interior Photographs

Roderick Angle: pages iv (bottom), 10, and 232
Michele Asselin: pages 148 and 169
Josef Astor: page 21
Myriam Babin: pages iii (middle), 38–42, and 153 (model only)
Rhoda Baer: page 174
Wes Bell: page 178
Larry Bercow: pages 4
Beth Bischoff: pages 68, 71, 73, 75, and 193
Nigel Cox: pages 70, 72, and 74
Jim Cummins/Stock Market: page 224
Michael Cuno: page 192
Robert Fleischauer: page 16
Foto Fantasies: page 81 (background only)
Todd France: pages 61, 64, 65, and 67
Gadge: page 226
Robert Gerheart/Rodale Images: page 240
Aaron Goodman: page 81 (model only)
Mitchel Gray: pages iv (top), 62, 63, 66, 83, 86, 87, 89–94, 98–103, 108–11, 116–22, 127–34, and 139–45
John Hamel/Rodale Images: pages 196 and 225
John Iacono/SI/Timpix: page 238
Index Stock: page 45 (model only)
Svend Lindback: page 207
Steven Lippman: pages iii (top), 9, 190, 203, and 228
Blake Little: pages vi and 60
Mitch Mandel/Rodale Images: pages iv (middle), 52, 53, 177 (first, second, and fifth), 184–88, 194, 200, 201, 204, 205, and 208–23
Lou Manna: pages 170 (sugar-free muffin and pineapple), 171 (fig bar and cantloupe), and 173 (tart and raspberries)
T&D McCarthy/Stock Market: page 78
Dennis O'Clair/Tony Stone Images: page 182
Joseph Oppedisano: pages 31–37
Rodale Images: pages 158 and 177 (fourth)
Z. Sandmann/Stock Food: page 153 (pizza)
Mark Seelen: pages iii (bottom) and 55–58
Anthony Verde: pages 45 (clothing only) and 175
Jessica Wecker: pages iv (top) and 164–68
Timothy White: page 46
Kurt Wilson/Rodale Images: 170–73 and 177 (third)

Illustrations

Kelly Alder: page 7
Paul Corio: pages 11–13
Paul Gilligan: page 224
David Pierce: pages 24 and 26–28
Chris Sharp: pages 76 and 77
Steve Wacksman: pages iii and 79
Sam Whitehead: page 15

Index

Underscored page references indicate boxed text. **Boldface** references indicate photographs or illustrations.

A

Abdominal fitness. *See also* Muscle building
- evaluating, 2–3
- exercise(s), 62–63, 66, 138–47, 208–9
  - scheduling, 85
- strategies for improving, 5–7, 60–61, 64–65, 67
- tracking, 157

Abductor/adductor moves, 195, **215**
Abrasions and lacerations, 237
Ab roller, 26, **26**
Aerobics. *See also* Sports
- drinks for, 159
- in Ian King workout, 87, 138
- strength training and, 184

Alcoholic drinks, 22, 37, 77, 162
Alternating front lateral raise, **221**
Alternating press with dumbbells, 197, **221**
Ankles, exercises for, **215–20**. *See also* Exercises
Ankle sprain, 235
Antioxidants, 164, 165
Appetite control, 154, 165
Arms, exercises for, **209–13**. *See also* Exercises
Arthritis, 11, 238
Assisted pullup/dip machine, 26, **26**
Asthma, 233

B

Back, exercises for, **214–15**. *See also* Exercises
Back extension, 62, **214**
Balance exercises, 49, 235
Bananas, 25
Barbell lunge, **34**, **73**
Barbell preacher curl, **35**
Bar rollout, **122**
Basketball, 182–89, 227
Beach volleyball, 225
Beef, 151, 153
Beer, 3, 151, 162, 175
Bench dip, **120**, **129**, **143**
Bench press
- close-grip, 49, **108**, **121**, **129**
- before date, 77
- decline dumbbell, **34**
- dumbbell, 62
- for
  - arms, wrists, and hands, **210**
  - basketball, 184
  - bicycling, 194
  - golf, 197
  - running, 206
- for Ian King workout, **90**, **102**, **108**, **116**, **144**
- incline, 27, **73**, **131**
- machine, **75**
- in $100 workout, **71**
- in simplest total-body workout, 32, **32–33**
- wide-grip, **102**, **116**
  - incline, **131**
  - with legs up, **116**

Bent-over row, 32, **33**, **71**, **145**, 194, **214**
Biceps curl, **71**, **73**, 77, **89**, **99**, **133**, 194, 209
Bicycling, 25, 184, 190–95, 224
Blood glucose, 156
Blood pressure, high, 11
Blueberries, 25, 164
Box hop, 183, **184–85**
Bread, whole grain, 151, 164–65, 167
Bridge, 41, **41**, 56, 66, **66**, **93**
Broccoli, 151
Bruises, 237
Butter, 150
Butterfly machine, 26, **26**

C

Cable crunch, 66, **66**
Cable row, 62
Calcium, 150–51
Calf raise, **75**
- on leg-press machine, **35**, **119**
- seated, **110**
- standing, 63, **63**, **71**, **92**, **132**

Calisthenics, 25
Calories burned during
- chores, 13
- vacations, 80–81

Carbohydrates
for energy, before working out, 23, 156
in
food, 153, 164, 165, 176
sports drinks, 22, 159, 160
for muscle building, 156, 163
Carioca drill, **184**
Chair dip, 41–42, **42**
Cheese, 151
Chicken, 151, 153, 165–66, 167
Chinup, 40, **40**, **98**
Cholesterol levels, 156, 165
Clam, 63, **63**
Cleats, 226
Climbing wall, **24**, 25
Close-grip bench press, 49, **108**, **121**, **129**
Clothing, for exercise, 30, 45, 206, 239
Coffee, 14, 37, 162
Colas, 162
Collarbone, broken, 236–37
Concentration curl, 194, 197, **210**
Cooldown, after exercising, 42
Cortisol, 20, 22, 165
Cottage cheese, 164
Crossover crunch, **208**
Crunch, 26, 42, **42**, 184, 195, 197, 199, **208**
cable, 66, **66**
crossover, **208**
oblique, 66, **66**, **209**
reverse, 62, **139**
side, **93**
Swiss-ball, **73**
reverse, **130**
side, **132**
weighted, **71**, **75**
Cycling twist, **139**

D

Dancing, 81
Deadlift, **73**, **100**, **109**, **134**, 184, 199, 206, **223**
one-leg, **91**
stiff-legged, 27, **118**
wide-grip, **118**
stiff-legged, **101**
Decline barbell triceps extension, **35**
Decline dumbbell bench press, **34**
Decline knee-up, **109**
Diabetes, 224
Diet, 6, 163–68
Dip, 41–42, **42**, 49, 58, **58**, 62
bench, **120**, **129**, **143**
Drinking, 22, 25, 32, 37, 158–62
Dumbbell bench press, 62
Dumbbell curl, **75**
Dumbbell fly, **117**
Dumbbell lateral raise on an incline, **34**
Dumbbell lunge, **75**, 184, 198, 206, **216**
Dumbbell power clean and press, **144**
Dumbbell shoulder press, 62
Dumbbell stepup, 198, 206, **216**
Dynamic lunge, **101**

E

Eating
for fat loss, 6, 174
habits to break, 154
for muscle building, 163–68, 174
in restaurants, 177
workouts and, 23, 25, 37, 77, 156
writing down specifics about daily, 6–7, 157
Eggs, 150, 153, 164, 166
Endurance training, 197
Energy drinks, 162
Exercise equipment
alternatives, **34–35**, 34-35
bicycling accessories, 195, 227
evaluating, 8–10, 43
for sports, 226–27
types of
bikes, 28, 191, 193
free weights, 27, **32–35**, 70
home gym, 70, 70 –71, 72, 72 –73, 74, 74 –75
jump rope, 38–39, 70
rehab, **24**, 25
stairclimber/arm crank, 28
treadmill, 28
weight machines, 26
weight-training accessories, 32
Exercises. *See also* Stretch(es)
abductor/adductor moves, 195, **215**
alternating front lateral raise, **221**
alternating press with dumbbells, 197, **221**
back extension, 62, **214**
barbell lunge, **34**, **73**
barbell preacher curl, **35**
bar rollout, **122**
bench dip, **120**, **129**, **143**
bench press (*see* Bench press)
bent-over row, 32, **33**, **71**, **145**, 194, **214**
biceps curl, **71**, **73**, **77**, **89**, **99**, **133**, 194, 209
box hop, 183, **184–85**
bridge, 41, **41**, 56, 66, **66**, **93**
cable crunch, 66, **66**
cable row, 62
calf raise (*see* Calf raise)
carioca drill, **184**
chair dip, 41–42, **42**
chinup, 40, **40**, **98**
clam, 63, **63**

Exercises *(cont.)*
close-grip bench press, 49, **108**, **121**, **129**
concentration curl, 194, 197, **210**
crossover crunch, **208**
crunch (*see* Crunch)
cycling twist, **139**
deadlift (*see* Deadlift)
decline barbell triceps extension, **35**
decline dumbbell bench press, **34**
decline knee-up, **109**
dip, 41–42, **42**, 49, 58, **58**, 62, **120**, **129**, **143**
dumbbell bench press, 62
dumbbell curl, **75**
dumbbell fly, **117**
dumbbell lateral raise on an incline, **34**
dumbbell lunge, **75**, 184, 198, 206, **216**
dumbbell power clean and press, **144**
dumbbell shoulder press, 62
dumbbell stepup, 198, 206, **216**
dynamic lunge, **101**
forearm curl, 197, 199, **211**
front lateral raise, **221**
front squat, **118**
grip strengthener, 197, 199, **212**
hanging knee raise, **117**
hanging leg raise, 66, **66**
heel raise with seated-leg-press machine, 206, **220**
hip lift, **101**
hip/thigh extension, **92**
inclined pushup, 198
incline dumbbell curl, **127**
incline press, 27, **27**, **73**
jackknife, 66, **66**
jumping drills, 189
jumping jacks, 38–39, 198
jumping rope, 38–39
jump shrug, **142**
jump squat, **140**
knee raise, **117**
knee-up, **109**
lateral pulldown (*see* Lateral pulldown)
lateral raise (*see* Lateral raise)
leg curl, 26, **35**, 63, **63**, 184, 194, 206, **217**
leg extension, **62**, 63, **217**
leg press, **34**, 194, **217**
leg raise (*see* Leg raise)
lunge (*see* Lunge)
lying dumbbell row, **92**
lying triceps extension, 73, **128**, 194, 197, **212**
lying vacuum, 56, **93–94**
machine bench press, **75**
machine row, **75**
machine shoulder press, **75**
modified V-sit, **140**
moon walking, **185**
narrow dumbbell squat, **218**
neutral-grip lateral pulldown, **121**
neutral-grip pullup, **121**
nonlockout squat, **145**
oblique crunch, 66, **66**, 93, **209**
oblique twist, 197, 199, **209**
one-arm dumbbell row, 194, 197, **215**
one-leg curl, **75**
one-leg deadlift, **91**
one-leg partial squat, **91**
overhand lateral pulldown, **98**, **110**, **141**
overhand seated row, **99**
overhead triceps extension, **134**
parallel-grip seated row, **108**
power clean and press, **144**
preacher curl, 27, **27**, **35**, **111**, **133**
pullover, **90**
pullup (*see* Pullup)
pushup (*see* Pushup)
reverse crunch, 62, **130**, **139**
reverse forearm curl, 197, **211**
reverse-grip biceps curl, **122**
reverse lunge, **40**, 40–41
reverse pushup, 41, **41**
reverse wrist curl, **127**, 194, **213**
rope triceps extension, **133**
Russian twist, **119**
seated calf raise, **110**
seated hammer curl, 128
seated row (*see* Seated row)
shoulder extension, 197, **221**
shoulder press (*see* Shoulder press)
shrug (*see* Shrug)
side lateral raise, 197, **222**
side raise on bench, **110**
situp (*see* Situp)
slow curlup, **94**
squat (*see* Squat)
standing calf raise, 63, **63**, **71**, **92**, **132**
standing heel raise, **219**
standing leg curl, **35**
static lunge, **91**
step-back lunge, **71**
stepup (*see* Stepup)
stiff-legged deadlift, 27, **27**, **101**, **118**
straight-leg raise, 184, **219**
Swiss-ball (*see* Swiss-ball exercises)
T-bar row, **73**
tender-trap strengthener, 58, **58**
toe raise, 184, 197, 206, **220**
toe touches, **140**
triceps extension (*see* Triceps extension)
triceps pressdown, 77, **103**
triceps pushdown, **75**

tuck and roll, 236–37
twisting situp, **103**
underhand-grip seated row, **117**
underhand lateral pulldown, **98**, **141**
underhand seated row, **99**
upright row, 62, **71**, **103**, 199, **222**
walking, 49, 80
walking lunge, 56, **142**
wall squat, **39**, 40
waving hands like clouds, 59
weighted chinup, **98**
weighted crunch, **71**, **75**
weighted pullup, **111**
weighted situp, **111**
wide-arm pushup, **39**, 39–40
wide-grip bench press, **102**, **116**
with legs up, **116**
wide-grip biceps curl, **133**
wide-grip deadlift, **118**
wide-grip incline bench press, **131**
wide-grip lateral pulldown, **131**
wide-grip pullup, 131
wide-grip seated row, **130**
wide-grip stiff-legged deadlift, **101**
wide-grip upright row, **71**
wide-stance squat, **73**
windmill lunge, **143**
wrist curl, **127**, 194, **213**
wrist roll, 197, **213**
wrist-to-knee situp, **100**
Zottman curl, **128**
Exercising. *See also* Sports; Workouts
before date, 76–77
improving, 20–23
after injury, 233–37
medical checkup before, 11
simplifying, 30–36
when traveling, 80–81
for weight loss, 6

F

Faintness or dizzy spells, 11
Fasting, 6
Fat, dietary, 150, 151, 153, 163, 168, <u>176</u>
Feet, exercises for, **215–20**. *See also* Exercises
Finger, jammed, 238
First-aid kit, 195, 240
Fish, 151, 153
Fishing, 227
Fitness, 13, 48–49
Flexibility, 48, 50–54, 79, 184, 197. *See also* Stretching
Food labels, 155
Football, 79, 226
Forearm curl, 197, 199, **211**
Frisbee, 227
Front lateral raise, **221**
Front squat, **118**
Fructose, 160
Fruits, 151–56

G

Glucose, 160, 161, 224
Golf, 196–201
Grip strengthener, 197, 199, **212**
Gym specifications, 29, <u>44</u>

H

Hamstring injury, 233
Hands, exercises for, **209–13**. *See also* Exercises
Hanging knee raise, **117**
Hanging leg raise, 66, **66**
Headache during workout, 19
Heart disease
checking for, during annual exam, 15
exercising and, 11
preventing, through
diet, 151, 153, 163, 165
exercise, 224
Heart rate, checking, 49
Heel raise with seated-leg-press machine, 206, **220**
Hip lift, **101**
Hips, exercises for, **215–20**. *See also* Exercises
Hip/thigh extension, **92**
Horse riding, 81
Hunger, controlling, 154, 156
Hydrogenated fat, <u>176</u>
Hypertrophy programs, 78
Hypoglycemia, 161

I

Ian King workout, 84–147
Ibuprofen, 233–35
Ice cream, 157, <u>175</u>
Immune system, 160
Inclined pushup, 198
Incline dumbbell curl, **127**
Incline press, 27, **27**, **73**
Injury prevention, 230–39
Inline skating, 81, 225
Insulin, 151, 156
Internet site about fitness, <u>78</u>
Interval training, 184, 203, 206
Iron, 151

J

Jackknife, 66, **66**
Juice, 151, 156, 161–62
Jumping drills, 189
Jumping jacks, 38–39, 198
Jumping rope, 38–39
Jump shrug, **142**
Jump squat, **140**
Junk food, <u>174</u>

K

Knee injury, 238
runner's knee, 234–35
Knee-up, **109**

L

Labels, on food, 155
Lacerations and abrasions, 237
Lateral pulldown, 26, 62, **73**
  neutral-grip, **121**
  overhand, **98**, **110**, **141**
  underhand, **98**, **141**
  wide-grip, **131**
Lateral raise, 27, **27**
  alternating front, **221**
  dumbbell, on an incline, **34**
  side, 197, **222**
Lat-pulldown machine, 26, **26**
Leg curl, **35**, 63, **63**, 184, 194, 206, **217**
Leg-curl machine, 26, **26**
Leg extension, **62**, 63, **217**
Leg press, **34**, 194, **217**
Leg raise
  with ankle weights or dumbbells, 206, **218**
  hanging, 66, **66**
  straight, 184, **219**
Legs, exercises for, **215–20**. *See also* Exercises
Lettuce, 151
Lunge
  barbell, **34**, **73**
  dumbbell, **75**, 184, 198, 206, **216**
  dynamic, **101**
  reverse, **40**, 40–41
  static, **91**
  step-back, **71**
  windmill, **143**
Lying dumbbell row, **92**
Lying triceps extension, **73**, **128**, 194, 197, **212**
Lying vacuum, 56, **93–94**

M

Macadamia nuts, 153
Machine bench press, **75**
Machine row, **75**
Machine shoulder press, **75**
Magnesium, 151, 165
Maltodextrin, 156, 160
Massage therapist, 44
Mayonnaise, 150
Medical checkup, 11, 14–15
MH List of
  best sporting goods, 226–27
  first-aid supplies, 240
  heathful ethnic foods, 177
  tips for thorough medical checkup, 14–15
  vacation workouts, 80–81
MH Quiz about
  athletic performance, 180–81
  diet, 150–51
  exercise motivation, 18–19
  physical fitness, 48–49
  sports injuries, 230–31
  waist size, 2–3
Milk, 23, 150–51, 153, 161–62, 164, 166
Minerals, 155–56, 160
Modified V-sit, **140**
Monounsaturated fat, 153, 163, 165, 176
Moon walking, **185**
Multivitamins, 164
Muscle building
  abdominal, 66
  diet for, 6, 163–68, 174
  in home gym
    advanced level, 73, **73**
    beginner level, 71, **71**
    intermediate level, 75, **75**
  in Ian King workout
    abdominal, 138–47
    aggressive routine, 97–106
    arms, 126–37
    shaping up, 88–96
    strength training, 107–14
    pectorals, 115–26
  lower-body, 62–63
  problems
    inflexibility, 50–51, 54
    stress, 165
    too much cardiovascular exercise, 44
  upper-body, 62
  vegetarianism and, 176

N

Narrow dumbbell squat, **218**
Nausea during workout, 19
Neutral-grip lateral pulldown, **121**
Neutral-grip pullup, **121**
Nonlockout squat, **145**
Nose, broken, 236
Nutrients, 153–56
Nutritionist, 44

O

Oatmeal, old-fashioned, 153, 164, 166
Oblique crunch, 66, **66**, **93**, **209**
Oblique twist, 197, 199, **209**
Olive oil, 153, 164–65
Omega-3 fatty acids, 151
One-arm dumbbell row, 194, 197, **215**
One-leg curl, **75**
One-leg deadlift, **91**
One-leg partial squat, **91**
Oranges, 164–65
Overhand lateral pulldown, **98**, **110**, **141**
Overhand seated row, **99**
Overhead triceps extension, **134**

P

Pain
  in back, 239
  from
    golf, 197
    inflexibility, 50–51, 54

in knees, 238
playing in spite of, 231
vs. soreness, 79
Parallel-grip seated row, **108**
Pastrami, 151
Peanut butter, 156
Pears, 151
Peppers, 151
Periodization workout schedule, 183 -84, 183
Polyunsaturated fat, 168, 176
Pork, 153
Potassium, 25, 160, 168
Potato, 151, 167, 168
Power clean and press, **144**
Preacher curl, 27, **27**, **35**, **111**, **133**
Protein, 150–51, 153, 164, 176
Protein bars, low-fat, 175
Protein shake, 23, 156, 165, 167
Pullover, **90**
Pullup, 26, 49, **141**, 184, 199, 206, **212**
neutral-grip, **121**
weighted, **111**
wide-grip, **131**
Pushup, 49
inclined, 198
reverse, 41, **41**
wide-arm, **39**, 39–40

R

Red peppers, 151
Reverse crunch, 62, **130**, **139**
Swiss-ball, **130**
Reverse forearm curl, 197, **211**
Reverse-grip biceps curl, **122**
Reverse lunge, **40**, 40–41
Reverse pushup, 41, **41**
Reverse wrist curl, **127**, 194, **213**
Rib, fractured, 235
Rice, whole grain, 168
Rope triceps extension, **133**
Rotator cuff, torn, 234
Runner's knee, 234–35
Running, 184, 202–6, 239
Russian twist, **119**

S

Salmon, 166–68
Saturated fat, 176
Scuba diving, 81
Seafood, 151, 153
Seated calf raise, **110**
Seated hammer curl, 128
Seated row, 77
underhand, **99**
wide-grip, **130**
Seated vertical-rowing machine, 26, **26**
Sets
back-off, 79
compound, 78
drop, 22
giant, 78
strip, 97, 115, 126
superset, 78, 126
triset, 78, 126
21s, 126
warmup, 79, 97, 107, 115, 126, 198
work, 79, 97, 107, 115, 126
Sex, improving, 3, 49, 76–77
Shadow boxing, 57–58
Shoulder
dislocated, 237
exercises for, **221–23**
Shoulder extension, 197, **221**
Shoulder press, 89, **102**, **111**, **120**, **132**, **142**
dumbbell, 62
machine, **75**
Shrug, **73**, **90**
jump, **142**
Side lateral raise, 197, **222**
Side raise on bench, **110**
Situp, 49, **139**
Swiss-ball, **134**
weighted, **111**
wrist-to-knee, **100**
Skating, inline, 81, 225
Slow curlup, **94**
Snacks, 156–57, 175, 195
Soccer, 224, 238
Sodium, 22, 160
Softball, 226
Soy protein, 153
Speed training, 192
Spinach, 151
Sports. *See also* Workouts
basketball, 182–89
bicycling, 190–95
football, 79
golf, 196–201
performance test, 180–81
tennis, 80–81
Sports drinks, 159–62
Sprinting, 79, 184
Squat
before date, 77
for
abdominal fitness, **62**, **63**
basketball, 184
bicycling, 194
golf, 197
hips, legs, ankles, and feet, **219**
front, **118**
in Ian King workout, **100**, **109**, **130**
jump, **140**
narrow dumbbell, **218**
nonlockout, **145**
one-leg partial, **91**

Squat *(cont.)*
  in simplest total-body workout, 32, **32**
  wall, **39**, 40
  wide-stance, **73**
Standing calf raise, 63, **63**, 71, **92**, **132**
Standing heel raise, **219**
Standing leg curl, **35**
Static lunge, **91**
Step-back lunge, **71**
Stepup, **62–63**, 63, **119**
  dumbbell, 198, 206, **216**
Stiff-legged deadlift, 27, 27, **101**, **118**
Straight-leg raise, 184, **219**
Strength training. *See* Weight training
Stress fractures, 236
Stretch(es). *See also* Exercises
  abdominal, 56
  ankle, 235
    pull, **204**
  back primer, **200**
  bow-and-arrow stance, 57, **57**
  calf, **53**
    raise, **86**
  chest, **86**
  elbow, 198, 234
  gluteals, **86**
  groin, **53**, **205**
  hamstring, **53**, **86**
  hand-and-arm builder, **201**
  hip, **52**
    hip-flexor, 58
  horse stance, 57, **57**
  iliotibial bands, 234
  leg stretcher, **201**
  lower-back, **52**
    twister, **200**
  neck, **200**
  quads, 234
  shoulder, **52**, **200**
    front, **86**
    rear, **86**
  side twister, **201**
  simple, 36, **36**
  spinal twists, **205**
  straight-knee calf, **205**
  thigh, **53**
  toe touches, **204**
  total-body, **204**
  towel, 56, 234
  triceps, **86**
  upper-back, **86**
  wrist builder, **201**
Stretching
  for
    flexibility, 50–54, 79
    golf, 198, 200–201
    injury prevention, 86, 231
    running, 204
    soccer, 224
  after injury, 233–37
Supplements, 156, 164
Swimming, 225
Swiss-ball exercises
  bridge, 66, **66**
  crunch, **73**
    reverse, **130**
    side, **132**
  jackknife, 66, **66**
  situp, **134**

T

Tai chi, 49, 54, 59
T-bar row, **73**
Tea, herbal, 161–62
Tender-trap strengthener, 58, **58**
Tendinitis, 233–34
Tennis, 80–81, 226–27
Tennis elbow, 234
Testosterone, 20, 76, 153, 165
Thiamin, 151
Toe raise, 184, 197, 206, **220**
Toe touch, **140**
Tomato sauce, 150
Torso, exercises for, **223**. *See also* Exercises
Trainer's Forum on
  back pain, 239
  cardiovascular/aerobic exercise vs. weight training, 13
  exercise plateau, 44
  getting in shape to play weekend sports, 79
  inline skates, 225
  jammed finger, 238
  overtraining, 238
  personal trainers, 12
  playing sports when sore or injured, 238
  runner's clothing, 239
  scheduling workouts around irregular job hours, 43
  sets, 78
  snacks, 174, 175
  stretching to prevent injuries, 224
  swimming, 225
  switching sports, 225
  timing of meals, 174
  vegetarianism and muscle building, 176
  volleyball strategies, 225
  weight lifting after 50, 224
Training logs, 6–7, 15, 43
  Ian King workout
    phase 1, 95–96
    phase 2, 104–6
    phase 3, 112–14
    phase 4, 123–25
    phase 5, 135–37
    phase 6, 146–47

Triceps extension, **89**, **212**
  decline barbell, **35**
  lying, **73**, **128**, 194, 197
  overhead, **134**
  rope, **133**
Triceps pressdown, 77, **103**
Triceps pushdown, **75**
Tuna, 153, 164–66
Turkey, 165 –66
Twisting situp, **103**

U

Underhand-grip seated row, **117**
Underhand lateral pulldown, 98, **141**
Underhand seated row, **99**
Upright row, 62, **71**, **103**, 199, **222**
Urine, 159–62, 231, 233

V

Vegetables, 153, 155
Vegetarian protein sources, 176
Vitamins, 150–51, 154–55, 165
Volleyball, 225

W

Walking, 49, 80
Walking lunge, 56, **142**
Wall squat, **39**, 40
Warming up, 22, 79
  for
    basketball, 186–87
    golf, 198
    Ian King workout, 97, 107, 115, 126
    injury prevention, 231
  before stretching, 51
Water, to combat dehydration, 153–54, 158–59, 231–33
Waving hands like clouds, 59
Weighted chinup, **98**
Weighted crunch, **71**, **75**
Weighted pullup, **111**
Weighted situp, **111**
Weight gain
  diet for muscle building and, 163–68
  reasons for, 2–3
  strategy for, 157
Weight loss
  diet for muscle building and, 166–67
  eating for, 174
  when eating out, 177
  food substitutions for, 170–73
  goals for, 19
  in Ian King workout, 88
  problems
    bad eating habits, 154
    hunger, 154, 156
    no visible progress, 44
    thirst, 161
  strategy for, 5–7, 157
Weight training. *See also* Muscle building
  accessories, 32
  aerobics and, 184
  drinks for, 159
  after 50, 224
  food for, 153
  for
    basketball, 182–89
    bicycling, 194–95
    golf, 197–201
    running, 204–6
  hints and tips for, 79
  to increase metabolic rate, 44
  pain after, 239
  periodization schedule for, 183 –84, 183
  stances for, 57, **57**
  workouts for, 107–14
Whole grains, 153
Wide-arm pushup, **39**, 39–40
Wide-grip bench press, **102**, **116**
  with legs up, **116**
Wide-grip biceps curl, **133**
Wide-grip deadlift, **118**
Wide-grip incline bench press, **131**
Wide-grip lateral pulldown, **131**
Wide-grip pullup, 131
Wide-grip seated row, **130**
Wide-grip stiff-legged deadlift, **101**
Wide-grip upright row, **71**
Wide-stance squat, **73**
Windmill lunge, **143**
Wine, 77, 162
Workouts
  abdominal, 62–63, 66
  customizing, 48–49
  before date, 76–77
  drinking before and after, 22, 25, 32, 37, 158–62
  eating before and after, 23, 25, 37, 77, 156, 174
  in home gym
    advanced level, 73, **73**
    beginner level, 71, **71**
    intermediate level, 75, **75**
  Ian King
    abdominal, 138–47
    arms, 126–37
    muscle-building, 97–106
    pectoral, 115–26
    shaping-up, 88–96
    strength-training, 107–14
  injury prevention and, 230–37
  log of, 6–7, 15, 43
  lower-body, 62–63
  partners for, 10, 19, 36
  performance level of, 11, 33–34
  periodization schedule for, 183 –84, 183

Workouts *(cont.)*
personal trainers for, 8, 12, 44, 59
problems during
difficulty breathing, 233
hangover, 22
intimidation, 10
irregular work schedule, 43
lack of visible progress, 44
not stretching and warming up, 22–23, 231
overtraining, 238
stress, 20–22
switching programs too often, 35–36
unbalanced strength, 48–49
scheduling, 22, 23, 32–33, 85
simplifying, 30–37
tracking, 36
when traveling, 38–42
upper-body, 62
varying, 85–87, 183, 225
Wrists, exercises for, **209–13**. *See also* Exercises
wrist curl, **127**, 194, **213**
wrist roll, 197, **213**
Wrist-to-knee situp, **100**

Y

Yoga, 25, 49, 54
Yogurt, low-fat, 25, 150

Z

Zinc, 151, 155–56
Zottman curl, **128**